DIVERSITY MANAGEMENT IN PRACTICE

DIVERSITY MANAGEMENT IN PRACTICE

A CROSS-CULTURAL & MULTI-DISCIPLINARY
ANNOTATED BIBLIOGRAPHY
ADDRESSING POLICY AND WELL-BEING

EDITED BY

Susanne Küchler &
Sandra Wallman

Coordinated by
ROSSELLA LO CONTE

Sustainability Diversity

sus.div
:....eurodiv

sussex
ACADEMIC
PRESS

2 4 6 8 10 9 7 5 3 1

First published in 2009 by
SUSSEX ACADEMIC PRESS
PO Box 139
Eastbourne BN24 9BP

and in the United States of America by
SUSSEX ACADEMIC PRESS
920 NE 58th Ave   Suite 300
Portland, Oregon 97213-3786

British Library Cataloguing in Publication Data
A CIP catalogue record for this book is available from the British Library.

Library of Congress Cataloging-in-Publication Data
Diversity management in practice : a cross-cultural & multi-disciplinary
annotated bibliography addressing policy and well-being / edited by Susanne
Küchler and Sandra Wallman.
p. cm.
Includes bibliographical references and indexes.
ISBN 978-1-84519-317-1 (h/c : alk. paper)
1. Ethnicity—Bibliography. 2. Diversity in the workplace—Bibliography.
I. Küchler, Susanne. II. Wallman, Sandra.
Z7164.C81D58 2009
[HF5549.5.M5]
016.6583008—dc22

2009018796

Mixed Sources

Product group from well-managed
forests and other controlled sources
www.fsc.org Cert no. SGS-COC-2482
© 1996 Forest Stewardship Council

FSC

The paper used in this book is certified by The Forest Stewardship Council (FSC),
a non-profit international organization established to promote the responsible
management of the world's forests. Products carrying the FSC label are
independently certified to assure consumers that they come from
forests that are managed to meet the social, economic and
ecological needs of present and future generations.

Typeset and designed by SAP, Brighton & Eastbourne.
Printed by TJ International, Padstow, Cornwall.
This book is printed on acid-free paper.

Contents

Acknowledgements

This volume was produced under the auspices of the SUSDIV (Sustainable Development in a Diverse World) collaborative Network of Excellence (NoE) funded by the European Commission and administered by FEEM (Fondazione Eni Enrico Mattei).

We are happy to acknowledge the participation of our network partners and others who contributed so generously to this collection. It goes without saying that all of this rests on the life stories of people around the world whose experience of their own and others' diversities are the bedrock of this bibliography.

List of Abbreviations

ADEA	Association for the Development of Education in Africa
ASQ	*Administrative Science Quarterly*
CEE	Central and Eastern European countries
CIPCA	Centro de Investigación y Promoción del Campesinado
EBLUL	European Bureau for Lesser Used Languages
EIB	Intercultural bilingual education (Spanish acronym)
EO	Equal opportunity
EPRA	European Public Real Estate Association
EU	European Union
EUMC RAXEN	European Monitoring Centre on Racism and Xenophobia
FDI	Foreign direct investment
FTSE International	*Financial Times* London Stock Exchange
GATT	General Agreement on Tariffs and Trade
GDP	Gross domestic product
GIEIF	Global Infrastructure Equity Index Fund
GLPEPF	Global Listed Private Equity Passive Fund
GREEIF	Global Real Estate Equity Index Fund
GSOEP	German Socio-Economic Panel
GTZ	Deutsche Gesellschaft für Technische Zusammenarbeit
HBR	*Harvard Business Review*
ICD	Intercultural dialogue
ICML	International Conference on Minority Languages
JEP	*Journal of Economic Perspectives*
JEL	*Journal of Economic Literature*
LARA	Louvaine Area Residents' Association
LDI	Liability Driven Investment
LMLS	Language maintenance and language shift
LTCM	Long-Term Capital Management
MD	Managing Diversity programme
MNF	Multinational firm
MOST	Management of Social Transformations
NAREIT	National Association of Real Estate Investment Trusts
NFP	National Focal Point
NGO	Non-governmental organization
NMC	Non-member country

OECD	Organization for Economic Cooperation and Development
R&D	Research and development
RLS	Reversing language shift
SUS.DIV	Sustainable Development in a Diverse World
TNC	Transnational corporation
UIE	Unesco Institute for Education
UNDESA	United Nations Department of Economic and Social Affairs
UNESCO	United Nations Educational, Scientific and Cultural Organization

Introduction

Diversity is not a new phenomenon. It is an essential feature of human societies, but its prominence as an area of enquiry ebbs and flows. In these days of the early 21st century, diversity is again a public issue – sometimes political, sometimes economic, but commonly something that needs to be measured, controlled, *managed*. Recent events have contributed to heating up the discourse – new migrations, boundary changes, drought in Africa, worldwide recession among others. "Fortress Europe" has been constructed as a reaction to new anxieties, indeed, as a defence against the perceived threat of diversity itself.

The most media-visible dimensions of diversity are race and ethnicity: many of the bibliographic entries in this volume directly address cause and effect of conflict, competition or stand-off between groups of people characterised by these kinds of differences. But morphology and culture are certainly not the only bases for discrimination, exclusion or privilege; other differences which make a difference to the life chances of individuals and groups of people are also addressed in the contributions. Diversities of class, gender and age are steadily significant. Age becomes ever more so. In more affluent settings the classic demographic pyramid begins to invert; more people are living longer, fewer are born. In other settings, notably in the third world, as much as half the population is under fifteen years old. Economic disparities are exacerbated by this demographic contrast. It is the engine driving migration flows and interdependencies between east and west, south and north, creating a package of problems that are too readily seen in raw terms of racial or cultural parameters.

The significance of diversity is neither transparent nor static. Not transparent because there are so many factors involved in definitions and identities; not static because the meaning of difference varies with context and context shifts with time, place and situation. Situations in which diversities of different kinds are "overlaid" are especially hard to manage. The remnant population of a declining inner city area is often, for plain economic reasons, combined of old whites and young blacks. Is the tension between them about race or about age? The observer wants a categorical single dimension answer; the actor[s], on the contrary, have multi-dimensional lives, identities and priorities; the boundaries they manage are necessarily fuzzy.

— ❖ —

The current preoccupation with diversity is reflected in policy declarations at all levels. Most apposite, possibly most influential among them, is UNESCO's *Universal Declaration on Cultural Diversity* (2001). Many of the entries in this bibliography pre-date the UN declaration, but its formation statements guide our efforts here. Two of its Articles focus the debate most effectively. One states that: "cultural diversity is as necessary for humankind as biodiversity is for nature" (Art.1); and the other that diversity is "one of the roots of development understood not simply in terms of economic growth, but also as a means to achieve a more satisfactory intellectual, emotional, moral and spiritual existence" (Art. 3). In this vision, cultural diversity becomes a new form of capital, embodied in both material (monuments, historical sites) and immaterial cultural assets (languages, traditions and lifestyles). It is accumulated through generations and can enhance economic growth and human welfare. However, in investigating diversity, scholars and practitioners alike face three major considerations:

❖ Cultural diversity is a dynamic, adaptive process, undergoing continuous evolution and enrichment.

❖ The full potential of cultural diversity is not achieved by the simple juxtaposition of cultural differences and identities. Culture, understood as everyday relational practices, is never linear and fully coherent, but rather adaptive, inventive and open-ended.

❖ The effect of cultural diversity is context dependent: it is embedded in specific social, economic and political relations that create power structures in society. Culture and cultural diversity concepts should not be used to obscure existing power relations, but rather as a means to understanding how power relations are reflected and enacted through the cultural channel.

These considerations remain central to the SUS.DIV project, and have inspired the preparation and publication of this volume.

The Network

This cross-cultural and multi-disciplinary annotated bibliography has emerged out of a collaborative network on the sustainability of diversity, titled *Sustainable Development in a Diverse World* [acronym SUS.DIV]. It is funded by the European Commission as part of its Sixth Framework Program, designed to support Networks of Excellence (NoE) over a five-year period (2005–2010).[1] The SUS.DIV network integrates resources and expertise on diversity/ sustainability issues. In order to maximise its contribution to policy, policy-makers and practitioners have been actively involved throughout - a commitment reflected in the range of contributions to this bibliography.

The network brings together 32 different institutions from Europe, Asia and the Americas, making a total of 110 participants. The institutions are from 16 different nations, and the participants come from 29 different countries; many are living and working away from their homeland. The network covers disciplines as diverse as anthropology, psychology, economics, sociology, political sciences, art and economic history, architecture, law, urban and regional studies, geography, and linguistics.

The network addresses four particular challenges:

❖ *The challenge of sustainable development*
The World Commission on Environment and Development (1987) defines *sustainable development* as that which "meets the needs of the present without compromising the ability of future generations to meet their own needs". The European Strategy for Sustainable Development adopted in Gothenburg in 2001 defines diversity as an essential element of a society which is capable of delivering a better quality of life for us, our children, and our grandchildren.

❖ *The transition towards a knowledge based society*
The OECD (1996) defines the knowledge economy as "directly based on the production, distribution and use of knowledge and information". In the knowledge economy, knowledge creation, creativity and innovation represent the real engine of growth. 'Diversity heritage' may represent an important asset in the transition to a knowledge economy.

❖ *The process of globalisation*
Globalisation increases confrontation and exchange amongst different economic activities, lifestyles, consumption patterns and other forms of cultural expression. The most frequent criticism of globalisation concerns the danger of cultural homogenisation and the destruction of local and national diversities. However, globalisation may also encourage the re-emergence of identities previously suppressed in the name of national homogeneity.

❖ *The process of European integration and enlargement*
The enlargement of the EU to include parts of the former communist world has heightened awareness of different historical experiences, different visions of the state and the market, different modes of production, different technologies and economic specialisations. Deeper integration among current EU member states has put diversity on to the political agenda. Policy issues, once the responsibility of independent states, are now subject to centralized decision making. Public goods' provision and welfare services are now matters of contention, aggravated in some European cities where the presence of foreign migrants is newly visible.

The Volume

This annotated bibliography responds to the challenges set out above. Its broad scope offers a vital tool for those conducting primary research in topics related to migration and population. It also aims to be an inspiration for practitioners in the field of diversity management and policy implementation. This volume meets the need, recognised by the European Commission, to evaluate approaches to integration and the management of diversity.

Policy arenas that will benefit directly from this collection include:

❖ *Policies towards immigrants*: How should immigration be regulated? Which policies and practices will stimulate interactions of cultures and contribute to innovative and creative behaviour? How can reunification of families and the formation of cultural communities be best encouraged?

❖ *Economic policies*: How can the position of minorities and new immigrants to the labour market be improved without jeopardising the host community? How might the labour market take better advantage of the skills and knowledge of immigrants? How should decisions about the distribution of regional funds be made? These funds have marked relevance for labour mobility and therefore have an impact on population distribution.

❖ *Educational policies*: Under which conditions should 'culture-specific' schools be encouraged? To what extent should bilingualism be promoted? Which policies and practices might stimulate interactions of cultures and contribute to innovative and creative behaviour?

One of the major features of this annotated bibliography is that it provides a bridge across the linguistic and intellectual traditions that currently set scholars and practitioners apart from each other. It brings together short reviews of items identified by network partners, associated scholars and practitioners, as key to their work in the diversity arena. The language of the volume is English, but its range includes European and non-European countries and their associated languages in translation. Readers who are normally restricted to anglophone publications are here given access to cross-linguistic and cross-nation perspectives.

Items annotated in the publication cover both classical and contemporary perspectives, allowing those concerned with *Diversity Management in Practice* to communicate more readily. In every case reviews are written in English; where appropriate the original language title is also given (only half a dozen of the 47 contributors has English as a mother tongue). A number of contributors have identified motion picture films, videos and novels as sources of inspiration and understanding. These reviews enhance understanding of the variety of ways in which diversity is recognised, and of the way these recognitions are applied in interaction.

Selections are personal as well as professional. The editors have encouraged individuality of style within an otherwise strict framework. These are therefore not conventional reviews. In effect, this bibliography demonstrates the variation in approaches to and definitions of diversity across disciplines and languages; it also allows insight into individual concerns and experience.

Each contributor has identified up to five items that have contributed to their separate efforts to understand, analyse or manage diversity. The collection contains 172 entries of between 300 and 500 words. It includes academic books and articles, journalistic and conference reports, novels, and fictional, video or documentary films. Each review specifies the subject, the main discipline, the location where the study was conducted, the type of diversity at issue and up to five keywords. These details are collated in four comprehensive indexes set at the end of the book, under the headings *Subject index; Main Discipline index; Geographic Area index; Diversity-type index*. The indexes are designed to be used in combination, allowing the reader easy navigation through the variety of themes and contributions.

Diversity Management in Practice is recommended to researchers, students and teachers, people dealing with diversity training programmes and strategies, local political institutions and voluntary organisations, European Networks of Excellence, and those working on Diversity as it affects other fields of research. Its insights apply to diversity issues in Europe and the United States, but also outside Anglophone academic institutions and political contexts. A list containing addresses and contact details of the authors and institutions involved in the writing and collection of the reviews is provided on pages 00-00.

Note

1   The network is co-ordinated by Fondazione Eni Enrico Mattei (FEEM) under the scientific leadership of Katholieke Universiteit Leuven (K.U.Leuven). www.sus.div.org

The Reviews

Xavier Albó, 1999. *Iguales aunque diferentes* (La Paz: Ministerio de Educación–UNICEF–CIPCA), 134 pp.

English Translation of the Title: *The Same but Different.*

Keywords: *interculturality, cultural pluralism, linguistics policy, intercultural policy, bilingualism*

The book provides a brief synthesis of cultural diversity in Bolivia, the main concepts for analysing and acting upon it with an intercultural approach, and an outline of the most relevant public policies for doing so. One of the most interesting and useful parts is the section on intercultural concepts (pp. 83–99), strongly embedded in the Bolivian context, which allows a localized understanding of those policies. Within the distinction between formal and substantive theories, this conceptual discussion is closer to the latter: a conceptual proposition based on a specific reality. Though the text is described as addressing intercultural issues in symbolic realms, such as education and culture, a number of the proposed concepts can be used for the analysis and understanding of intercultural relations in more material realms like rural development. A useful distinction is made between the concepts of interpersonal and structural *interculturality* (pp. 88–90), capturing the personal and social dimensions of the intercultural phenomenon. The section on interpersonal interculturality is far more in-depth than the structural one.

A missing aspect in the discussion of both concepts is the issue of power, which, though mentioned in passing in the structural interculturality concept, is not elaborated fully. This scant reference to power in the structural dimension and its absence in the interpersonal dimension is perhaps an expression of a more structural, rather than relational, vision of power. A useful element is the distinction between five basic types of interculturality (pp. 85–87) to describe everyday intercultural relations. These types range between two poles: a *negative* and a *positive* interculturality. The first refers to attitudes and relations characterized by the negation of others, and the second to attitudes and relations characterized by the full acknowledgment and respect of others. Between these two extremes are intermediate types such as *dependent, bonding* and *tolerant* interculturality. A discussion of how power is built within these different types of intercultural relations might have enriched this typology. These distinctions have nonetheless allowed us to build a matrix of intercultural situations in a study on the impact of intercultural relations on sustainable rural development in Bolivia.

José Fernando Galindo-Cespedes
Centre for Research and Promotion of Peasantry, Cochabamba, Bolivia.

Alberto Alesina & Eliana La Ferrara, 2005. "Ethnic Diversity and Economic Performance", *Journal of Economic Literature* 43: 762–800.

Keywords: *ethnic diversity, economic performance, immigration, developed countries, developing countries*

This paper surveys and assesses the literature on the positive and negative effects of ethnic diversity on economic policies and outcomes. Conflict of preferences, racism and prejudices often lead to policies that are both odious and counterproductive for society as a whole. The oppression of minorities may lead to political unrest or even civil wars. But a diverse ethnic mix also brings about variety in abilities, experiences and cultures that may be productive and may lead to innovation and creativity.

The paper proposes a simple economic model in which public good provision is lower in fragmented societies while productivity may be positively related to variety. The authors exhaustively support the former statement; however, the picture is complex in regard to the relation between productivity and variety. It is somehow easy to highlight economic failures of fractionalized societies, but this is not a general phenomenon. In rich democratic societies growth and productivity improve with diversity, the USA being one of the most significant examples. But within the developing world, similar levels of ethnic diversity are associated with conflict and inter-ethnic cooperation. Theoretical progress might be achieved with the incorporation into the model of more realistic institutional features that would distinguish cases in which the economy actually manages to take advantage of the potential benefits of variety in production.

The focus of the paper is on communities of different size and organizational structure, such as countries, cities in developed countries, and villages and other groups in developing countries. The endogenous formation of political jurisdictions is also considered and several open issues in need of further research are highlighted, such as the endogenous formation of ethnic identity.

This article is a milestone in economic research on diversity. By presenting diversity as a complex multidisciplinary phenomenon, involving various social science disciplines such as economics, sociology and anthropology, it claims that in order to analyse diversity it is necessary to look at the broader picture. It suggests thinking about important issues, e.g. the measurement of diversity, and it discusses the policy implications of diversity.

Although dealing largely with USA data, this paper stimulates discussion on ethnic diversity in other parts of the world. In fact, while the USA has been a melting pot throughout most of its history, Europe has been much more ethnically homogeneous so far, and only with the recent opening of borders within the European Union and its expansion to the East, in addition to increasing migration from Africa and other neighbouring areas, have member countries started to become more heterogeneous. Multi-ethnicity will be one of the major challenges for Europe in the near future.

Carlo Fiorio
Eni Enrico Mattei Foundation and University of Milan, Milan, Italy.

Tariq Ali, 2002. *The Clash of Fundamentalisms: Crusades, Jihads and Modernity* (London: Verso), 428 pp.

Keywords: *diversity, culture, fundamentalism, modernity, politics*

The Clash of Fundamentalisms entwines a secular history of Islam, a biography of Tariq Ali and his family (who played an important role in the political life of Pakistan), and an analysis of the political destiny of a region that stretches from the Arab lands to South Asia. This recent book comes after the 9/11 attack on New York's Twin Towers and is intended to dismantle the rhetoric of *good* and *evil* which followed it, where *good* stands for USA and its allies and *bad* stands for Saudi Arabia and other rogue states, and the idea that cultures or civilizations are monoliths in opposition to one another. But the rise of modern Islamic fundamentalism seems to be the answer to the imperial fundamentalism of the USA.

Ali writes about Palestine and Israel, Zionism, the Ottoman Empire, the origins of Wahhabism, Pakistan, Afghanistan, Kashmir and USA imperialism, to end with a "Letter to a Young Muslim", a passionate condemnation of every attempt to use religion as a justification for war and the destruction of diversity and the *other*. It is important not to confuse the individual with the social and cultural background in which he or she has grown up.

One of the most impressive insights into diversity that Tariq Ali stresses in this book is that one can be an atheist and be part of an Islamic culture at the same time: it is possible to belong to a certain culture without being a believer. The view of cultural diversity as a *clash of civilizations* (as in Samuel Huntington's view) is clearly opposed by Ali, who argues that the building of a monolithic image of Religion and Culture leads to ethnic cleansing and war. In fact, he remembers the time of the Partition, when Pakistan was founded to provide the Muslim élites of India with power, and how once-peaceful neighbours turned into aggressive religious fanatics.

Maria Alessia Montuori
Psychoanalytic Institute for Social Research, Rome, Italy.

Hassana Alidou, Aliou Boly, Birgit Brock-Utne, Yaya Satina Diallo, Kathleen Heugh & H. Ekkehard Wolff, 2006. *Optimizing Learning and Education in Africa – The Language Factor: A Stock-taking Research on Mother Tongue and Bilingual Education in Sub-Saharan Africa* (Paris: Association for the Development of Education in Africa), 186 pp.

Keywords: *mother-tongue education, literacy, bilingual/multilingual education, Africa*

This report, commissioned by a consortium of development agencies, ADEA, UIE and GTZ, was intended as one of a range of studies on language education in Africa to be presented to the ministers of education at the ADEA 2006 Biennial Meeting in Libreville, Gabon. The Report comprises a comprehensive evaluation of the current range of language education policies, models and interventions in both the formal and non-formal sectors. These include second/foreign language only (i.e. subtractive models); initial mother-tongue medium followed by transition to English, French or Portuguese (also known as early exit models); and very late exit/additive bi(tri)lingual programmes.

Since the UNESCO "Report on the Use of the Vernacular Languages in Education" in 1953, development agencies have invested considerable resources in education policies and programmes in which there is an early exit from the mother tongue to one of the international languages as the primary medium of teaching and learning. Educational achievement of school pupils across the continent has been disappointing and the majority of students exit from the school system prior to secondary school. The research evidence shows that most studies of language programmes on the continent are seriously flawed in regard to the validity and reliability of the data. In particular, much of the research includes weak, self-reported data and does not demonstrate the medium- to long-term efficacy of the different approaches. The research team concludes that such research needs to monitor student achievement at least into the sixth year of school.

The significance of this study is that it departs from the 1953 UNESCO report and offers education policy-makers and providers the evidence that one to three years of mother-tongue (home or local language) medium is insufficient for meaningful education for most school pupils. It draws attention to the teaching and learning conditions which facilitate successful literacy and numeracy development and includes a dimension on the cost-effectiveness of mother-tongue-based programmes in relation to those which are foreign- or second-language dominant. The primary implication is that the data point towards the need for extended use of local and regional languages for at least six to eight years of education. The evidence has implications for linguistically diverse education systems in other parts of the world and it is consistent with similar research in North America during the 1990s. The ADEA-UIE-GTZ research has sparked other related or follow-up studies in Ethiopia, South

Africa, South-East Asia and the Indian subcontinent, each of which confirm the educational value of indigenous languages and diversity.

Kathleen Heugh
University of South Australia, Research Centre for Languages and Cultures, Adelaide, Australia.

Maurizio Ambrosini, 1999. *Utili invasori: L'inserimento degli immigrati nel mercato del lavoro italiano* (Milano: F. Angeli), 281 pp.

English Translation of the Title: *Useful Invaders: Immigrant Inclusion in the Italian Labour Market.*

Keywords: *labour market, self-employment, informal economy, immigrants, territorial heterogeneity*

The purpose of this book is to study the issue of immigrant employment in Italy and overall to analyse strategies for employing immigrants in the labour market and in different occupational paths. According to Ambrosini, Italy has specific characteristics that make it very different from other European countries: the Italian labour market is much segmented, with strong territorial diversities and immigration flows that are extremely heterogeneous. The combination of these realities creates many paths to insertion in the labour market. It happens through both regular and informal channels, with the aid of ethnic groups, which could represent a resource but in some cases leads towards occupational segregation.

An important path is linked to the informal economy: Italy has a large submerged (black) economy that inevitably attracts weak, uncertain and in many cases irregular people as immigrants. This always represents a first possible way of insertion and survival for foreigners, but may finish in a spiral of marginalization and outrage. Another possible road is represented by self-employment, which is rapidly growing in immigrant communities. This choice covers very different projects, providing refuge for people excluded from the labour market in firms integrated within the national manufacturing sector. The most common strategy is dependent employment, which includes the factories of the industrial districts, domestic service in metropolitan areas and agricultural jobs in the Southern region of Italy. Ambrosini shows a country where immigrants are *useful invaders*, because they act in a complementary and not competitive way with respect to natives in the labour market. Immigrants in fact perform occupations rejected by Italians, they represent a cheap workforce for local firms operating in the labour-intensive traditional sector (shoes, clothes), and help to fill gaps in the social system (for instance, elderly care).

The book offers a useful base for studying the Italian case, where new and quick migratory flows have to be inserted in a fragmented and always informal labour market. Here is a scene characterized by diversity: diversity of the subjects is enlarged by territorial heterogeneity, and it creates a large range of paths and occupational typologies that Ambrosini is able to specify, describe and understand. The book presents many stimulating typologies of informal labour, self-employment (exotic, ethnic, intermediary, open, refuge) and occupational paths (some precarious and irregular, others regular and stable), classified in respect of the economic and cultural benchmark of the referring group. In this way it helps with an understanding of the main characteristics of the diverse Italian labour market and society.

Gabriele Morettini
Marche Polytechnic University, Department of Social Sciences, Ancona, Italy.

Benedict Anderson, 2006. *Comunità immaginate: Origini e fortuna dei nazionalismi, translated by Marco Vignale* (Roma: Manifestolibri), 238 pp.

English Translation of the Title: *Imagined Communities: Reflections on the Origin and Spread of Nationalism.*

Keywords: *nationalism, ethnicity, civil society, communities*

Anderson's book explores the historical roots of nationalism as both an ideological mechanism and a cultural movement. Actually, the title itself, "Imagined Communities", summarizes the basic thesis of the work: nationalism is a fruit, an invention, of the mind of its supporters. The determination of a (self-styled) national community is not therefore the result of the observation of objective historical evidences, but the enhancement and re-elaboration of particular elements linked to the ethnic and cultural origins of the community/nation. A useful comparison of these positions can be made with the work of Ernest Gellner in *Nations and Nationalism* (1983).

Anderson analyses nationalism using a global perspective, beyond the European case, brought into focus mainly by previous scholars of this issue. This enlarging of the field of research allows him, for instance, to point to the Creole nationalism of Central America as the first historical expression of nationalism: a *political* nationalism, born from and fed by the rejection of the motherland and by the diffusion of the ideals of the Enlightenment at the end of the eighteenth century. This phenomenon is followed by the *linguistic* nationalism of the nineteenth and twentieth centuries, and by the *official* nationalism characteristic of the monarchies in the Old Continent, but also of those in Asia, which at the end of the nineteenth century discovered (and imagined) their national identity. Finally, Anderson analyses a fourth type of nationalism, that of the twentieth century, which sums up the main characteristics of the previous three forms.

This work is particularly useful for the study of social and cultural diversity in contemporary history as far as it was, and is still today, empathized and exploited by nationalisms. These latter – in Anderson's vision – believe they will find their *raison d'être* in supposed historical and cultural roots, considered the bases of the national conscience of a people (see chapters 2 and 3). Whoever does not share these roots is regarded as a stranger, a diverse *other*, unable to take part in the imagined community. The history of the last two centuries has shown that at times these dynamics stay within the limits of patriotism, and at other times they produce racism and repression.

Roberto Giulianelli
Marche Polytechnic University, Department of Social Sciences, Ancona, Italy.

José Andrés-Gallego, 1993. *Storia generale della gente poco importante: L'Europa e l'America intorno al 1789*, translated by Gianfranco Ciabatti (Milano: Sansoni, 1993), 306 pp. [Original Title: José Andrés Gallego, 1991. *Historia general de la gente poco importante*, Madrid: Editorial Gredos s.A.]

English Translation of the title: *General History of Unimportant People: 1789 Europe and America.*

Keywords: *occupational groups, border social groups, social control*

Unimportant people living in the Western world around 1789 were not necessarily poor and destitute. So Andrés Gallego's work is not only a history of the daily life of the humble people of that time, but it is also an attempt to make a general (though concise) comparison between the old and newborn world in terms of economic conditions, cultural habits, ways of life and thinking, as well as in terms of the reciprocal relations with the law and the State of all those who were not organically part of that supreme law and state. It is not only the peasants who have their space in the book, but also the guild master, the nurse, the magistrate, the criminal, the youngest of a noble lineage, the fool and many others. All, with their own manners, capabilities and opportunities, bear the problems of feeding, birth rate and control, education and professional training, sexual ethics, and death. It is a humanity that cannot rely on great power and that sees the decline of the *ancien régime* culminating in revolution *par excellence*, in France at the end of the eighteenth century.

The work covers a wide range of *social relationships* (the importance of the woman in the social hierarchy and in the choice of consort; the relevance of lineage and the evolution of family structures; the social and familiar consequences of sexual rigour; the development of individualism; the neighbour-hood and fear, devotion, heresy and Satanism; feast); *economic organizations* (the consumer revolution, the debate on living standards and the effect of the family on the economy; the distribution of property; legality and illegality; servants and slaves; compulsory labour and personal services in feudalism; hunters, peasants, artisans, and farm-hands; the bourgeoisie and the revolution of professionals; the conditions of labour); and *power relations* (local government and popular deputation; free Commons and fights for local power; the instruments of power, including laws and courts; submission to the written law; taxes as the germ of the revolution; the states, i.e. class; families, corps, loyalty, orders; a harmonious and respectful society, including protection, beggary, charity; violence, crimes and revolts; and the leaders of protest).

Regarding the issues of social diversity and sustainability, the book can be considered as a sort of inventory of the forms of diversity in the *ancien régime* societies and economies in a phase of epochal crisis when the old equilibrium was about to dissolve.

Ercole Sori
Marche Polytechnic University, Department of Social Sciences, Ancona, Italy.

Pol Antràs, Mihir A. Desai & C. Fritz Foley, 2007. "Multinational Firms, FDI Flows, and Imperfect Capital Markets", *National Bureau of Economic Research* Working Paper 12855: 3–32.

Keywords: *model of monitoring multinational firms' activity, financial contracting, investor protection*

The paper demonstrates that when firms want to exploit technologies abroad, multinational firms' (MNF) activity and foreign direct investment (FDI) flows arise endogenously, so that monitoring is problematic and financial frictions exist. It also provides a model in which product developers have a comparative advantage in monitoring their technologies abroad. The model shows the degree to which MNF's activity is financed by capital flows, the extent to which multinationals take ownership in foreign projects and the scale of operations abroad. The article attempts to unify MNF's activity and FDI flows while examining financing decisions and production in the foreign market. This means that foreign entrepreneurs can choose to *behave* and enjoy no private benefits, or to *misbehave* and take private benefits during the contracting period.

Managing misbehaviour and the associated private benefits can be manifested by choosing to implement the project in a way that generates perks for the manager or his associates. Usually the benefits are for the entrepreneur, which is why any branch of MNF in a certain country should have good investor protection (monitoring entrepreneurs) in order not to divert funds from the firm.

At the contracting stage the inventor and the foreign entrepreneur negotiate a contract that stipulates the terms under which the entrepreneur will exploit the technology developed by the inventor. It is presumed that an optimal contract is such that all the payoffs are positive and thus the agent can become an equity share holder of the inventor's firm. Non-verifiable monitoring and FDI is needed when the transaction of the technology is a market transaction, and when the payment of a flat fee for the use of the transformed technology meets the criteria of FDI.

The survey concentrates on the activities of American MNFs and their affiliates and covers the period 1982–99. The article pays attention to those firms which conduct more research and development (R&D). They usually deploy new technologies that require unique monitoring, and are companies important to external funders. It explains that "multinational parents" should hold bigger ownership stakes in affiliates located in countries with weak investor protection. The model predicts that the MNF's activity will be greatest in countries with stronger investor protection. Furthermore, the model suggests that ownership liberalizations should be larger in host countries with weak investor protection.

For my own work, the analysis and the main findings of the article are interesting, especially with respect to how the scale of the MNF's activity is positively related to the quality of investor protection and capital market development. The article focuses on R&D companies which are the generators of FDI quality and so are useful for economic development, but which are attracted mainly from countries with a high level of technological and investment potential.

Evgenia Vladimirova-Krasteva
Economic and Investment Bank (part of KBC Group), Sofia, Bulgaria.

Kurt April & Marylou Shockley (eds.), 2007. *Diversity: New Realities in a Changing World* (New York: Palgrave Macmillan), 380 pp.

Keywords: *pluralism, multiculturalism, leadership, stewardship, social change*

This book is a collection of provocative articles on a range of experiences in a variety of countries and continents. Authors include academics, consultants, managers in both the public and the private sectors, journalists and students. Organized around the six facets of diversity – looking at, expanding, embedding, creating, preparing for and realizing new realities – the book is a survey of real-life situations and experiences from countries as diverse as China, India, South Africa, the USA, Holland and Northern Europe, among many others.

Analyses, proposals and case studies are rather pragmatic: while describing experiences from around the world, they offer examples, advice and notes of caution to practitioners while challenging theorists to put on new lenses.

The world, the authors claim, is far messier than theory can capture or portray. There is a need for people to assume an activist role in questioning dominant paradigms and "expanding our realities of inclusion" (p. 79). The authors advocate plural constructivism in philosophy and leadership/management. They push for the creation of new ideas and practices in the marketplace that help think about diversity in new ways while adding to the current facets of diversity. They assert that the path is full of tensions, confusion, frustration and helplessness, all of which we need to manage with open minds and stewardship. In this sense, they advocate a new culture of learning and learning organizations.

Referring to efforts to instil diversity in the Dutch police force, Philomena Essed speaks to the need for full commitment and inclusiveness in the development of social and cultural sensitivity. In the conclusion to the book, editor Kurt April identifies three historical foci of diversity: an initial "legalistic approach" (p. 358) (early to mid-twentieth century), "valuing diversity" (p. 358) (late twentieth century) and "managing diversity" (p. 358) (early twenty-first century). Today, he claims, "the 'inclusion' philosophy has been expanded beyond a mere cultural focus" (p. 362) into a "self-leadership philosophy" (p. 364) that calls for individuals to be stewards of diversity.

The book provides a great overview of diversity from multiple perspectives, particularly of practitioners. Perhaps its major contribution is the realization that diversity speaks many languages, is practised in many ways and is understood differently by different people throughout the world, and that today's quest for diversity is only a beginning. Along these lines, the book calls for practices and theories that continuously push the envelope into new ways of thinking and practice throughout the world, hoping that they themselves reflect the diversity we seek and produce a true world of diversity.

John J. Betancur
University of Illinois at Chicago, Department of Urban Planning and Policy, Chicago, USA.

Ali S. Asani, 2003. "Creating Tradition through Devotional Songs and Communal Script: The Khojah Isma'ilis of South Asia", in Richard M. Eaton (ed.), *India's Islamic Traditions, 711–1750* (New Delhi: Oxford University Press), pp. 285–310.

Keywords: *syncretism, devotional songs, provenance, script, tradition*

The religious beliefs and practices of the *Khojah Isma'ili* community of South Asia give them a distinctive identity within Islam. Supposedly converted from the Hindu Lohana community of India, they consider the Aga Khan (a direct descendant of the Prophet Muhammad) their spiritual leader and follow the Shi'i path of Islam. Their actual practices are, however, syncretic. Though Shi'i, Sunni *mullahs* and *qazis* perform some of their important rituals, and though Muslim, the Hindu god Vishnu is part of the Sufi masters' (lit. old person) religious consciousness. As followers of Sufi traditions, they have deep reverence for Pirs who guide and guard them through the challenges of life. *Ginan*, the unique Khojah prayer song, is an important part of their worship ritual. Though influenced by Hindu devotional poetry and music and sung in different North Indian ragas, these are far more than prayer songs; they *are* the prayer and hence are sacred – all the more so because they are composed by Pirs; to sing them is almost like being in the Pir's presence. Since it is associated with a Pir, the authorship of the *ginan* is important, but it is a complex and controversial issue. The last line of the song gives the composer's name, the *bhanitas*, but instead of mentioning the actual composer's name, *bhanitas* are often attributed to famous Pirs of earlier centuries. Going by this, the *ginans* would seem to be of much older origin than an analysis of their structure would indicate.

Why would the composer's actual name be withheld? The author suggests that the older names were used because *bhanitas* of Pirs with religious authority over centuries would give the compositions a weight, an authority, an anchor, that a later composer's name would not provide. It is the reviewer's experience that this is often done in Indian classical music texts as an expression of humility or as an acknowledgment that everything emanates from the Master. Besides, in an oral tradition, the concept of an original is open to question.

The script of the *ginan*, the Khojki, is an interesting field of study. There is considerable discussion on why Khojki, a rather limited local script of mercantile origin, was used for writing the *ginan*. One view is that since Khojki was the predominant script in the areas where Khojahs lived in large numbers, its use made religious knowledge accessible to a larger number of people. In addition, a common script gave the Khojahs of different areas a common identity. The exclusive script also kept Khojah religious literature within their own boundaries and guarded it against intrusion or possible persecution from outsiders.

For researchers in the field of diversity, multiculturalism, coexistence and syncretism, this is an important article. It will also benefit those working on transmission and safekeeping of knowledge, sacred or secular. The complexity of provenance that the author discusses is of special interest to one studying the North Indian *khyal* form, where texts are mired in controversy as to their period, authenticity, style and authorship.

Alaknanda Patel
Centre for Development Alternatives, Ahmedabad, India.

Colin Baker, 2001. *Foundations of Bilingual Education and Bilingualism* (Clevedon [England]; Buffalo [NY]: Multilingual Matters), 496 pp.

Keywords: *bilingualism, education, multilingualism*

This volume is an updated review of the fields of bilingualism and bilingual education. It contributes to the study of linguistic and cultural diversity. This is the fourth edition of the work, which has become a classic in the field of bilingualism, and contains nineteen chapters. The early chapters focus on bilingualism and provide a very informative and comprehensive summary of research in the field. They deal with different aspects of bilingualism such as language planning, becoming bilingual at different ages and the effects of bilingualism on cognitive development. Baker summarizes different theoretical positions and the results of research in the field and discusses complex positions and controversies in a very clear way. The second half of the book focuses on bilingual education and is more relevant for the study of diversity, because it looks at the way diversity can be dealt with in the school context. Baker proposes a typology of bilingual education with strong and weak types, depending on the aims of the school and the use of the different languages in the curriculum.

An important aspect of bilingual education discussed in this volume is the acquisition of literacy skills by speakers of different languages. Examples of different bilingual situations in different parts of the world are provided, but there is a whole chapter devoted to bilingual education in the USA. There are also chapters on other aspects of bilingual education such as assessment, identity or special needs. A very interesting chapter that can be related to sustainable development is chapter 17, "Bilingualism and Bilingual Education as a Problem, Right and Resource". The last chapter of the book deals with the new challenges of bilingualism in the modern world.

The volume is written in a very reader-friendly style and it can be used as a textbook. There is a list of headings at the beginning of each chapter and a list of key points, suggested activities and study activities. Many tables and charts are also included. This volume is very useful for the understanding of diversity in schools. The identification of different types of bilingual education and their effectiveness has been particularly useful in developing the *Continua of Multilingual Education*, on which I am currently working. This proposes a model to analyse the different types of multilingual schools, taking into account linguistic distance and the diversity of languages used in the socio-linguistic context and in close social networks including the family.

Jasone Cenoz
University of the Basque Country, Donostia-San Sebastián, Spain.

Vladimir Balaz & Alan M. Williams, 2001. "Capital Mobility in Transition Countries of Central Europe: Macroeconomic Performance Factors and Structural Policies", *Journal of Economics* 02/2001: 242–271.

Keywords: *Foreign direct investment (FDI), privatization, transition economies.*

The paper examines the influence of financial sector development and privatization on foreign direct investment (FDI), portfolio investments and other forms of investment. The global financial landscape for the CEE (in particular the Czech and Slovak republics, Hungary and Poland) has changed significantly during the period 1989–97. It is related to five main factors: liberalization of international capital transactions; regulatory reforms of capital markets both in developed and underdeveloped countries; improvements in the macro-economic performance and prospects for short-term returns from financial investments; rapid progress in communication technologies and the search for alternative sources for higher yields by the portfolio managers of large institutional investors; and privatization and structural economic policies in many emerging countries such as those in Central Europe. Indeed, investment decisions are based on profit/risk factors which are different in different macro-economic approaches.

It is obvious that foreign investors expect dividends or interest yields, portfolio diversification, capital gains or combinations thereof. However, we can assume that they are not always governed by rational considerations and that they could affect capital asset pricing and capital market behaviour. The factors recognized by capital asset pricing are internal (pull factors) and external (push factors).

The first refers to economic and social developments in emerging markets. The second refers to developments in international markets and can be expressed through the differences in rates of return on alternative investments in international markets and those in the host country. The two factors are linked and have an inverse relationship. Substantial among internal factors are credit-worthiness indicators which embody debt to exports and GDP ratios. Privatization in the CEE was a large-scale process of redefining property rights. FDI is more likely to be directed to economies with relatively high development levels (GDP per capita) and relatively developed financial systems (ratios of broad money to GDP). FDI investors have longer-term targets and were less influenced by interest rates and trade balances. Portfolio investors were a diverse group, ranging from large pension funds to insurance companies with relatively stable yield policies. The other investments were also a broad variety of flows, ranging from official aid, provided by international financial institutions, to speculative sales/purchases on the banking and securities markets.

I find that this article reveals multiple facets of capital penetration and its effects on economic changes, development and diversity. In summary, we can say that most of the approaches and analyses of capital mobility and credit-worthiness indicators attempt to capture the macro-economic differences in a large range of countries. However, it is somewhat difficult to do so because every country has its own economic specification. The article also identifies the factors which were significant in attracting capital flows in transition economies.

Iskra Christova-Balkanska
Institute of Economics, Bulgarian Academy of Sciences, Sofia, Bulgaria.

Ayo Bamgbose, 2000. *Language and Exclusion: The Consequences of Language Policies in Africa* (Hamburg and London: LIT Verlag, Münster), 151 pp.

Keywords: *language policy and planning, language education, language as a resource*

Ayo Bamgbose, one of the most respected scholars of African languages, traces language policy on the continent from colonial times to the present and shows how the Western occupation and partition of Africa was accompanied by language policy which excluded African languages from high-level functions in politics, the economy and education. Although African languages have been used in early primary education, upper primary and secondary education tends to be conducted in one of the former colonial languages. Since most children are unable to develop sufficiently strong literacy skills and learn enough of the international language in early primary, they make little sense out of the upper primary curriculum. Bamgbose suggests that this is a significant factor in the attrition rate of more than 50 percent of pupils by the end of secondary school across the continent.

Bamgbose devotes a chapter to the notion of language (linguistic diversity) as a resource and makes recommendations for further language policy and planning on the continent. Unfortunately, the rationale for linguistic diversity upon which he focuses remains as pertinent today as it was nearly a decade ago.

This book is an invaluable resource for postgraduate studies on the negative effect of inappropriate language policy on the educational outcomes of school pupils in developing, particularly African, contexts. I have included it as essential reading for participants in a training of trainers programme for senior education officials and teacher educators in African countries. Bamgbose is able to draw from his decades of scholarly work and ground-breaking research to produce a concise and readable analysis of the social, educational and economic importance of the use of diverse languages in education. UNESCO's Education for All framework and goals cannot be achieved until the issues regarding linguistic access to education are met in developing countries, and this is ably demonstrated in this volume.

Kathleen Heugh
University of South Australia, Research Centre for Languages and Cultures, Adelaide, Australia.

Fredrik Barth (ed.), 1969. *Ethnic Groups and Boundaries: the Social Organization of Culture Difference* (Bergen: Universitetsforlaget; London: Allen & Unwin), 153 pp.

Keywords: *ethnicity, social anthropology, social organization, culture*

The book *Ethnic Groups and Boundaries* represents the results of a symposium held at the University of Bergen from 23 to 26 February 1967. There are seven essays published, but the most important part of the publication is Fredrik Barth's general introduction. Barth articulates a statement that the core of contemporary ethnic composition of the world is not based on cultural differences among people, but on the organization of society. He criticizes anthropological reasoning that rests on the premise that cultural variation is discontinuous: every (ethnic) unit keeps its own culture; geographical and social isolation have been considered critical factors in sustaining cultural diversity. He rejects such causality and suggests that ethnic boundaries persist despite a flow of commodities and personnel across them, and proves in the book that ethnic distinctions do not depend on an absence of mobility, contact and information. Interaction of social systems does not automatically lead to their liquidation through change and acculturation; cultural differences can persist despite inter-ethnic contact and interdependence.

The social processes of exclusion and incorporation of individuals and groups of people are important for the persistence of separate ethnic units. This strong statement has substantial consequences for empirical research of ethnic diversity and sustainability. Primary emphasis is given to the fact that ethnic groups are categories of ascription and identification by the actors themselves. The question of why the ethnic groups persist in this way could be answered by the study not of culture difference, but of processes of interaction among ethnic group members and ethnic boundaries maintenance.

The Barthian statement also has an important message for local politicians and decision-makers concerning the way ethnic diversity is organized. The cultural peculiarities are a secondary product and express interpersonal ties and loyalties among people in family, church organizations, the state, etc. They also express economic and political ties and interests. The collected essays illustrate these processes.

Fredrik Barth supports his statements by empirical study on social organization and boundary maintenance between Pathans in Afghanistan and Pakistan and the Baluch tribes. Harald Eidheim refers to boundary maintenance between the almost assimilated but stigmatized Sami (Lapps) and Norwegians. Gunnar Haaland describes processes between Furs and Baggaras in Western Sudan. Jan-Petter Blom presents his results from the study of peasant communities in Norway; Karl Erik Knutsson from ethnic groups in Southern Ethiopia; Henning Siverts from Southern Mexico; Karl G. Izikowitz from Laos. The collection proves, on the one hand, some universality of the pilot Barthian statement and, on the other hand, the variability of single manifestations of ethnic boundary-creating activities. In social anthropology, *Ethnic Groups and Boundaries* has been one of the most influential books of the last fifty years. The notion of how ethnic diversity is organized and maintained enables us also to understand the social processes involved.

Zdenek Uherek
Institute of Ethnology of the Academy of Sciences of the Czech Republic, Prague, Czech Republic.

Harald Bathelt, Anders Malmberg & Peter Maskell, 2003. "Clusters and Knowledge: Local Buzz, Global Pipelines and the Process of Knowledge Creation", *Progress in Human Geography* 28, 1: 31–49.

Keywords: *clusters, knowledge exchange, local buzz, global pipelines*

This paper is concerned with the spatial clustering of economic activity and its relation to the spatiality of knowledge creation in interactive learning processes. It first questions the view that *tacit knowledge* transfer is confined to local milieus, whereas *codified knowledge* may roam the globe almost unhindered. The paper argues that substantial (transaction) costs are related to obtaining and applying codified knowledge as tacit knowledge, and it subsequently highlights the conditions under which all kinds of knowledge can be exchanged locally and globally. It claims that active interaction is not necessary for knowledge to be exchanged among actors within the cluster, as this is largely automatic.

An essential distinction is made between learning processes taking place among actors by just being in the proximity of each other in the cluster – *buzz* – and the knowledge attained by consciously investing in building channels of communication – *pipelines* – to selected providers located outside the local milieu. It argues finally that the coexistence of high levels of local buzz and many non-local or global pipelines may provide firms located in outward-looking and lively clusters with a string of particular advantages regarding innovation and knowledge creation not available to outsiders. Firms and clusters where the local buzz and the knowledge entering through the global pipelines are successfully combined will be the best-performing firms and clusters.

This paper shows, among other things, how different kinds (diversity) of information are necessary for optimal firm performance with respect to learning and innovation. First of all, knowledge created in a familiar context, usually easier and faster to process at the receiving end, is important for expanding the existing body of knowledge. However, this should be combined with new information or knowledge created in a completely different context, outside the box for the receiving end. It may take longer to grasp this information, but it will lead to new combinations of knowledge, and thus to innovation.

Steven Knotter
IDEA Consult, Brussels, Belgium.

Ulrich Beck, 1992. *Risk Society: Towards a New Modernity*, translated by Mark Ritter (London: Sage Publications), 260 pp.

Keywords: *reflexivity, modernity, risk, sustainability*

Risk Society: Towards a new Modernity deals with two interrelated core issues: reflexive modernization and risk. Beck's thesis is that we are witnessing not the end, but the beginning of modernity – that is, modernity beyond its classical industrial design: "Just as modernisation dissolved the structure of feudal society in the nineteenth century and produced industrial society, modernisation today is dissolving industrial society and modernity is coming into being" (p. 10). He refers to a three-stage periodization: pre-modernity, simple modernity and reflexive modernity. Simple modernity is coextensive with industrial society, reflexive modernity with risk society. The principle of industrial society is the distribution of goods, while risk society is characterized by the production and distribution of dangers. Techno-economic progress is increasingly overshadowed by the production of irreversible risks. Gradually, these risks become globalized: unlike the occupational hazards of the past, they can no longer be limited to certain localities or groups; they create transnational and non-class-specific global hazards.

Reflexive modernization implies modernity radicalized against the categories of the classical industrial setting. After all, the concept of industrial society rests upon a contradiction between the universal principles of modernity – civil rights, equality, functional differentiation – and the exclusive structure of its institutions, in which these principles can partially be realized. Although at a certain level of modernization social agents become more individualized, at the same time modernity itself imposes constraints of a traditional kind due to the semi-religious status of modern science. Its cultural form is scientism, which demands identification of social actors with particular social institutions and their ideologies in rational frames of modern social control. One of the effects of this is the exclusion of reflexivity from the political and social interactions between experts on the one hand and social groups on the other. A reflexive learning process would have recognized the conditions underpinning the scientific conclusions and would have compared these conclusions with different forms of knowledge held by the general public. This reflexive learning process implies negotiation between different epistemologies, different discourses and cultural institutions.

Beck's plea for reflexivity is extremely valuable in relativizing and thereby re-evaluating modernity and modernization. Rather than reverting to a kind of utopian evolutionism typical of simple modernization approaches, he presents a more realistic and balanced view by drawing attention to major dangers that are no longer limited in time and space. Neither does he revert to doom-mongering, pointing out that these threats can be dealt with by becoming more reflexive. An interesting and fruitful thought is his localization of this reflexivity in concrete and specific criticisms of science. He thus links the theme of reflexive modernization to the reflexive learning process. Reflexive modernization tries to reconcile the tension between human indeterminacy and the tendency to objectify and naturalize our institutional and cultural productions. In this respect, he points to a fruitful and important – yet frequently ignored – source of reflexivity: the discourses of non-intellectual lay public groups in risk conflicts.

Selma M. van Londen & Arie de Ruijter
Tilburg University, Faculty of Social and Behavioural Sciences, Tilburg, The Netherlands.

Marino Berengo, 1999. *L'Europa delle città: Il volto della società urbana europea tra medioevo ed Età moderna* (Torino: Einaudi), 1040 pp.

English Translation of the Title: *The Europe of Cities: The Face of European Urban Society between Middle and Modern Age.*

Keywords: *occupational groups, ethnic minorities, religious minorities, border social groups, social control*

Berengo focuses his attention on the pre-industrial town where daily meetings and interactions among individuals were more intense than in the rural areas, and where the forms of organization of collective life were largely and necessarily experimental. The aim of the book is to present the virtually infinite variety of ways through which this happened, analysing some of its aspects. The geographic setting of the work is Western Europe, from Portugal to

Poland, and from the North Sea to the Mediterranean. Its chronological borders are variable and change from the beginning of the twelfth century to the Thirty Years War (1618–48) or to the Westphalia Peaces (1648), depending on the argument at issue. In this long time span, urban space is the privileged seat of public life, sometimes more free and open, sometimes more compressed by the power outside the city. After that period, the regional and national states recognized towns as special places of life and identity.

Rather than examining single towns or their physical configuration, the book deals with urban society in a comparative way. Pre-industrial people who lived in the city, breathed its air and attended its institutions – from corporations to city magistracies and councils – could not be wrong: artisans or burgomasters, priors or jurymen, even servants, all recognized with certainty the reality of the town. Berengo's book is particularly interested in urban typologies (capitals, subject towns) and the relationship between town and countryside; institutions and the government, with special regard to the forms of social distinction and the ruling groups (patricians, nobles); the structure of employment and organizations (guilds, corporations) of artisans and liberal arts; the ethnic, religious and behavioural minorities (*mudejares, moriscos,* Jews, merchant colonies, students); marginality (the poor, vagrants, prostitutes), deviance and the related structures of social control (hospitals, prisons, brothels, courts).

In terms of social diversity and sustainability, the pre-modern city presents some elements of reflection for the contemporary global society. Globalization causes a reduction of power and identification capacity for the national state. This process is parallel to an economic, institutional and cultural polarization between international and supernational spaces, on the one hand, and small homelands, local economies and town governments, on the other. If this is true, then the experience of the pre-industrial city in the integration, control and government of various forms of social diversity in the frame of the urban community becomes relevant once again.

Ercole Sori
Marche Polytechnic University, Department of Social Sciences, Ancona, Italy.

Homi K. Bhabha, 1994. The Location of Culture (New York & London: Routledge), 285 pp.

Keywords: *multiculturalism, post-colonialism, cultural theory, identity theory, postmodernism*

This collection of essays, written over a nine-year period from 1985 and published in 1994, sets forth Homi Bhabha's sustained effort to conceptualize an alternative way of negotiating cultural difference – one that avoids the apparent failings manifest in the way the West has traditionally related to its *other.* In this respect the work is a key text in the corpus of social criticism. Moreover, its celebratory treatment of emergent identities and marginal cultural forms provides a productive resource for diverse cultural practice.

Throughout these densely layered essays the theorist telescopes as problematic the apparently unilinear and monadic understanding with which *alterity* (otherness) has traditionally been approached. Each essay exhibits Bhabha's adept handling of diverse sources – including canonical and anti-canonical literature, performance art, colonial texts, localized historical accounts and contemporary post-colonial and post-structural theory. Such breadth helps to furnish a critique of broad epistemic scope, by showing that this problematically singular way of approaching diversity is both unethical, in its historically contingent complicity with colonialism, and untenable, for such static conceptions of identity have been superseded by models of hybridized and diasporic selves recently emerged from the dark borders of modernity.

Post-colonial critiques of Western mono-culturalism abound: what is useful in *The Location of Culture* is the affirmation of productive cultural practices that accompanies its critique. Proceeding in the critical and ethical tradition of thinkers such as Walter Benjamin, Frederic Jameson, Edward Said and Jacques Derrida, Homi Bhabha adopts what he understands to be an active role in fostering diverse forms of cultural production from the margins. In this regard the texts presented in this volume play, dually, a diagnostic and an obstetric function with respect to the birth of a new orientation towards genuine and complex diversity in the socio-cultural sphere. This dual functionality is effected through textuality: the ability to articulate and genuinely approach hybrid forms of identity is brought forth through the affirmative act of reading, writing and rewriting of texts. Crucial to such textual acts is the notion of liminality: understood both as a principle central to the problematic malfunctioning of nomadic hegemony, and as a notion that orients the excentric position from which post-colonial discourse is articulated.

It is in the foregrounding of a liminal space from whence to enunciate – the border-zone host to the *others* of centuries of colonial violence and disenfranchisement – that Homi Bhabha delivers his most productive and useful contribution to the notion of diversity. In contrast to the static and totalizing tendency of colonial paradigms of ethnography and quasi-scientific anthropology, he offers a way of approaching alterity that is neither unreflective nor reactionary with regard to its engagement with the hybridity, partiality and contingency of identity and culture. And it is in this regard, where Bhabha envisages an alternate space of cultural expression that is at once both ethical and necessary for the cultural survival of migrant and minority identities, that one is most likely to find contributions fruitful to the study of diversity.

Jasper Jack Cooper
Interdisciplinary Centre for Comparative Research in the Social Sciences, Paris, France.

Guido Bolaffi, Raffaele Bracalenti, Peter Braham, & Sandro Gindro (eds.), 2003. *Dictionary of Race, Ethnicity and Culture* (Thousand Oaks, London and New Delhi: Sage Publications), 355 pp.

Keywords: *race, ethnicity, culture*

Race, ethnicity and culture are complex issues of key relevance in multiple disciplines. However, the usage and meaning of terms may vary as disciplines employ unique terminology that takes into consideration factors such as place, culture and time. Expressions and usage or modes of conveying meaning differ from place to place and to some extent mirror the different levels of awareness or sensitivity within a group or society towards key issues. The choices made thus embody local culture, the discipline (when used by scholars), and political and social awareness.

This edited volume, which includes contributions from anthropologists, sociologists, psychologists, lawyers, biologists and philosophers, provides an overview of key issues, concepts and ideas related to race, ethnicity and culture used in Europe and America. Each entry provides a history of the term and its development or etymology, indicates connections with other entries and discusses its current relevance. The volume addresses the contradictory and at times problematic usages of some terms and provides insight and clarity into both common and less frequently used terms. The book also offers extensive indexing and cross-referencing that make it easy to connect related terms and explore a concept or debate in greater depth even at this cursory level.

The volume serves as a valuable tool to students and scholars across disciplines interested in issues of race, ethnicity and culture who are new to the subject or seek a broad understanding of different key terms and concepts. The breadth of the terms and disciplines included ensures that the volume has something of interest for a wide range of scholars, bringing together knowledge that would not otherwise be readily accessible for those focusing on race, ethnicity and culture in their work. This aspect of the volume reflects the increase in multidisciplinary work, the collaboration across disciplines and the sharing of ideas that increasingly characterize the research being carried out in recent years.

Vanja M. K. Stenius
Psychoanalytic Institute for Social Research, Rome, Italy.

George J. Borjas, 2003. "The Labour Demand Curve is Downward Sloping: Re-examining the Impact of Immigration on the Labour Market", *Quarterly Journal of Economics* 118, 4: 1335–1374.

Keywords: *immigration, economic performance, United States Immigration Reform Act, low-skilled wages*

This paper focuses on a single question which is of paramount importance in the labour economics literature as well as for economic policy: Do immigrants harm or improve the employment opportunities of native workers?

This paper develops a new approach to estimating the labour market impact of immigration by exploring the variation in supply shifts across education and experience groups. This approach is in contrast with the local labour market approach and reaches different conclusions about the impact of immigration on the labour market.

The paper uses data drawn from the 1960–90 *USA Census*, as well as the 1998–2001 *Current Population Surveys*, and assumes that workers with the same education but different levels of work experience participating in a national labour market are not perfect substitutes for each other. It turns out that immigration – even within a particular schooling group – is not balanced evenly across all experience cells in that group, and the nature of the supply imbalance changes over time. This fact generates a great deal of variation across those groups and over time, which helps to identify the impact of immigration on the labour market. Most importantly, the size of the native workforce in each of the skill groups is relatively fixed, so that there is less potential for native flows to contaminate the comparison of outcomes across skill groups.

The paper shows evidence that immigration has indeed harmed the employment opportunities of competing native workers. The empirical analysis indicates that immigration lowers the wage of competing workers: a 10 percent increase in supply reduces wages by 3–4 percent. The wage impact differs dramatically across education groups, with the wage falling by 8.9 percent for high-school dropouts, 4.9 percent for college graduates, 2.6 percent for high-school graduates, and barely changing for workers with some college qualifications.

This paper is instructive as an alternative way of assessing immigration impacts on the labour market. The advantage of this approach is that it can potentially reveal the impact of immigration even when the local markets approach cannot because of intercity mobility or trade. However, it lacks a clear counterfactual approach which constitutes probably its main disadvantage.

Inferences from the macro-time-series approach rely on assumptions about trends in factors like the degree of skill bias in recent technological change. Nonetheless, it is an important contribution as it shows how economic research, even when based primarily on real data, can reach debatable conclusions when it makes heavily dubious assumptions.

Carlo Fiorio
Eni Enrico Mattei Foundation and University of Milan, Milan, Italy.

Pierre Bourdieu, 1984. *Distinction: A Social Critique of the Judgment of Taste*, translated by Richard Nice (Cambridge, MA: Harvard University Press), 613 pp.

Keywords: *class, cultural taste, distinction, diversity*

Bourdieu analyses the processes by which the making of cultural distinctions articulates and legitimizes forms of power and control rooted in economic inequalities. Distinction is generated by learned patterns of cultural consumption which are internalized as natural cultural tastes and used to justify forms of social domination. As such, taste is a deeply ideological category: it functions as a marker of class in the double sense of a socio-economic category and of a particular level of quality. The cultural tastes of dominant groups are given institutional form, and subsequently their taste for this institutionalized culture is held up as evidence of their cultural and, ultimately, social superiority. What is cultural (i.e. acquired) is presented as natural (i.e. innate) and, in turn, is used to justify existing social relations. In this way, art and cultural consumption fulfil the social function of legitimizing social differences, social exclusion and social hierarchy.

Bourdieu calls the operation of such distinctions the *ideology of natural taste*: the view that genuine appreciation can only be attained by an instinctively gifted minority armed against the mediocrity of the masses. In particular, the distinction between high (official) culture and popular culture is important. In this context, popular culture is seen as inferior, as a residual category, left over after high culture has been defined. The historical creation of a unique space for Culture with a capital C, above and beyond the social, for Bourdieu serves the purpose, or at least has the consequence, of reinforcing and legitimizing class power as cultural and aesthetic difference. Obviously, the meaning of *Distinction* does not lie in proving the self-evident notion that different classes do not have different lifestyles and different tastes in culture, nor does it lie in Bourdieu's claim that culture is used as a weapon in the struggle for access to and exploitation of scarce resources. This is nothing new, let alone revolutionary.

The relevance of *Distinction* for research lies in the emphasis, among the dominant classes, on the distinction between those with high economic capital and those with high cultural capital. Bourdieu has thus drawn attention to the perpetual struggle of those with high cultural capital to raise the social value of the competences involved. It is for this reason that they will always put up resistance as (a part of) society advocates and moves towards cultural democracy. One of the consequences of this, as Bourdieu observes, is that "aesthetic intolerance can be terribly violent . . . the most intolerable thing for those who regard themselves as the possessors of legitimate culture is the sacrilegious reuniting of tastes which taste dictates shall be separated . . . At stake in every struggle over art there is also the imposition of an art of living" (p. 57).

Selma M. van Londen & Arie de Ruijter
Tilburg University Faculty of Social and Behavioural Sciences, Tilburg, The Netherlands.

John Breuilly, 1995. *Il nazionalismo e lo stato*, translated by Umberto Livini (Bologna: Il Mulino), 524 pp.

English Translation of the Title: *Nationalism and the State.*

Keywords: *nationalism, nation, political history, religions, ethnicity*

Breuilly analyses the origins and historical developments of nationalism and of the movements inspired by it with special attention to Europe, but enlarges his investigation also to other continents, in particular Asia. The main characteristic of his approach is that nationalism is not considered in the frame of the research of any national identity, or of the defence of any class interest or particular social economic equilibrium, but is assumed as one of the most relevant political forms of early modern and contemporary history, strictly connected to the emergence of the state. The book is divided in three parts. The first outlines the social and ideological bases of nationalism. The second and third deal with different case studies analysed on the basis of the types (official, ethnic, social nationalism) and the roles (unification, independence, reform) played by some of the major nationalistic movements of the nineteenth and twentieth centuries.

Breuilly stresses how nationalism, in its different forms and historical embodiments, makes one of its major characteristics social and cultural diversity. The various main nationalisms of Western and Asiatic history are based generally on three principles, determining the ideal borders of the nation and so deciding who is inside it and who is not: (a) the principle of the uniqueness of the national community, (b) the principle of the right of the nation to have its own state, and (c) the principle of the nation as a corps of citizens. Through such a conception of the nation, nationalism has stated its right to existence, using history, ethnic elements, language and religion to select the members of any national community. This inclusion/exclusion mechanism led also to the political and human aberrations (genocides, wars, etc.) of the nineteenth and, all the more, of the twentieth century. In this sense, Breuilly's work provides useful analytical instruments to deal with social and cultural diversity and its sustainability in contemporary history.

Roberto Giulianelli
Marche Polytechnic University, Department of Social Sciences, Ancona, Italy.

Wendy Brown, 2006. *Regulating Aversion: Tolerance in the Age of Identity and Empire* (Princeton and Oxford: Princeton University Press), 268 pp.

Keywords: *toleration, identity, citizenship*

Brown opens the book asking, "How did tolerance become a beacon of multi-cultural justice and civic peace at the turn of the twenty-first century?" (p. 1). Introduced in the West as a virtue, tolerance is supposed to diffuse tension and decrease conflict across divides. Yet, as the author shows, tolerance assumes abjection of the tolerated and a position of superiority on the part of the tolerant party. Confronting the uncritical use of this term to advocate diversity, she explores the aspects of depoliticization, power, governmentality, equality and naturalization of difference included in the term and its practice. While used to depoliticize, the discourse of tolerance is conveniently used to "enshrine that which cancels" (p. 34), to mark "inassimilability to a hypostasised universal" (p. 71), or to "legitimate the state in late modernity" (p. 103).

The author points to the use of tolerance in different ways depending on what is at stake. In a careful analysis of the Simon Wiesenthal Centre Museum of Tolerance in Los Angeles, she shows how the exhibits use a universal call for tolerance "to stage a political position while appearing to promulgate only unimpeachably good values" (p. 148). At root are the divisions between *we* the civilized West and *they* the barbarian *Other* and "tolerance as a civilisational discourse" (p. 202). Although condemning the assumptions of tolerance and its use in particular struggles of the tolerated, the book closes on a positive note, calling for a pairing of the discourse of tolerance "with a language of power, social forces, and justice" (p. 204).

I found this analysis very powerful in its disclosure of the paternalistic and manipulative nature of tolerance and, for our case, the ways in which it is used to maintain unequal diversity. I wish, however, that the author had expanded on her call at the end for a form of tolerance based on justice and the struggle for equality. We might go down the easy route of accepting that tolerance is better than nothing. At the same time, however, the book does not seem to agree with such a minimalist solution that would ultimately serve the very purpose she despises.

John J. Betancur
University of Illinois at Chicago, Department of Urban Planning and Policy, Chicago, USA.

Luigi Campiglio & Raul Caruso, 2007. "Where Economics has been headed? Multiple Identities and Diversity on Economic Literature. Evidence from Top Journals over the Period 2000–2006", *Institute of Economic Policy*, Munich Personal Research Papers in Economics (RePEc) Archive (MPRA) Paper No. 6797: 1–19.

Keywords: *diversity in economic literature, multiple identities, richness*

The article firstly applies to the concept of diversity, extensively used in biological, ecological and information sciences, to analyse economists' work between 2000 and 2006. On the one hand, the main goal of the research is to describe the evolution of economic literature. We pay special attention to generalist journals like the *American Economic Review, Econometrical, Journal of Political Economics, Quarterly Journal of Economics*, etc., which are committed to publishing top-quality contributions from all fields of economics and which have significant impact on different subdisciplines within economies.

Diversity in economic literature is measured on the basis of sample journals and the entire Econlit database. Among them, *Journal of Economic Perspectives* (JEP) is the most diverse, because it examines several goals in economic research and analysis, and it offers its readers an accessible source for state-of-the-art economic thinking. The key idea of the article is that all published economic journals have multiple identities, captured by *Journal of Economic Literature* (JEL) codes. The idea of multiple *identities* is similar to the concept of named goods. The latter represents a good owned by an agent which can be distinguished from the same good when it is owned by a different agent. In economics, every article becomes a different good under a different JEL code. That means that every article retains multiple identities, which contribute to the variety and richness of economic literature.

I believe this is a very useful article because it reveals the diversity in economic literature. Every article has multiple identities and different aspects which are captured in the JEL code. The code acts as a measure of diversity in the field of economics. Special attention is paid to the best-known journals, which have published articles making a special contribution to the economic sciences.

Evgenia Vladimirova-Krasteva
Economic and Investment Bank (part of KBC Group), Sofia, Bulgaria.

David Card, 2005. "Is the New Immigration Really so Bad?", *National Bureau of Economic Research* (NBER) Working Paper 11547 (August): 1–44.

Keywords: *immigration, economic performance, United States Immigration Reform Act, integration, low-skilled workers competition*

This article, focusing on the USA, deals with the effects on the labour market of main immigration waves in the last century. Interestingly, it shows that economists' perceptions of USA immigrants based on empirical data analysis have shifted from mainly positive in the 1970s to rather negative more recently. Early research, looking at immigration at the beginning of the twentieth century, found that immigrant men earned as much as natives, despite having less education, and concluded that investments in on-the-job training made up for the gap in formal schooling. The shift in perceptions has closely tracked changes in the national origin of immigrants to the USA, often attributed to the 1965 Immigration Reform Act, and a widening gap between the language and culture of natives and immigrants. Concerns over immigration have also been heightened by the decline in low-skilled wages in the USA and the belief that some of this may be due to immigrant competition.

This article reviews the most recent results on USA immigration, and asks two key questions: Does immigration reduce the labour market opportunities of less skilled natives? Have immigrants who arrived after the 1965 Immigration Reform Act been successfully assimilated? Overall, evidence that immigrants have harmed the opportunities of less educated natives is scant. On the question of assimilation, the success of the USA-born children of immigrants is a key yardstick. By this measure, post-1965 immigrants are doing reasonably well. Even children of the least educated immigrant origin groups have closed most of the education gap with the children of natives.

This paper is important as it shows that a careful research design is crucial for driving results which might have strong policy implications, as in the case of immigration policies. It is approachable to non-specialized readers as it describes basic descriptive statistics and shows the educational composition of recent and less recent immigration in the USA. The discussion about the two main approaches used in economics for estimating the impact of immigration on native workers is instructive: the first is the local labour market approach, which relates differences in the relative structure of wages in different local labour markets to differences in the relative supply of immigrants; the second is a time series approach, relating changes over time in immigrant densities to economy-wide measures of relative labour market outcomes.

This paper stimulates thinking not only about immigrant earnings, but also about immigrants' education and assimilation in hosting societies. While, according to past evidence, few of the 40 percent of immigrants to the USA with low schooling will catch up with average earnings of natives, most of their USA-born children will do so, showing the strong intergenerational progress of immigrants' children. An inclusive society that allows immigrants' children to acquire education to the levels of natives' children is a key element in the sustainable development of that society. Lessons from the USA literature provide potentially valuable lessons to researchers in other contexts.

Carlo Fiorio
Eni Enrico Mattei Foundation and University of Milan, Milan, Italy.

Stacy Churchill, 1986. *The Education of Linguistic and Cultural Minorities in the OECD Countries* (Clevedon: Multilingual Matters), 175 pp.

Keywords: *linguistic minorities, education, policy*

This publication contains the outcomes of an in-depth analysis of central governments' policies vis-à-vis the teaching of minority languages inside the educational system of member states of the OECD (Organization for Economic Cooperation and Development). Churchill provides a very challenging comparative analysis in which he develops several categorizations, typologies and continua that have influenced many researchers. In the context of these efforts to preserve and promote minority languages, education is perceived as a field of paramount importance. The perspective of the Churchill study takes the political aspect as its starting point. The policies that have been developed for the education of linguistic and cultural minorities in the member states of the OECD are the object of investigation. He includes a large range of linguistic minorities, divided into three main groups: (1) *indigenous peoples* such as the Sami, the Australian aboriginals and the Maori; (2) *established minorities* such as the Catalans, Bretons and the Canadian Francophones; (3) *new minorities*, covering groups perceived to have migrated recently to their current place of residence.

The main goal of his study is a review of the different types of policy instruments available for the education of linguistic minorities, and the consequences of the choice of different instruments. He claims that, "The minority issue is so powerful, emotionally and socially, that the policy-making ground-rules are transformed; the present study opens up entirely new perspectives of policy-development" (p. 21). Churchill's study is a significant contribution to existing knowledge in the area of problems of minority languages.

The book is not just a synthesis of information gathered in over thirty case studies. Churchill takes us one step further as he has developed a coherent framework for the analysis of policy development for minority education. The theoretical framework which he proposes is consistent and worthwhile. His approach has stood the test of time and is still worth reading, although the data for most cases have long become outdated.

Durk Gorter
University of the Basque Country, Donostia-San Sebastián, Spain.

Simone Cinotto, 2001. *Una famiglia che mangia insieme: Cibo ed etnicità nella comunità italoamericana di New York, 1920–1940* (Torino: Otto Editore), 458 pp.

English Translation of the title: *A Family That Eats Together. Food and Ethnicity in the New York Italo-American Community, 1920–1940.*

Keywords: *migration, ethnicity, integration, family, entrepreneurship*

Through a case study of the Italo-American community in New York in the 1920s–1930s, the book analyses the social and economic origins of the role played by food, eating practices and related rituals in the origin of the collective identity of Italians in the USA. Cinotto shows how food culture, as a symbol of ethnic membership, satisfies specific necessities of life, respectability and visibility of the new Americans coming from Italy. The Italian community in New York is analysed in a moment of transition, after the end of the big immigration flow caused by the Quota Act in the mid-1920s. In that phase, there was a growing separation between the alien immigrant generation and the native Italo-Americans. Instead of remaining in the cultural limits of the old world, the ethnic Italo-American cuisine appeared as a result of hybridization and the selective incorporation of elements, resources and meanings coming out of the American experience and assuming its own characteristics of unity and tradition.

The issues presented by the author include the role of food in building up a peculiar Italo-American ideology of home, family and community; the plot of interests based on the significant Italo-American presence in the food market and the role of entrepreneurs in promoting ethnicity; and the invention of the Italian restaurant as place of narration and *mise en scène* of a popular Italian image. The whole story has largely been told using the words of the immigrants and their offspring. Cinotto's food history is therefore a sort of prism through which it is possible to observe the process of Americanization of two generations of immigrants. Adopting a viewpoint between history and anthropology, he takes an interesting look at several aspects of everyday life, town and historical transformation.

As to the questions of diversity and sustainability, the book influenced the researchers in Ancona concerning the issue of ethnic entrepreneurship, showing that the process of migrant integration does not produce total deprivation of the original cultural habits, but a sort of creative hybridization which has a role of intermediation among the different generations, and between the ethnic community and the indigenous society. The hybrid born out of these processes can represent an economic resource for entrepreneurial activities and paths of social promotion. It can be supposed that at the root of the recent success of Italian food, in all its various versions such as "traditional", "Slow food" and "quality", the experience of Italian migrant communities has a role.

Ercole Sori
Marche Polytechnic University, Department of Social Sciences, Ancona, Italy.

Centro de Investigación y Promoción del Campesinado (CIPCA), 1991. Por una Bolivia diferente: Aportes para un proyecto histórico popular (La Paz: CIPCA), 261 pp.

English Translation of the Title: *For a Different Bolivia: Contributions for a Popular Historical Project.*

Keywords: *society, rural communities, indigenous communities, rural development, territorial organization*

This is a collective book that systematizes and debates for the first time in Bolivia an alternative proposal of state and society stated from the perspective of the indigenous people who make up the majority of its population. The first part (pp. 17–74) presents a proposal made up by CIPCA's team, after two years of workshops with a number of indigenous groups and leaders on issues such as Bolivia as a pluri-national state, food security, territory for indigenous people, socialism and capitalism, intercultural bilingual education and popular media. The second part (pp. 75–149) synthesizes the discussions and comments of thirty-two persons all deeply engaged with and knowledgable about those issues. The last section compiles a number of documents and maps regarding some of the specific topics.

All of this was born from developments occurring in the country during the last two decades. Published before the Popular Participation Law (1994) that decentralized the distribution of resources and decision-making at the municipal level, this work has had a strong impact on peasant and indigenous social organizations, as well as on institutions that work in rural development and political parties concerned with the well-being of rural communities. In fact this book was a landmark in the process of drafting, from a bottom-up approach, overall policies for inclusion of peasant and indigenous sectors. A number of crucial topics which are now at the centre of public debate about the process of change in Bolivia – such as land tenure, social and political participation, local management of the territory and type of state (pluri-national) – were already stated in this document in 1991.

Within the current context, when the challenge of building a more inclusive and democratic society in Bolivia is moving from the *mestizo-criollo* élites to indigenous and peasant sectors now in power, a reading of this text is necessary for two reasons: first, because of its anticipation of processes currently under way; and second, because of a sense of recovery of a country's visions stated by indigenous and peasant sectors, at that time in a subordinate position. So its reading in this context could provide indigenous and peasant sectors with a way of bringing together both bottom-up and top-down thinking and acting.

The methodology of drafting this collective document expresses an array of visions from different social and intellectual sectors in Bolivia, and as such it is an interesting example of how to combine research and action to state alternative proposals of state and society from the perspective of groups excluded from political decision-making. In this sense, the book is an interesting example of action-research in developing contexts like Bolivia, where research faces the challenge not only of understanding cultural diversity, but also of putting forward proposals of cultural inclusion for excluded majorities.

José Fernando Galindo-Cespedes
Centre for Research and Promotion of Peasantry, Cochabamba, Bolivia.

Stanley Cohen, 1972. *Folk Devils and Moral Panics: The Creation of the Mods and Rockers* (Oxford: Martin Roberston), 224 pp.

Keywords: *folk devils, moral panics, moral entrepreneurs, subcultures, grounded theory*

Cohen's classic study of the Mods and the Rockers in 1960s Britain both presents us with a brilliant study of grounded theory and provides us with the concept of moral panics. Originally published in 1972, the work explores how the media and moral entrepreneurs focus on a particular issue or group of persons, labelling them as representing a threat to societal values. Cohen refers to the group thus labelled as *folk devils*; they are essentially vilified scapegoats for real or perceived social ills.

As originally conceptualized by Cohen, moral panics are characterized by five key indicators: a heightened level of *concern* in regard to the perceived threat; *hostility* towards the group seen engaging in the behaviour; *consensus* or agreement within society as to the nature of the threat; *disproportion* in that the threat or menace is perceived as being greater than it actually is; and finally *volatility* in that moral panics, by definition, erupt suddenly. Moral panics and the creation of folk devils are not limited to any specific group or threat. The term has been used – both correctly and incorrectly – to define various phenomena over the past thirty-odd years. As such, Cohen's thinking has encouraged scholars and researchers to consider old and new events in the light of generated differences in the sense that the media, policy-makers and the community have defined the menace and the characteristics of the responsible group or persons. Cohen has encouraged generations of scholars to explore crime, delinquency, social disorder and other potential threats as constructions in which differences are amplified and exaggerated. In such cases the actual distinctions between groups or individuals lose their relevance, whereas imagined differences and the imagined threat determine societal response.

The vilification of a folk devil becomes the order of the day and justifies reactions that potentially do more public harm than good. Cohen's work encourages us to reconsider the creation of different groups, of *us* versus *them*, in the light of social processes that tend to exaggerate or distort differences and draw distinctions that otherwise might not exist.

Vanja M. K. Stenius
Psychoanalytic Institute for Social Research, Rome, Italy.

Amelie Constant, Liliya Gataullina & Klaus F. Zimmermann, 2006. "Ethnosizing Immigrants", *Institute for the Study of Labor* (IZA) Discussion Paper No. 2040 (Bonn): 1–22.

Keywords: *ethnicity, ethnic identity, acculturation, migrant assimilation, migrant integration*

This article provides a new type of measurement of the ethnic identity of immigrants and explores its evolution in the host country. The *ethnosizer* is a measure of the intensity of a person's ethnic identity, constructed from information on the following elements: language, culture, societal interaction, history of migration and ethnic self-identification. The paper examines a two-dimensional concept of the ethnosizer, giving immigrants four classifications: integration, assimilation, separation and marginalization.

The findings of this paper indicate that females, Muslims, those with schooling in the home country and those of older age at the time of entry have the most persistent ethnic identity, while young immigrants are most assimilated or integrated. The article investigates migrant ethnicity and the evolution of ethnic identity in Germany. The most interesting part of this work is that the authors have tested their model using empirical analysis; they have conducted a survey addressing 1,400 immigrants, excluding the German-born and focusing on the effects of adjustment among first-generation immigrants.

The ethnosizer is tested in a two-dimensional model distinguishing between integration, assimilation, separation and marginalization of migrant ethnic identity. Using data from the German Socio-Economic Panel, the various measures are calibrated and their relationship to age, age of entry, religion, educational level and ethnic origin are investigated. This article, testing the proposed ethnosizer (one- and two-dimensional) models against empirical research, provides insight on *ethnic identity* and *ethnicity*, assuming that both these notions become meaningful after migration.

The article is focused on immigrant populations in Germany and mainly first-generation immigrants, and the findings indicate differences that may exist in the perception of ethnic identity between immigrants. The aspects explored include the sex of immigrants, their religious beliefs (especially focusing on the differences between Muslims and Christians), and completed and incomplete schooling received in the home country. The conclusions from this research indicate that females are more apart from the native German ethnicity than males and this is caused by a low attachment concerning language use and cultural aspects. Catholics adapt more readily to the ethnicity of the host country; Muslims, on the other hand, adjust less readily.

Tonia Damvakeraki
National and Kapodistrian University of Athens, Athens, Greece.

Davina Cooper, 2004. *Challenging Diversity: Rethinking Equality and the Value of Difference* (Cambridge and New York: Cambridge University Press), 235 pp.

Keywords: *values, collective identity, inequality, power, social pluralism*

Centring on the ways in which values exist and operate and how these dynamics relate to "maintenance and contestation of inequality" (p. 5), this book examines the relationship between equality and diversity, specifically how we recognize something as a social relation of disadvantage and oppression, how equality applies to those in charge, and how it intersects with values such as freedom. To carry this analysis out, the author uses three examples illustrating the politics of diversity: stigmatization of smokers, disputes over the establishment of eruvs that allow Jews to carry out the Sabbath outside their homes, and same-sex marriage.

In inviting *us* to affirm difference, argues Cooper, the politics of diversity fails to define relations of inequality and ways of determining the legitimacy of claims of disadvantage. She then proposes a conceptualization of politics including structural asymmetries of power, how they circulate through the values they are attached to and how principles of inequality relate to social dynamics such as capitalism. Based on these insights, the last chapters of the book focus on how to undo inequality. Cooper sees the need to accord privilege to the establishment of new practices that can be routinized to the point of turning them into common sense.

This is a unique approach to the issue of diversity because it ties up analysis and implications, specifically practical ways to advance the cause of equality. I also found it unique in that it addresses the question of the legitimacy of diversity claims. Are all diversities equal? Are all claims of disadvantage and oppression legitimate? What is the best way of dealing with "groups whose desires, choices or identities are perceived as socially harmful" (p. 4)? Along with the three examples of the politics of diversity which Cooper cites, practical dilemmas abound. What of the good liberal who wants to be tolerant of other cultures, but cannot stomach everything they do or believe (women's rights, female circumcision, forced marriage, etc. are frequent areas of contestation)? Remember also the dilemma of the right of exit: governments may protect the rights of a minority group, but what of the minority group member as an individual – the one who doesn't want to follow the rules, to stay in?

John J. Betancur
University of Illinois at Chicago, Department of Urban Planning and Policy, Chicago, USA.

Jonathan Coppel, Jean-Christophe Dumont & Ignazio Visco, 2001. "Trends in Immigration and Economic Consequences", *Organisation for Economic Co-operation and Development* (OECD) Economics Department Working Paper No. 284: 1–32.

Keywords: *migration, ageing, labour markets, development*

This paper reviews immigration trends and their economic impacts in a number of OECD countries. While migration systems present similarities across countries, institutional arrangements vary widely and impact on the size and composition of migration flows. Some of the main factors driving immigration are briefly discussed. The paper also considers the economic, fiscal and social implications of immigration. It is suggested that immigration can confer small net gains to the host country. However, the benefits are not necessarily evenly distributed and some groups – in particular those whose labour is substitutable with immigrants – may lose, calling for a smooth working of labour and product markets in OECD countries.

The paper also claims that, while migration can partly offset slower-growing or declining OECD populations, it cannot by itself provide a solution to the budgetary implications of ageing populations. Finally, the authors touch on some development issues, such as the potential gains from emigration in source countries and the role that host/destination countries can play in reducing immigration pressures through more open markets and greater transfers of technology.

Apart from reviewing recent trends in international migration, there are further insights into the impacts of immigration on four very important themes linked to migration and diversity of migrant populations in OECD countries. More specifically, the research of this paper presents (1) the consequences of immigration for labour market performance and the role that immigration can play in easing skilled labour shortages in specific sectors; (2) the budgetary impacts of immigration; (3) the extent to which immigration is the answer to the ageing and declining OECD countries' populations; (4) the potential consequences of migration on economic development in the country of origin.

Overall, this paper presents a number of diversity aspects found in the migrant populations, but also explains the potential effects that they might have in the general development of the host country in terms of labour market performance, education and skills levels as well as social aspects such as ageing, skills shortage and brain-drain.

Lena Tsipouri
National and Kapodistrian University of Athens, Athens, Greece.

Patricia Cortes, 2008. "The Effect of Low-Skilled Immigration on U.S. Prices: Evidence from CPI Data", *Journal of Political Economy* 116, 3: 381–422.

Keywords: *immigration, native and immigrant workers substitution rates, low-skilled wages*

This paper contributes to the immigration literature by estimating the impact of low-skilled immigration on prices, wages and the purchasing power of natives. It exploits the large variation across USA cities and through time in the relative size of the low-skilled immigrant population to estimate the causal effect of immigration on prices of non-traded goods and services.

By using appropriate econometric techniques, it shows that, at current immigration levels, a 10 percent increase in the share of low-skilled immigrants in the labour force decreases the price of immigrant-intensive services, such as housekeeping and gardening, by 2 percent. A simple theoretical model and some wage estimates suggest that wages are a likely channel through which these effects take place. However, wage effects are significantly larger for low-skilled immigrants than for the median low-skilled native, implying that the two are imperfect substitutes. Estimation results, based on USA data from the consumer price index, imply that the low-skilled immigration wave of the period 1980–2000 increased the purchasing power of high-skilled workers living in the thirty largest cities by an average of 0.32 percent, and decreased the purchasing power of the typical native high-school dropout by a maximum of 1 percent and that of Hispanic low-skilled natives by 4.2 percent. The author concludes that, through lower prices, low-skilled immigration brings positive net benefits to the USA economy as a whole, but generates a redistribution of wealth.

This paper is an innovative piece of research as it looks at the gains that immigration brings to the native population, focusing in particular on prices, which very few authors have addressed before. The study of the benefits from immigration is important because the contrast between benefits and costs informs decisions about immigration policy. Because of the focus on city-level outcomes, this paper only looked at prices of non-traded goods and services. However, low-skilled immigration is also likely to have effects on the prices of traded goods, but these will occur at an aggregate, national level. This paper inspires some theoretical and empirical exploration of this issue in order to have a broader assessment of the effects of low-skilled immigration.

Carlo Fiorio
Eni Enrico Mattei Foundation and University of Milan, Milan, Italy.

Florian Coulmas (ed.), 1991. *A Language Policy for the European Community: Prospects and Quandries* (Berlin: Mouton de Gruyter), 311 pp.

Keywords: *European Community, language policy, multilingualism, national languages, minority languages*

This collection of sixteen articles edited by Florian Coulmas is an important contribution to the thinking and reflection about the language problems and challenges at the level of the European Community (now European Union, EU) as a whole, the member states, and some of the regions in Europe. It can be considered the first ever holistic publication on the subject of language policy for the EU. The contributions deal with multilingualism in the meetings at European level, along with legal aspects and the language policies of member states. Ample attention is also given to linguistic diversity in regard to regional as well as immigrant minority languages. The opening chapter by Coulmas contains important reflections on national languages, language use inside European institutions, language education for European citizens and the protection of minority languages. It provides an historical overview and uses economic cost-benefit analysis to explain those developments.

The book is an early effort at analysing what happens in the EU in regard to linguistic diversity, multilingualism and language policy. Its relevance has become clearer over the years as the interest and importance given to the development of language policy has grown, at the level of Europe itself, as well as in the member states and the regions. Today the EU has a commissioner and a directorate that deals with multilingualism; its policy in the area of languages has developed accordingly.

This publication has been an important inspiration for my own work in understanding the value of language diversity. The book has done good work as a catalyst for policy-makers, and has helped to strengthen and enrich policies for a truly sustainable diversity of all languages in Europe. After sixteen years the same publisher produced a follow-up to the original collection. See G. Extra & D. Gorter (2008), *Multilingual Europe: Facts and Policies.*

Durk Gorter
University of the Basque Country, Donostia-San Sebastián, Spain.

Norbert Cyrus, 2005. "Active Civic Participation of Immigrants in Germany", Country Report prepared for the *European research project POLITIS*, Oldenburg, pp. 1–75.

Keywords: *civic participation*

Civic participation of immigrants is a relevant issue in the general debate on immigration and integration in Germany. Several studies – some of them commissioned by public authorities – examine aspects of civic participation. The main focus here is on the impact of immigrant associations on integration. The research field, however, does not involve all immigrants – that would include ethnic Germans – but only foreign nationals. By this focus, naturalized immigrants are omitted while foreign nationals born in Germany are included. Accordingly, in order to get information on active civic participation of immigrants, the research findings require a closer re-evaluation.

The current article attempts a better understanding of the conditions for immigrant civic participation, focusing on the demographic developments and key events that shaped the composition and social situation of the present immigrant population. Furthermore, the study depicts the immigration and integration policy that provides the framework for immigrants' participation. The level of participation of immigrants in civic organizations and associations is assessed, and the dispute over negative and positive impacts of participation is recapitulated. Overall, the study provides significant information and data concerning major immigrant groups from non-EU countries, their residence status, migration and migrant policy, legal framework and institutional setting for immigrant participation. There is specific focus on aspects regarding basic citizens' rights, voting rights, participation in political parties, representation in local decision-making, membership in German associations, representation in workers' councils and the right to assemble and establish associations. The author provides significant insights with regard to the reasons or expectations leading immigrants to active engagement in civic organizations or associations in the host country, and also on specific ethnic group behaviours.

Tonia Damvakeraki
National and Kapodistrian University of Athens, Athens, Greece.

Antonia Darder & Rodolfo D. Torres, 2004. *After Race: Racism after Multiculturalism* (New York: New York Academic Press), 189 pp.

Keywords: *race, racism, intersectionality, capitalism*

After Race seeks to explain why a change of perspective in the debate on race and racism is needed. According to this book, skin colour should not continue to be central in such a debate. In spite of that, the authors don't reject the centrality of race as an ideology, or the role of racism as a "powerful, structuring and hegemonic force" (p. 2). Moving away from a colour-centred race approach, they argue that the white/black paradigm is only a limited aspect of a broader social phenomenon which can lead to further research challenges. Both the theory that biological races do not exist and the theory that the concept of race is socially and culturally constructed need to be overcome in such a way that multiple racisms can be addressed. We should note that this text distances itself from the Critical Race Theory and the intersectionality argument incorporated in it, which presents the idea of class as merely one of a number of grounds overlapping each other and multiplying inequalities.

The book maintains that the significance of racism in the capitalist USA society cannot be understood without an underlying comprehension of class inequality. It raises many provocative issues, among which is a criticism of the widespread separation between politics and economy in the race debate. Even if the book deals with a rethinking of race in USA society, it provides readers with a fresh view on the race debate over the last decades and proposes new approaches available overseas as well. Written by different scholars, this book provides the reader with a polyphonic and critical reflection. Even if its content can be better appreciated while bearing in mind the liberal approach to diversity, the ongoing debate on multiculturalism and the studies on intersectionality within the Critical Race Theory, I recommend this book to everyone who wishes to acquire a critical understanding of racism.

Barbara Giovanna Bello
State University of Milan, Cesare Beccaria Department of Law, Milan, Italy.

Oswald De Andrade, 2008. "The Cannibal Manifesto", translated by Leslie Bary, *Latin American Review* 14, 27: 35–47, **&**
Jean Baudrillard, 2008. *Carnaval et cannibale: Suivi de Le Mal ventriloque* (Paris: Herne), 98 pp.

Keywords: *cannibalism, Baudrillard, globalism, resistance, appropriation*

In 1928, the Brazilian modernist poet Oswaldo de Andrade composed *The Cannibal Manifesto* in which he ironically claimed, "Tupi [cannibalistic Indians of Brazil] or not Tupi that is the question . . . I am only interested in what's not mine, the law of men, the law of the cannibal." Andrade's manifesto was a radical attempt simultaneously to reaffirm the power of native Brazilian traditions and to propose an anti-colonial paradigm insisting that Brazilians *eat the colonist* and their socio-cultural capital, taking what they need and spitting out what is toxic. Andrade formulates a dialectical strategy of resistance which inverts the poles of the virile colonist and the docile natives, one which asks that the primitive ingest the technology and advances of the modern as a means of overcoming the colonial binary itself. For Andrade, only cannibalism unites us – socially, economically, philosophically. Cannibalism is counter-assimilation and a politics of primitive metabolism, which would revel in its savage past and combine native materials with the worldview and scientism of colonial forces. Hence the new modern Brazilian primitivist had the right codification of vengeance for transforming taboo into totem, and it was only in normalizing the taboo that a rich cosmopolitan mosaic culture could be imagined.

As early as 1928, Andrade and what would become the Brazilian *Anthropophagic movement* were envisioning a utopian form of global cosmopolitanism where the oppressed, empowered by their own savagery, could appropriate the models of the colonist by eating him and thus forge a series of hybrid identities that were Olympian in their scope and singular in their constitution. However, such a utopian vision would soon itself be eaten by the monolith of the global itself.

Recently, Jean Baudrillard returned to the politics of *anthropophagi* in his essay "Carnival and Cannibal", where he opposes cannibalistic counter-appropriation to the carnival of the global. *Carnivalization,* as a process, is the exportation of the religious, technical, economic and political values of the Occident throughout the world, one that proceeds by way of an immense farce and transforms the globe into a space of pure masquerade and simulation. In the play of carnival and cannibal, neither term prevails. The Occident, according to Baudrillard, carnivalizes itself by creating its own global museum of parodies of every culture. Moreover, the cannibal does not create a singularity, but is whitened and absorbed into the carnival itself, in an immense anthropological derailment where every species loses itself in the masquerade.

In the homogenizing of difference in the global carnival there no longer exists the *agôn* of power and counter-power, but rather only the interminable play of appearances which are at once "cultural" and absorbed into the mass simulation of roots and authenticity. In other words, it is the demiurge of global that ingests all identity and spits it back out in a simulated and already metabolized form. Cannibalism thus remains a powerful metaphor for reflection on diversity as both a site of resistance and a space of banal heterogeneity that conspires with the carnival.

S. Romi Mukherjee
Interdisciplinary Centre for Comparative Research in the Social Sciences, Paris, France.

Edward De Bono, 2000. *Six Thinking Hats* (London: Penguin), 175 pp.

Keywords: *method, lateral thinking, emotions, constructive thinking, creativity*

De Bono's book is not directly related to diversity as such, but to the concept that thinking is a human resource which needs to be improved through proper methodologies. In particular the author suggests a very simple and useful tool to clear possible confusion between emotions and logic, creativity and information: the six hats method. These hats are mental hooks which define different ways of thinking and bring a contribution to the whole thinking. Each of them has a different colour: white, red, black, yellow, green and blue. Each chapter of the book gives a summary of each thinking hat. Since its development, this method has been used across ages and cultures. It is very suitable as part of intercultural training in order to awaken participants' awareness about cross-cultural or multicultural situations.

How is this book linked with the diversity issue? Through this method people learn to wear each hat strategically in a problem-solving perspective and to work constructively with others who have different points of view, different cultures, diverging working attitudes and styles. I personally became inspired in my work as trainer in international training programmes. Participants are usually fascinated by this user-friendly tool and enjoy using hats as symbols which indicate roles. Sometimes the use of real hats or coloured paper hats can help the learning process. In a way the idea of different hats underlines the value of diversity among people. Diversity in thinking (different hats) can enhance creativity and innovative solutions. Through this book, people with different cultural, educational, scientific and business backgrounds can learn to bring different frames of reference to a problem and find a better understanding. The book includes practical examples, together with tips for implementation. This is a handy resource for everyone who is interested in exploring conflict resolution strategies, as well as gaining new ideas for training activities.

Barbara Giovanna Bello
State University of Milan, Cesare Beccaria Department of Law, Milan, Italy.

Antoine De Saint-Exupery, 1997. *The Little Prince* (Great Britain: Mammoth), 78 pp.

Keywords: *worldview, mindfulness, education, cultural bias*

"It is only with the heart that one can see rightly; what is essential is invisible to the eye" (p. 68). *The Little Prince* is a book about a child's view of the world as he travels through different planets where he meets a fox, a snake, a rose and several adult characters. It is narrated in the first and third voice, which creates a shift between the world as seen by the child, and the child as seen by the adult. This duality makes *The Little Prince* what is usually described as a children's book for adults.

The story recounts the encounter of the author with a young prince in the Sahara. The boy's curiosity about the world and his views of life and human nature are both simple and profound. *The Little Prince* gives the reader a lesson on the simplicity of life as seen through the unbiased and pure heart of a child. *The Little Prince* claims to have come from B612, an asteroid discovered by a Turkish astronomer. The scientist is said only to have acquired credibility about his discovery when he abandoned his traditional outfit and adopted a European costume (by force of the law) when presenting his discovery for the second time to the International Astronomer Congress. The author then reflects on this event in the following manner: "If I have told you these details about the asteroid, and made a note of its number for you, it is on account of the grown-ups and their ways. When you tell them that you have made a new friend, they never ask you any questions about essential matters. They never say to you, 'What does his voice sound like? What games does he love best? Does he collect butterflies?' Instead, they demand: 'How old is he? How many brothers has he got? How much does he weigh? How much money does his father make?' Only from these figures do they think they have learned anything about him" (pp. 15–16).

It is precisely this logic of questioning that makes *The Little Prince* an inspiring piece in my own life and work. As a child, *The Little Prince* was another friend who had similar questions, a child who saw himself different from adults but wanted to build a bridge to reach them. Now that I am an adult, and I work as a lecturer in intercultural communication and personal leadership, *The Little Prince* is an example of how our worldviews and interactions largely determine the way we define reality and how we create meaningful relationships with others. The views offered to us by the scientific world are not free from cultural biases and single-mindedness. *The Little Prince* is a constant reminder that *seeing with the heart* is something education should strive for, along with mindfulness and curiosity about the measurable reality. By bridging these, we could bring more sensibility to future professionals who, like the Little Prince, are open minds in search of true meaning in their lives and reasonable understanding of their work and their impact on the planet.

Manuela Hernández-Sanchéz
The Hague University, Academy of European Studies and Communication Management, The Hague, The Netherlands.

Philippe Descola & Gísli Pálsson (eds.), 1996. *Nature and Society: Anthropological Perspectives* (London: Routledge), 310 pp.

Keywords: *communalism, eco-cosmology, nature-culture, reciprocity, sustainability*

In *Nature and Society: Anthropological Perspectives* the nature–culture dichotomy is the core theme. The contributors focus on the deconstruction of the nature–culture dualism, drawing from cultural anthropology, anthropological case studies, biology, ethno-biology, sociology of science and recent research on ethology and the origin of humankind. Of special interest is Pálsson's "Human-environmental relations: orientalism, paternalism and communalism" (pp. 63–82). Situating the nature–society dichotomy in an ethnographic and historical perspective, he argues that in medieval Europe there was no radical separation of nature and society. Medieval man thought of himself as an integral part of the natural world. However, by the end of the Renaissance, man had become disconnected from nature. Nature became a quantifiable, three-dimensional, rationalized, controlled and objective universe. Since then, Western man has come to distinguish different models of the relationship between man and the environment: orientalistic exploitation, paternalistic protection and communalism.

From the point of view of orientalism, the intellectual heir of the Renaissance and the Enlightenment, the environment is just a means to serve humankind. This view suggests that people are masters of the natural environment and can make use of it according to their needs and whims. It is characterized by negative reciprocity.

Paternalism is characterized by protection and good stewardship, rather than by exploitation. Humans act in the name of nature. They must approach nature with care. In this view too, nature is objectified, so that there is a clear divide between the Western world, which is disconnected from nature, and primitive cultures and peasant societies, which often think of human-environmental relationships in terms of protection and balanced reciprocity.

In the early 1990s, the new paradigm of communalism or contextualism came to the fore. Unlike orientalism and paternalism, communalism rejects the dichotomy of nature and culture. The communalism view emphasizes the intimate personal relationships of humans and their natural environment, expressed in generalized reciprocity. Man is defined as a participant in nature. Nature is an ecosystem that includes humans. This is founded on a vision of oneness with nature, unification with the great chain of being. The idea of communalism reflects the cosmological idea of pre-Renaissance times, of ancient kingdoms and of many hunting, gathering and fishing societies which are being completely marginalized in a globalizing world. The cosmologies of some of these cultures are true eco-cosmologies (p. 185), implying sustainable human-nature relatedness, and necessary for sustainability.

Pálsson's article is important in that it addresses the deconstruction of the nature–culture dichotomy. His plea for the dialogic paradigm of communalism is very appealing: "The paradigm of communalism, with its emphasis on practice, reciprocity and engagement . . . provides an avenue out of the modernist project and current environmental dilemmas" (p. 78). Through the concept of eco-consciousness as conceptualized in communalism, man becomes conscious of his dependence on nature. Indirectly, unintentionally and unknowingly, many primitive societies have taught mankind that symbiosis, balance, harmony and moderation are essential values for sustainability and thus for the quality of life in general.

Selma M. van Londen & Arie de Ruijter
Tilburg University, Department of Social and Behavioural Sciences, Tilburg, The Netherlands.

Jared M. Diamond, 1997. *Guns, Germs and Steel: The Fates of Human Societies* (New York and London: W.W. Norton & Company), 480 pp.

Keywords: *diversity, environment, organizations, technology, farm economy*

The aim of this book is to offer a short history of the world in the last 13,000 years. Diamond's analysis starts from the strong differences between countries, with European superiority well represented by the arrest of powerful Atahualpa, the Incas' emperor, caged in his kingdom, in front of his huge army, by a small handful of Spanish conquistadors. The main topic is therefore to understand why Atahualpa was targeted by the Europeans, while they did not go to Madrid to defeat Carlo V. Differences in development are always explained in terms of a presumed cultural superiority of European people which is connected to biological factors or innate capabilities. Diamond definitely rejects this idea; on the contrary, he suggests a vision connected to external and sometimes chance elements: the current superiority of some areas is caused by a set of geographical, meteorological and environmental conditions that favour Euro-Asiatic continents.

The issue is the availability of domesticated animals and plants, which help the transition from a society of hunter-gatherers to an agricultural society characterized by higher food productivity. More food means strong population growth, the opportunity to dedicate time and energy to activities which are not immediately productive (technology, military life, writing) and the capacity for building a more complex social and political organization. The change to a farming economy starts a virtual process which makes possible the strong social, cultural and military development of the population.

Other societies were crushed by the military (guns) and technological (steel) power of Europeans, but also by new germs, developed in the overpopulated farm villages, that in some cases (for example smallpox for American Indians) represented an element of destruction more catastrophic than the guns themselves. Europe was favoured by crucial factors like the availability of domesticated plants and animals and the lack of geographical barriers, permitting a widespread and persistent flow of ideas and people. Development is therefore not connected with any presumed biological superiority, but with a set of opportunities, sometimes random, that are combined in a favourable way.

The book owes its success both to the original and ambitious thought it proposes, and to the popular style in which it is written..The book is pervaded by the idea of diversity, to which Diamond tries to give an innovative long-range and interdisciplinary definition (combining archaeology, ecology, palaeontology, geography, genetics and social sciences). Diversity does not depend only on innate factors, but is strictly connected with geographical and environmental conditions. Diamond conveys a positive evaluation of diversity:

it represents an important motor for evolution – only the circulation of ideas, people and technology permits a long period of sustainable growth.

Gabriele Morettini
Marche Polytechnic University, Department of Social Sciences, Ancona, Italy.

Héctor Díaz-Polanco, 2007. *Elogio de la Diversidad: Globalización, Multiculturalismo y Etnofagia* (Mexico, Buenos Aires and Madrid: Siglo XXI Editores), 223 pp.

English Translation of the Title: *Praising of Diversity: Globalization, Multiculturalism and Ethnofagia.*

Keywords: *multiculturalism, globalization, social/economic/political aspects*

Winner of the International Essay Award, this book examines the claim that globalization homogenizes societies across the globe both economically and culturally. Contrarily, on the economic end, the author argues that globalization has increased inequality, while threatening the survival of the planet along with human sustainability. On the cultural end, he claims that actually multiculturalism has become a selling point and has been manipulated to depoliticize politics and economics so as to make room for their *free* operation away from the politico-democratic process: "multiculturalism celebrates difference as a 'cultural' matter while dissolving the inequality and hierarchy that differentiated identities themselves include and struggle to express and overcome" (p. 174).

Contradicting postmodernist claims that meta-theories are dead, the author argues for the need for meta-theories that help identify the new methods capitalism uses in cultural control and its manipulation of diversity. Against liberal universalisms, he proposes a dialogue to develop a new common terrain of equal diversity against the totalizing claims and impositions of so-called Western culture. Examining what he calls the adversaries of diversity – i.e. liberalism, Kant, Rawls and communitarianism – the author argues that the debate over diversity is about the "necessary conditions for construction of a just and democratic society of solidarity" (p. 190). He proposes diversity as a meta-principle to guide the process of change.

This book is about the political economy of diversity. I found particularly useful the criticism of multiculturalism as a product of neo-liberalism, in part detracting from the issues of distribution and social justice, in part a new version of universalism as it dictates which differences are admissible and which are not, which can be tolerated and which not. Along these lines, while pretending to abandon the call for assimilation, multiculturalism seeks to liberalize minority cultures; while allowing them to keep selected features, it expects them to accept the basic liberal principles and to avoid challenges to the ruling and liberalizing – "formerly civilising" (p. 177) – nature of Western culture. The call to abandon the multicultural proposal is rather challenging to those who see it as the new path to a global society of difference. As proposed, multi-culturalism is part of the effort to "reduce the space of freedom to the individual leaving aside the claims of groups and classes" (p. 83). Ultimately, the author agrees with Žižek that multiculturalism does not tolerate the true other: "we can get along with the ethnic *other* as long as it is deprived of the substance of its Otherness" (p. 182).

John J. Betancur
University of Illinois at Chicago, Department of Urban Planning and Policy, Chicago, USA.

Mary Douglas, 1987. *How Institutions Think* (London: Routledge & Kegan Paul), 146 pp.

Keywords: *social institutions, cognition and culture, organizational behaviour*

How Institutions Think sets out to clarify the extent to which thinking itself is dependent upon institutions. Human reasoning is often explained with a focus on the individual mind, but in this book the focus is on culture and its influence on individuals' ways of reasoning. Different kinds of institutions allow individuals to think different kinds of thoughts and to respond to different emotions. But institutions do not think by themselves; they are created by people through their interaction with each other and through the joint meaning they put on their social life. People need to squeeze each other's ideas into a common shape. This is a way to legitimate their ways of thinking, and it also creates shared ideas and ways of thinking, so-called institutions.

Douglas also discusses important questions of ethical principle and how institutions can be used to understand conflicts. According to her, when individuals disagree on elementary justice, their most insoluble conflicts are between institutions based on incompatible principles. Here she points out that the more severe a conflict, the more important it is to understand the institutions behind the actors' thinking.

The thinking in this book is of special interest as a tool when analysing organizations and workplaces, when trying to find obstacles or identify ways of implementing new orders. It is also of interest, for instance, when discussing discrimination, inclusion and exclusion at workplaces. Of importance here is how you can use the understanding of institutions as orders of thinking if you want to integrate new things within an organization or invite people with other ways of thinking into a group. Douglas's book contributes many different angles and interesting perspectives on these matters. To understand the institutions behind people's standpoints on some issues can be helpful when bridging differences. Institutions need to be considered with regard to organizations' approaches to thinking in institutionalized ways.

Angela Nilsson
University of Stockholm, Centre for Research in International Migration and Ethnic Relations, Stockholm, Sweden.

Thomas A. Dutton & Lian H. Mann, 1996. *Reconstructing Architecture: Critical Discourses and Social Practices* (Minneapolis: University of Minnesota Press), 329 pp.

Keywords: *architectural practice, architecture, society*

The making of architecture is instrumental in the construction of our identities, our differences, the world around us: much of what we know of institutions, the distribution of power, social relations and cultural values is mediated by the built environment. Historically, architecture has constructed the environments that house the dominant culture. The purpose of this book is twofold: (1) to reformulate the role of architecture in society as well as the specific understanding of architecture's capacity to further a progressive social transformation, and (2) to advance strategies for practice based on that reformulation.

The book was used to inform SUS.DIV projects in terms of the consideration of architecture as a social art. It presents seven key essays focusing on the suppression of the social in design; the feminist analyses in architecture; the bond between ecology and architecture; cultural pedagogy and architecture; the built environment and the African-American experience; the deconstruction of architecture and critical theory's real strategy. To create architecture is an inherently political act, yet its nature as a social practice is often obscured beneath layers of wealth and privilege.

The contributors to this volume question architecture's complicity with the status quo, moving beyond critique to outline the part architects are playing in building radical social movements and challenging dominant forms of power. Yet, as the essays in *Reconstructing Architecture* demonstrate, there exists a strong tradition of critical practice in the field, one that attempts to alter existing social power relations. Engaging the gap between modernism and postmodernism, each chapter addresses an oppositional discourse that has developed within the field and then reconstructs it in terms of a new social project: feminism, social theory, environmentalism, cultural studies, race and ethnic studies, and critical theory.

The activists and scholars writing within this book provide a clarion call to architects and other producers of culture, challenging them to renegotiate their political allegiances and to help reconstruct a viable democratic life in the face of inexorable forces driving economic growth, destroying global ecology, homogenizing culture and privatizing the public realm. *Reconstructing Architecture* reformulates the role of architecture in society as well as its capacity to further a progressive social transformation.

Hisham Elkadi & Karen McPhillips
Deakin University, School of Architecture and Building, Victoria, Australia & University of Ulster, School of Architecture and Design, Belfast, UK.

Tim Edensor, 2006. "Reconsidering National Temporalities: Institutional Times, Everyday Routines, Serial Spaces and Synchronicities", *European Journal of Social Theory* 9: 525–545.

Keywords: *national temporalities, the everyday, object world, cognition*

This essay offers a critical review of existing theories of national temporality that are implicated in conventional conceptions of the nation and national identity, taking issue with dominant linear conceptions of the time of the nation which have overemphasized *official* histories, traditions and narratives. The author focuses on the neglected realm of the everyday as the temporal sphere in which national identity is continually reproduced, sedimented and challenged, arguing that we rely on the ordinary working interactional space of the here and now, which exists as a durable, collectively reproduced environment of reliable spaces, occasions, procedures and object worlds.

The essay distils the rich literature on time in ways most useful for the reader interested in how temporal quotidian orders constrain a multiplicity of possible experiences of place, by underpinning a common sense of *how things are* and of *how we do things* that connects persons at the local level. Following existing studies of the management and understanding of time which has been shown to depend upon an implicit, embedded and embodied form of social knowing, Edensor traces the existence of national synchronicities through timetabled routines of rituals and habits which specify when and where specific social practices should occur.

From the organization of household routines through mediatized timetables which have begun to take over many local festivities, ceremonies or forms of religious observance, to the time allocated to leisure and shared practices such as shopping, socializing and walking, temporal customs achieve national synchronicity and domesticate the foreign, by being absorbed into national routines.

The essay is rich in case studies which show how national borders remain affective and cognitive, despite a borderless Europe, precisely through everyday routines and practices surrounding work, family, leisure, socializing and cultural activities which stop at the border, while national schedules are transported globally through migration. But rather than being undermined in the process, national schedules, habits and routines are reconstituted in a new homely context by tapping into networks of people and information.

Susanne Küchler
University College London, Department of Anthropology, London, UK.

European Institute for Comparative Cultural Research (ERICarts), 2008. "Sharing Diversity, National Approaches to Intercultural Dialogue in Europe: Study for the European Commission", *European Commission, Directorate-General for Education and Culture* Report, March 2008.

Keywords: *European intercultural cooperation, cultural field, artists, intercultural strategies*

This report describes national approaches to intercultural dialogue (ICD) in a broader context and as an issue of policy in the sectors of education, culture, youth and sport. National policy approaches to ICD in the education sector range from a focus on civic education (throughout Europe) to intercultural education (in some countries). Across Europe, one of the main objectives of educational policy to promote dialogue is to provide resources for language learning.

The observations made in the study are useful for people working in the field of arts management. The study argues that diversity can be fostered at all stages of cultural/artistic production, distribution and participation: in the cultural field, good practices are those which involve a diversity of artists who synthesize different sources and traditions into new works, bring the public into a conversation, or trigger a change in the perception of and relationship to others. Artists, in particular, seem to be among the most important facilitators of ICD since their aspirations and passion can lead, not only to a change in attitudes, but also to a fresh, creative language in which this change is being expressed. The report highlights good practice in arts education projects: they can be generated proactively out of local circumstances and run by civil society organizations, or may be constructed in response to specific directives or funding programmes initiated by European or national, regional or local authorities. Individual or business initiatives which pursue social goals such as ICD are as important as publicly funded projects.

The study compares successful ICD projects which are reported to be found in *shared spaces*, both institutional and non-institutional. *Institutional spaces* appear to ensure equality of participation by all groups at governance (decision-making) levels and management (executive) levels, bringing the activities of minorities and migrants from the margins into mainstream organized spheres. An important aspect of institutional ICD activities is their potential to be sustained over time. *Non-institutional spaces*, on the other hand, such as neighbourhoods, streets, train stations, public parks, marketplaces, etc., but also virtual environments, are important spaces for intercultural dialogue that is likely to lead to innovative practices and new forms of expression.

The report concludes that for ICD activities to become part of the daily life experience, ICD needs to go beyond a mere tolerance of the *other*, as fostered by activities in institutional spaces, by means of nurturing creative abilities through innovative practice and new forms of expression.

Ljiljana Simic
Oracle – Network of European Cultural Managers, Brussels, Belgium.

Thomas Hylland Eriksen, 1993. *Ethnicity and Nationalism: Anthropological Perspectives* (London: Pluto Press), 179 pp.

Keywords: *social anthropology, ethnicity, nationalism, minorities, social processes*

This book is a successful synthesis of many foregoing attempts to build a general theory of ethnicity and ethnic relations. Thomas Hylland Eriksen utilizes a situationist point of view in it and he comes very close to constructivist approaches. From his point of view, ethnicity emerges and becomes relevant through social situations and encounters, and through the way people cope with the demands and challenges of life. This statement suggests also that ethnic diversity appears only in some specific situations.

Thomas Hylland Eriksen places the term *ethnicity* close to the terms *nationalism* and *politics*. He shows links between them. On the one hand, ethnicity is bound up with group stereotypes, and on the other hand, it appears in political arguments. Group membership and loyalties are confirmed and strengthened through stereotyping and articulation of conflict or competition. Thus articulation of ethnic differences indicates a state of society rather than the existence of stable groups. Ethnicity is not given but negotiated and created in processes of dichotomization and complementarization.

The author also shows that ethnicity is not the possession of poor unorganized people without any ideology, but of hierarchized groups that are able to negotiate their own status among other ethnic groups. In the modern world, to be an ethnic group also means to have museums, speakers, ethnographers, famous victims and the ability to use similar arguments like other ethnic groups. To be able to fulfil these criteria, some original culture may need to be lost.

In his book Eriksen also analyses theories of plural society and criticizes them for being ambiguous. He states that the theory of social and cultural pluralism is a clear example of what can be called an objectivist approach in ethnicity studies. Plurality can be both an advantage and a disadvantage, and to show it as a univocally positive political concept is unhelpful.

Thomas Hylland Eriksen makes an important step in the study of ethnicity in the modern and postmodern world. He shows the connection between ethnic diversification, nationalism, stereotyping and political goals. He shows that ethnic sentiments appear in some situations and disappear in others. He also does not insist on using such a term for describing related processes. Perhaps a wider term, such as *social identity*, would be truer to the flux and complexity of social processes, he suggests. Unfortunately, anthropologists do not use only their own concepts, but also the concepts of those natives involved. Therefore they cannot deliberately decide what words should be used and what should not.

Zdenek Uherek
Institute of Ethnology of the Academy of Sciences of the Czech Republic, Prague, Czech Republic.

Erik H. Erikson, 1963. *Childhood and Society*, 2nd edn (New York: W.W. Norton & Co. Inc), 445 pp.

Keywords: *identity, childhood, psychological development, ethnic group, family structure*

Research about diversity has always provoked questions about the real meaning of identity. In particular when taking into account ethnic diversity, identity has increasingly taken on the character of a dynamic notion: it is not *given*, but it is built through a process of continuous remodelling of the individual, which allows both for his stability and for his change in the course of time. In psychoanalysis, the notion of identity brought forward by Erik Erikson in *Childhood and Society* gives a paradigmatic example of this.

By treating several clinical cases and comparing the differences in child development in two groups of American Indians (Sioux and Yurok), Erikson highlights the interaction between individual development and social cultural systems, considering the multidimensionality of human development and applying Margaret Mead's comparative anthropological method. Identity assumes the form of a continuous and constant synthesis process among cultural contradictions, diverging social demands and the many-sidedness of personal pressures. All these factors are subject to a non-synchronous evolution: "To grow means to be divided into different parts which move at different rates" (p. 189).

Therefore it is a process lying between the individual and one's self, between individuals and the group they belong to, between the historical period and the individual history. This process is at the heart of both individuals and their community culture, which finds its roots in the past but stretches out towards the future: "A human being, thus, is at all times an organism, an ego, and a member of society and is involved in all three processes of organisation. His body is exposed to pain and tension; his ego, to anxiety; and as a member of society, he is susceptible to the panic emanating from his group" (p. 30). The opposition between identity and individual dispersion is particularly evident during adolescence, though it is present in the whole course – and in the evolution – of the experience of each individual: "[o]nly a gradually accruing sense of identity, based on the experience of social health and cultural solidarity at the end of each major childhood crisis, promises that periodical balance in human life which – in integration of the ego stages – makes for a sense of humanity. But wherever this sense is lost . . . an array of associated infantile fears are apt to become mobilised: for only an identity safely anchored in the 'patrimony' of a cultural identity can produce a workable psychosocial equilibrium" (p. 371).

The outcome is a conflict among the different needs arising within the relation between the individual and the world. This conflictual dimension certainly implies a constant effort, which involves an unavoidable and sometimes dramatic uneasiness. No identity can develop outside society – and outside the roles and prototypes that it offers – but a "sane" individual is called to constantly compare these roles with his ego's needs for development, thus contributing to the upkeep of the social process. Though it is not recent, the contribution of *Childhood and Society* is still useful for the study of modern social orders, which are characterized by quick changes and confront the individual with increasingly ambiguous and contradictory ideals.

Attilio Balestrieri & Raffaele Bracalenti
Psychoanalytic Institute for Social Research, Rome, Italy.

Josef Estermann, 1998. *Filosofía Andina: Estudio intercultural de la sabiduría autóctona Andina* (Quito: Abya-Yala), 359 pp.

English Translation of the Title: *Andean Philosophy: Intercultural Study of Andean Indigenous Wisdom.*

Keywords: *Andean philosophy, Andean culture, Andean cosmo-vision, ethics, Andean theology*

This book outlines key concepts and a working agenda for an Andean philosophy, a field of study aimed at the description and understanding of the indigenous rationality of Andean societies (mainly Bolivia, Ecuador and Peru). From an intercultural perspective, an approach that conceives the world and rationality as culturally determined (p. 311), it addresses topics such as cosmology, anthropology, ethics and theology, contrasting the Andean and the Occidental approaches to key aspects of each topic. The book has the virtue of having put together a broad range of reflections on Andean thought and practice dispersed in various disciplines such as Latin American philosophy,

Andean history, Andean anthropology and critical development studies, providing them with a unified framework within the epistemic project of building an Andean philosophy, or ethno-philosophy. This work is part of an intellectual effort underway in various regions of the world (Africa, Latin America and Asia) that aims to recover and give voice to forms of thought and action silenced and subordinated by the colonization process.

The text is novel in the way it names the concepts put forward. Appealing to a mix of Quechua and Greek terms, the author uses terms such as *Pachasofia* (cosmology), *Runasofia* (anthropology), *Ruwanasofia* (ethics) and *Apusofia* (theology), which are useful tools to articulate another type of thought: an intercultural thinking. These neologisms act as *sensitizing concepts* to approach social reality in a different manner.

Besides the discussion of key philosophical concepts, such as reality, rationality and substance (subject), the text provides a number of insights into cultural diversity in Andean societies. Andean rationality is defined in symbolic and ritual terms rather than in logical or linguistic terms. This means that Andean people (*runa*) access the world not through rational means, but rather through non-rational capabilities (feelings, presentiments, etc). However, because of Occidental modernization processes underway in these societies, this kind of thinking and action is often seen as archaic, rather than as another type of rationality proper to these societies, or as expressions of extra-Occidental forms of modernity such as Andean modernity, Arabic modernity, or Bantú modernity. This is a particularly thorny issue faced by development agencies and projects working with indigenous and peasant communities, who often see this *other* rationality as an obstacle to be overcome, rather than something to be understood, dealt with and incorporated into more intercultural development approaches.

The book also provides interesting insights into the individual-collective issue. The assertion that in the Andean world language is more centred in verbs (actions) than in subjects (individuals) is an interesting clue to understanding the collective nature of these societies. For Andean philosophy the individual is nothing, something lost, if it is not part of a multiple network of relations. Those working in the field of rural development in these societies are often surprised to learn the local meaning of *poverty*: the poor are not those who lack material goods, but rather those who lack a dense network of relations.

José Fernando Galindo-Cespedes
Centre for Research and Promotion of Peasantry, Cochabamba, Bolivia.

European Monitoring Centre on Racism and Xenophobia (EUMC) & International Centre for Migration Policy Development (ICMPD), 2003. "Migrants, Minorities and Employment in Germany: Exclusion, Discrimination and Anti-Discrimination in 15 Member States of the European Union", *EUMC Comparative Study*, pp. 1–123.

Keywords: *ethnic inequalities, labour market*

This article is based on a comparative study of discrimination, exclusion and disadvantages of migrants and minorities in the employment sector, synthesizing fifteen national reports by the National Focal Points (NFPs) of the EUMC RAXEN network on the situation in the member states, as well as further research on the subject by the authors. The study follows a holistic approach to the question of discrimination in employment, analysing the relatively disadvantaged labour market position of migrants and minorities in broad terms, complemented by detailed inventories of the available evidence on discrimination. Despite signs of increasing diversity, national labour markets are still highly segmented along national or ethnic lines. Notwithstanding the fact that most member states have already long-established immigrant communities from non-EU countries, immigrants from outside the EU are still heavily concentrated in certain industrial sectors (e.g. manufacturing, construction), parts of the service sector (e.g. personal services, cleaning, catering, caring) and sectors that are subject to strong seasonal fluctuations (e.g. tourism and agriculture). Women with a migrant background are often restricted to certain segments of the labour market, such as personal and domestic services, cleaning, catering, health and care. As indicated, in the last few years all member states have stepped up their efforts in aiming to incorporate EU legislation on equality and anti-discrimination into national law. This has been translated into specialized public institutions to oversee the implementation. Furthermore, many member states have instituted new strategies to reinforce the labour market integration of migrants and minorities and to fight effectively against discrimination. Governments, social partners and NGOs have increased their involvement and active participation in a number of projects and initiatives aiming at furthering equality and fighting discrimination.

The article illustrates the difficulties, on a theoretical as well as on a practical level, of collecting and compiling comparable information about the situation of migrants and minorities in the labour markets of the member states. The study also provides an analysis of common and specific problems in data collection as well as some options and strategies for improved data comparability. Finally, the most important output of this study is that it concludes with a set of ten recommendations for the EU and its individual member states for further improving the situation.

Tonia Damvakeraki
National and Kapodistrian University of Athens, Athens, Greece.

Rainer W. Fassbinder (Dir.), 1973. *Angst essen Seele auf*, Germany.

English Translation of the Title: *Ali: Fear Eats the Soul.*

Keywords: *diversity, social class, migration*

Angst Essen Seele Auf is a film about a love story between Ali, a young Moroccan *Gastarbeiter* (guest-worker) living alone in Munich, and Emmi, an elderly, widowed German cleaning woman. Ali and Emmi have to face social proscription of their relationship: the harassment of neighbours, co-workers, local shopkeepers, and the disgust of family and friends. After returning from a trip in order to escape from this situation, they finally find themselves accepted – but only to the extent that returning them to their *proper* social roles allows them to be exploited once again by those around them. In a way, they find their personal relationship determined by many prejudices and assumptions which they had to face previously, playing out their *types* and becoming more like those who despised them.

As in a Bertolt Brecht perspective, Fassbinder gives a portrait of the characters aimed at removing the audience from the level of empathy to that of understanding the ways in which the characters' lives are determined by ethnicity, age and social class. The title, translated literally "fear eat up soul", is the ungrammatical way Ali describes the pain he is suffering in his relationship with Emmi, a pain which eventually manifests itself as an ulcerated stomach, a disease suffered by many foreign workers. This film shows how diversity can be multifaceted and involve different levels of perception by people involved in different kinds of relationships (friendship, love, parental, etc.). Shot in 1973, it is one of the first attempts to narrate diversity starting from a case of migration, in a way that is totally different from the usual mixed love stories where strong individual characters have to stand against a hostile and racist social environment. The stress of the film is on the different positions in society that drive somebody to accept or to refuse diversity (gender, age, ethnicity, etc.), rather than on individual and psychological characters.

Mario Alessia Montourii
Psychoanalytic Institute for Social Research, Rome, Italy.

William Faulkner, 1932. *Light in August* (Penguin Books), 480 pp.

Keywords: *identity, mestizo (meticcio)*

Thanks to the extraordinary intuitive capacity that can often be found in literature, *Light in August* manages to enlighten all the themes of the debate concerning diversity, through an epic synthesis that might be compared to that emanating from the voice of myths. The book takes into account identity signs and analyses what can make an individual so dramatically different: something that can also be found in the adherence to a cultural parameter, as contradicted as that might be and notwithstanding the intolerance towards it. However, the somatic and cultural element, configuring at the same time both diversity and identity – another formidable intuition fully explained by *Light in August* – is extremely plastic and oscillates from one side to the other, from the recognition to the denial of oneself and of the other: "Because the black blood drove him first to the negro cabin. And then the white blood drove him out of there, as it was the black blood which snatched up the pistol and the white blood which would not let him fire it . . . Then I believe that the white blood deserted him for the moment. Just a second, a flicker, allowing the black to rise in its final moment and make him turn upon that on which he had postulated his hope of salvation" (p. 424).

Those who find a relation with the diversity brought about by the protagonist of this book are able to sense it or feel obliged to see it, even when it is not immediately obvious: "Then yesterday morning he come into Mottstown in broad daylight, on a Saturday with the town full of folks. He went into a white barbershop like a white man, and because he looked like a white man they never suspected him . . . And then he walked the streets in broad daylight, like he owned the town, until Halliday saw him and ran up and grabbed him and said 'Aint your name Christmas?' and the nigger said that it was. He never denied it. He never did anything. He never acted like either a nigger or a white man. That was it. That was what made the folks so bad . . . it was like he never even knew he was a murderer, let alone a nigger too" (p. 331).

The social construction of diversity is stronger than the fact that Christmas is almost white, because the attribution of his mulatto identity makes him almost a black man. The same social construction is in the same way stronger than other people's cognitive capacity, as they are only able to see the black man even when they are faced by a man who is almost white. Faulkner's light is enlightening because it explains the whole range of dynamics concerning the perception of diversity, with a sharpness that makes this book one of the great representations of the human condition; a fully paradigmatic example, just like the jealousy of Shakespeare's Othello and the meanness of Molière's Arpagon.

Attilio Balestrieri & Raffaele Bracalenti
Psychoanalytic Institute for Social Research, Rome, Italy.

James D. Fearon (2003), "Ethnic and Cultural Diversity by Country", *Journal of Economic Growth* 8, 2: 195–222.

Keywords: *ethnic heterogeneity, cultural diversity, indicators, fractionalization, economic growth*

The article addresses the conceptual and practical problems involved in constructing an indicator of ethnic and cultural diversity for the purpose of cross-country comparison. Constructing such an indicator requires two steps. First, it is necessary to collect data on ethnic groups in different countries based on some appropriate listing or sample of ethnic groups. Second, it is necessary to synthesize all this information in an indicator that can then be used for cross-country comparison. Earlier articles in the economic literature dealt with these problems by first distinguishing groups according to fixed identity markers such as language or religion, and then using this information to construct a synthetic index that took into account the number of groups and the percentage of population in each group. (Statistically, the index measures the probability that two randomly chosen individuals belong to the same group.)

This article innovates in both areas.

First, it attempts a list of ethnic groups based on a process of "self-categorization", i.e. where people recognize the distinction of groups and anticipate that significant actions are or could be conditioned on belonging or not to a group. Short of carrying out cross-country surveys (asking people to identify themselves in the groups), the article relies on a number of sources to identify the groups in each country reflecting how people in the country divide the social terrain in ethnic terms. So doing, it identifies 822 ethnic groups representing not less than 1 percent of the population in 160 countries.

Second, it uses this information to construct an indicator of diversity that takes into account the cultural distance between the groups as well as the number of groups and their share of population. In particular, it uses the distance between the tree branches of two languages as a (imperfect) measure of cultural distance between the groups that speak them as a first language. The article shows that the latter index is imperfectly, but not negligibly, correlated (0.75) with the more widely used index that takes into account only the number and the population shares of ethnic groups. This is because in some areas, such as South American and African countries, a great number of ethnic groups speak relatively close languages, while in other countries a relatively small number of groups speak very different languages. This is the case in Cyprus, where the two ethnic groups speak Greek and Turkish, which are very different.

The article represents a substantial contribution to the empirical research on diversity. At a theoretical level, it tries (and shows that it is possible) to measure diversity by taking into account the complex and changing nature of cultural and ethnic identities. On a more pragmatic level, it brings a new dimension (the cultural distance between groups) into traditional measures of diversity that normally take into account only the number of groups and their relative population shares of groups.

Dino Pinelli
Eni Enrico Mattei Foundation, Milan, Italy.

Marcus Felson, 2002. *Crime and Everyday Life*, 3rd edn. (Thousand Oaks, London and New Delhi: Sage Publications), 224 pp.

Keywords: *crime prevention, routine activities*

Most theories of crime and criminality focus on the individual, on what leads someone to commit crimes and on how one can change the individual. In *Crime and Everyday Life* Felson makes a cogent argument for reconsidering how we think about crime in terms of its causes and potential means for reducing it by turning to situational crime prevention, specifically in the light of *routine activities theory*. Felson does not look for complex causes of crime within the individual, but examines our day-to-day activities, or routine activities, and how these facilitate the commission of crime through the convergence of three factors: a suitable target, a motivated offender and the absence of a capable guardian. The third edition of this new classic in criminology has been updated to reflect advances in technology and the preponderance of white-collar crime, but maintains its focus on how simple manipulations of the physical environment and daily activities – where people are at any given time – can greatly influence the crime.

In this clear and concise volume, Felson encourages us to think about crime in terms of things that one can manipulate, structural changes in daily activities and technological changes that lead to the widespread presence of small but valuable objects that make good targets for potential thieves. Hence it is the diversification of our lives, habits and objects that contribute to crime, or can be manipulated in such a way as to reduce crime either by removing the suitable target or by putting a capable guardian in place. Generally applied to property crimes, routine activities theory considers change and diversity as elements that are largely external to the psychology or social circumstances of the individual offender. The variables that can be manipulated are represented by factors such as time, visibility and the value of an object in relation to how easily it can be carried away.

Felson has been criticized for being overly simplistic, and for ignoring the psychology of the offender. These are valid criticisms, but the value of his work lies in the fact that he moves beyond the individual and the social and considers something more basic – our habits and how they contribute to the creation of situations where crime is or is not more likely to happen.

Vanja M. K. Stenius
Psychoanalytic Institute for Social Research, Rome, Italy.

Joshua A. Fishman, 2001. *Can Threatened Languages be Saved?* (Clevedon: Multilingual Matters), 503 pp.

Keywords: *language planning, linguistic diversity, minority languages, reversing language shift*

Joshua Fishman is a world leader in the field of language revitalization. His academic career spans over half a century. He is very productive and he has established different subfields of socio-linguistics, such as language mainte-nance and language shift (LMLS) or language and nationalism. In 1991 he published the book *Reversing Language Shift* (RLS). This was an extremely important contribution in the thinking about revitalizing minority languages and it established the subfield of RLS studies. The book contains studies on the development of thirteen cases of minority language groups. The follow-up to that book is *Can Threatened Languages be Saved?* In the introduction Fishman updates his theoretical basis for RLS in the case of minority languages.

This book is an evaluation of the first decade of RLS studies. He invited experts on the same thirteen communities from the first book and seven new communities to critically evaluate RLS theory. Each chapter examines the effects of ten years of RLS efforts in the language communities. The following language communities are dealt with: Irish, Frisian, Basque and Catalan (in Europe); Navajo, New York City Puerto Rican Spanish, both Secular and Ultra-Orthodox Yiddish in New York City, French in Quebec and Modern Hebrew (in North America); both immigrant and aboriginal languages (in Australia); Maori (in New Zealand); Otomi and Quechua (in Latin America); Oko (in Africa); Andamanese and Ainu (in Asia).

Particularly useful to my own work on Frisian has been Fishman's enlight-ened outsider view on this language that he mentions in the first book. His account has deepened my understanding of developments and diversity in the Frisian language group, as well as the dynamics of other minority languages. Also, one of the most important ideas in RLS theory that is highlighted in *Can Threatened Languages Be Saved?* is that the continued existence of a language can only be guaranteed by securing the intergenerational transmission of a language. This sounds obvious, but the fact that Fishman reiterated the point time and again has led to a greater awareness – for instance among policy-makers – that it is not only the school, or the modern mass media, or other typical policy areas that can make a language community sustainable in the long run. The family, the neighbourhood and the community as a whole are indispensable elements of a successful language policy that can sustain linguistic diversity. That is a valuable lesson to be learned from this book.

Durk Gorter
University of the Basque Country, Donostia-San Sebastián, Spain.

Ludwik Fleck, 1933. *Uppkomsten och utvecklingen av ett vetenskapligt faktum. Inledning till läran om tankestil och tankekollektiv*, translated by Bengt Liliequist (Symposium, Stockholm, 1997/1933), 167 pp.

English Translation of the Title: *Genesis and Development of a Scientific Fact.*

Keywords: *thought style, thought collectives, scientific knowledge, scientific concepts*

This book is about the way scientific knowledge comes into existence and develops. Ludwig Fleck, who is a medical doctor by training, shows from the example of syphilis how historical and social context influences scientific knowledge.

According to Fleck, every scientific fact and every scientific concept is the product of the history and the society in which they are created. And as those change, so also the science will change. To describe this he uses the concepts *thought style* and *thought collective*, and with these he tries to frame the importance of context, its conditions and determinations. Thoughts wander from individual to individual; all the time they are more or less remodelled as other individuals adapt their associations to them. The receiver of a message seldom understands the message exactly as the sender had in mind. After a series of such wanderings the original thought can be totally changed; this is what Fleck refers to as *thought collective*. The thought is both created by and shared by a collective which can consist of two or several hundred people. However, the thought is also restricted by its time and the dominant way of thinking. All concepts are bound by the reciprocal influence existing between them. You can therefore talk about a *thought style* determining the style of concepts: they are more or less bound together in a system. The author shows how researchers had the results from research in front of them many years before they actually saw them, because of their way of thinking. When their thought styles were changed, they were also able to see the results.

This book is especially inspiring to use when you think of limitations for change, for instance within organizations, because of predominant thought styles. It can be used to understand why some measures are not successfully implemented. If you take thought styles or thought collectives into account, it can help to understand what is going on and so to counteract the influence of prevailing thought styles.

Angela Nilsson
University of Stockholm, Centre for Research in International Migration and Ethnic Relations, Stockholm, Sweden.

Sigmund Freud, 1919. *Das Unheimliche*, translated by David McLintock (Penguin Classics), 161 pp.

English Translation of the Title: *The Uncanny.*

Keywords: *identity, ethnic group, gender, family structure*

Diversity brings with it the fascination of the new and unexpected, but at the same time it can provoke anguish. The fear of diversity – the cause of so much intolerance and hostility – has been examined by psychoanalysts, highlighting its most hidden or deepest triggers. A milestone for psychoanalytic research was *The Uncanny (Das Unheimliche)*, a small essay that Sigmund Freud wrote in 1919, in which he states that "*Unheimlich* is clearly the opposite of *heimlich, heimish, vertraut,* and it seems obvious that something should be frightening precisely because it is unknown and unfamiliar" (p. 124). When this sense of direction is lost, the world is no longer familiar (*heimlich*); it is no longer a person's home (*Heim*), but becomes the dwelling place for the unusual, the disquieting and the perturbing. Remembering also the second meaning of *heimlich*, which recalls all that is hidden and secret, Freud states that when all that should be hidden and secret (*heimlich*) is uncovered (*unheimlich*), one's own internal world is shaken, and what used to be familiar suddenly seems unusual: "for this uncanny element, is actually nothing new or strange, but something that was long familiar to the psyche and was estranged from it only through being repressed. The link with repression now illuminates Schelling's definition of the uncanny as 'something that should have remained hidden and has come to happen'" (p. 148).

This theme has been developed in particular by Julia Kristeva, who has looked through the main conceptualizations that have been expressed and the main positions that have been taken – most of all in the ambit of Western culture – towards foreigners, meant as main conveyers of diversity. Kristeva states: "In the fascinating rejection that the foreigner originates in us, we share an uncanny strangeness expressed by what Freud called 'the sense of depersonalisation', and which recalls our infantile desire and fear of the other. The foreigner is within us; and when we attempt to avoid the confrontation with the foreigner, we are fighting our unconscious – that 'improper' facet of our impossible 'own and proper' . . . After Stoic cosmopolitanism and religious universalist integration, Freud brings us the courage to call ourselves disintegrated in order not to integrate foreigners and even less so to hunt them out, but rather to welcome them to that uncanny strangeness, which is as much theirs as it is ours . . . an invitation (a utopia or very modern one?) not to reify the foreign, not to petrify him as such, not to petrify us as such . . . a cosmopolitanism of a new sort that, cutting across governments, economies, and markets, might work for a mankind whose solidarity is founded on the consciousness of its unconscious" (J. Kristeva, 1988,

Etrangers à nous-mêmes, Fayard, Paris; *Strangers to Ourselves*, translated by Leon S. Roudiez, 1994, pp. 191–2).

Attilio Balestrieri & Raffaele Bracalenti
Psychoanalytic Institute for Social Research, Rome, Italy.

Rachel M. Friedberg, 2001. "The Impact of Mass Migration on the Israeli Labour Market", *Quarterly Journal of Economics* 116, 4: 1373–1408.

Keywords: *immigration, wage differentials, employment growth*

The primary goal of this paper is the analysis of the impact of immigration on the labour market of the native Israeli population, exploiting a natural experiment such as the massive immigration from the former Soviet Union, occurring after 1989. Nearly one million Russians moved to Israel after 1989 and this extensive immigration increased Israel's population by 12 percent in the first half of the 1990s. In particular, the paper investigates whether changes in relative wages and employment across occupations occurred as a consequence of this Russian mass immigration.

In the presence of compensating movements of factors of production, in the long run the immigration will only influence the aggregate wage of the country, but not the relative wages of cities in that country. Given that movement across occupations is more constrained than movements across locations, an analysis of cross-occupation variation rather than cross-city variation would be more effective. This is the approach adopted here. Apparently, occupations that employed more immigrants experienced lower native wage growth and slightly lower native employment growth than others, and this may indicate an adverse effect of immigration on the native labour market. However, the instrumental variable estimations contradict this conclusion. At the occupation level, the mass migration of Russians to Israel has an insignificant effect on wage and employment growth of natives, whereas at the individual level it has a positive effect on hourly earnings. This last finding indicates that some complementarities exist between less-skilled native workers and immigrants, thus giving advantage to the former. Consistent with these results is the idea that the distribution of immigrants across occupations is not independent of relative market conditions, in that immigrants have disproportionately entered occupations with low wages, low wage growth and contracting employment. The inferior Hebrew-language skills of immigrants and the imperfect transferability of their human capital after arrival may have contributed to their entry into such low-paying jobs.

Cristina Cattaneo
Eni Enrico Mattei Foundation (Milan, Italy) and University of Sussex (UK).

Francis Fukuyama, 2007. *La fine della storia e l'ultimo uomo*, translated by Delfo Ceni (Milano: BUR), 432 pp.

English Translation of the Title: *The End of History and the Last Man.*

Keywords: *liberal democracy, totalitarism, historical development*

Together with Huntington's *Clash of Civilization*,[1] originally published as a reply to Fukuyama from a conservative viewpoint, *The End of History* can be considered one of the first, basic and relatively accessible conceptualizations of the positions taken by Western countries (most significantly the leading power, the USA) in the cultural-political debate as they face the world of globalization following the end of the Cold War. Although Fukuyama's essay is representative of a North American liberal-progressive vision, it also resonates with a large part of the socialist and social democratic reflections in Europe, with the fall of the Berlin Wall, for instance (although with different emphases and other analytical bases), emphasizing the issue of individual and social rights.

Far from postulating millenarian events, *The End of History* singles out the liberal democracy and its secular institutions – regulated market capitalism, multi-party organization of representation, the guarantee of *formal* rights for individuals – as the only form of laic universalism resulting positively from the tragedies of the twentieth century. On the other hand, apart from the optimistic observation that they have prevailed in the long term from the French Revolution onwards, Fukuyama does not hide the limits and imperfections of the existing liberal democracies, stating rather that they remain the unique, final, ideal horizon in the evolution of the organization of human society – at least at the present stage of development in political thought.

Like Huntington, Fukuyama does not deal directly with the question of diversity. It is implicit in his perspective, however, that the modern liberal democracy has the best chances to manage poverty, racism, sexism, etc., yet always partially and through progressive adjustments and negotiations. Though he seems to be worrying more about the risks of homologation connected to modernization – see in this regard his wide discussion of Nietszche's concept of *last (least) men* – Fukuyama considers democratic liberalism as the most evolved form of universalism able to integrate diversity, making it (also) a factor of creativity and renewal. The distance of this vision from Huntington's, where diversity is regarded almost exclusively as an element of conflict, gives a good demonstration of the polarity and range of the present Western discussion on these themes.

Francesco Chiapparino
Marche Polytechnic University, Department of Social Sciences, Ancona, Italy.

[1] Reviewed on page 92.

Néstor Garcia-Canclini, 1995. Consumidores y Ciudadanos: Conflictos Multiculturales de la Globalización (México: Grijalbo), 214 pp.

English Translation of the Title: Consumers and Citizens: Multicultural Conflicts of Globalisation.

Keywords: globalization, multiculturalism, cultural policy, cultural identity, multicultural conflicts

Based on previous empirical research work on cultural change in Mexico City and Latin America done in the 1990s, this book of essays addresses the processes of cultural identity construction in the region, and the multicultural conflicts generated by the tension between the construction of citizenship based on rights granted by nation-states, and the construction of citizenship based on consumption promoted, to a great extent, by global cultural industries. The author suggests that at the present time citizenship is constructed more as a function of consuming goods in private than as a function of collective participation. In other words, "social participation is organised through consuming rather than through exercising citizenship" (p. 15).

The text addresses key questions dealing with the nature of citizenship at the present time. Is there a non-neo-liberal path to becoming global? Can traditional forms of making politics within the nation-state framework be combined with emergent forms of citizenship in consuming communities? And how can cultural policies be stated within the context of strong influences of North American cultural industries?

This text is useful in a number of ways for cultural diversity studies in Latin America. First, it makes an explicit effort to bring into dialogue Latin American and Anglo-Saxon perspectives on cultural studies, a good sign of scientific diversity. Second, it makes good use of concepts to describe cultural tensions. For instance, the concepts of multi-ethnicity and multiculturality are useful for distinguishing social and political movements based on strong territorial ascriptions from those movements built on more fluid identity and territorial ascriptions. Third, it states interesting methodological guidelines for research.

For instance, the double-blind approach is particularly useful for Latin America, where cultural analysis can often be politically biased. Through the double-blind approach the analyst can often begin giving privilege to a particular point of view (for instance the indigenous point of view), but then move to the intersections of intercultural relations and the power dynamics embedded in them. Finally, this work provides interesting comparative insights for researchers working in non-urban contexts. For instance, though the author sees the notion of "multi-ethnic" as more appropriate to a period of nation-state stability, before globalization, the same diversity of Latin American nation-states means that the notion of "multi-ethnic" can still throw light on more traditional rural contexts at the present time. This is what the current political emergence of indigenous social movements is showing in the Andes.

José Fernando Galindo-Cespedes
Centre for Research and Promotion of Peasantry, Cochabamba, Bolivia.

Clifford Geertz, 1986. "The Uses of Diversity", *Tanner Lectures on Human Values* (Salt Lake City: University of Utah Press), Vol. 7: 253–75.

Keywords: *cultural relativism, ethnocentrism, exotic, values*

Already in the very first lines of the essay, Geertz quite incisively expresses a concern. The eagerness to know the most varied populations' ways of living and behaving has made anthropologists travel all around the world, but Geertz fears that anthropology is having to face "the possibility that the variety is rapidly softening into a paler, and narrower, spectrum" (p. 454) and calls for an immediate discussion on how it is that different values, and hence diversity, are to be justified.

After comparing the work of Lévi-Strauss and Rorty, Geertz gives his personal view of the issue, by deconstructing the intellectual meaning of diversity, its common sense and hidden facets, highlighting its positive and negative aspects, past convictions and future traps, and suggesting the need for a new angle of enquiry. The problem, Geertz argues, lies in the incapability of current intellectuals to find a compromise between embracing either cultural relativism or absolutism, and hence of assuming the we-are-we and they-are-they position, remaining deaf to the appeal of other values (p. 456). He argues that "an anthropology afraid of destroying cultural integrity and creativity, our own and everyone else's, is destined to perish of an inanition for which no manipulations of objectivised data sets can compensate" (p. 457).

According to Geertz, the greater our intellectual, emotional and moral space, i.e. the range of signs we can manage to interpret, the better we can understand how it is to be *them*, the clearer we become to ourselves (p. 459). So what is more ethnocentric: trying to understand the others so that in comparison we get to know ourselves more and better, or trying to understand the others just for the sake of knowing what it is like to be them?

Moral values are perhaps the most difficult to handle and recognize, but we all must be able to conceive difference: "it is not that we must love one another or die. It is that we must known one another, and live with that knowledge" (p. 463). The question is now how to deal with the puzzles of judgment to which disparate approaches to life give rise. Where do we locate ourselves? Where are the boundaries of *us* to be drawn?

As Geertz confesses, this essay has been an attempt to look at critically important intellectual issues from the angle of a working anthropologist. I believe this essay represents a frank and unpretentious attempt to propose a personal and intimate investigation into the meaning of diversity in its more holistic and profound sense. From a short but very engaging read, I learned that we have to be willing, ready and interested to express and accept difference in all its forms and manifestations, for this is the only way to keep society alive.

Rossella Lo Conte
University College London, Department of Anthropology, London, UK.

Bronislaw Geremek, 1992. *Uomini senza padrone: Poveri e marginali tra medioevo e età moderna* (Torino: Einaudi), 298 pp.

English Translation of the Title: *Men without masters: Poor and Marginal People between Medieval and the Early Modern Times.*

Keywords: *vagrants, migrations, gypsies, heretics, criminality*

The book outlines the scenario of poverty in Europe between the early Middle Ages and the early modern period, with poor masses pushed by famine to the urban centres since the countryside was unable to provide them with the means of minimal subsistence. They are beggars, driven out by the indifference and the suspicion of people unable to recognize them inside the known and shared hierarchies of the society; vagrants, excluded in contexts far from normal human relationships (the author describes, for instance, the struggle with vagrancy in Paris during the fourteenth and fifteenth centuries); criminals, the fruits of despair, need or survival instincts in a society ruled by violence, both in public and private life. Such complex characters, with their own ideologies and visions of the world, together with gypsies – who have been and are subject to repression since their arrival in Italy in the sixteenth century, heretics and others neglected by social institutions, are the focus of Geremek's work.

Men without masters, poor and vagrant, but free, victims of the social, political and economic transformations of the passage from the medieval to the early modern world. The poor are neglected by a rural world, where the land is dominated by aristocratic owners and by their atavistic rights, but at the same time they are the victims of emerging capitalism and its new élites, with its vertiginous movements of money and labourers. This multiform humanity, which is doomed perennially to defeat and exclusion – Geremek describes the emerging of exclusionary methods in Italy from the fourteenth to the seventeenth century – represents the largest part of the population. It has its own characteristics, its autonomy and its peculiar languages and codes. Thought marginal, these people constitute the major part, both active and passive, of the great transformations of the Western world during the early modern age. The church turns to them with its word and its assistance, but the first big manu-facturers are also interested in them, looking for low-cost labour, as are the armies of the first national states.

Geremek's essay helps us understand how, in a historical perspective, the various forms of diversity, with their dynamics and characteristics, can be func-tional in the maintenance and development of social and economic systems which are at the origins of those same diversities, giving in this way a peculiar meaning to the concept of sustainability itself.

Augusto Ciuffetti
Marche Polytechnic University, Department of Social Sciences, Ancona, Italy.

Sandro Gindro, 1991. *"Inconscio sociale e diversità"* in Sandro Gindro & Umberto Melotti, *Il mondo delle diversità* (Roma: Edizioni Psicoanalisi Contro), pp. 113–198.

English Translation of the Title: *The Social Unconscious and Diversity.*

Keywords: *identity, racism*

As a psychoanalyst, Sandro Gindro is interested in the functioning of the human mind and in the dynamics that construct it through its relationship with the other (the mind in relation). The starting point is the concept of the *social unconscious*, which the author distinguishes from the archetypes of the Jungian collective unconscious and from the primary fantasies transmitted as philo-genetic legacy described by Sigmund Freud, both considered unchangeable and meta-historical.

The social unconscious is the unconscious in which individuals, to the extent to which they belong to a social group, are immersed (this refers to the social group with which, at least in part, each individual identifies). Although it maintains some constants, the social unconscious is otherwise changeable over time and can vary from one group to the other. Thus the social uncon-scious is a dynamic structure that is collective in so far as it is shared by a group – which is more or less extended and whose boundaries are more or less rigid – rather than equal for everybody, and therefore *social*.

The interest of the essay *The Social Unconscious and Diversity* lies in the fact that diversity is described as a psychic need, not as a catalogue of elements of diversity. The social unconscious needs difference because diversity is also a reference point. This gives rise to the interest in diversity, which is taken as an element that contributes to the structuring of individuals' understanding of and relationship with the world. Since diversity is responsible for different ways of thinking – or elaborating experiences – the study of diversity and the analysis of the relationship with diversity allow the identification of all the elements, including the pathological ones, that set up the relationship with others, or with the Other.

In an attempt to dismiss the a-temporal and meta-historical approach to the description of the unconscious, Gindro emphasizes the historical and geographical elements that attribute peculiarity to the universality of human beings. It becomes apparent along this path that historically the diversity of skin colour and in particular the physical feature of black skin stands as some sort of obsession held by white people or Western culture. Although the author's contribution is not a real dissertation on relativism and universalism, it spreads some light on the problematic relationship with diversity, providing interpretation tools that go beyond the uninspired opposition between relativism and universalism.

Attilio Balestrieri & Raffaele Bracalenti
Psychoanalytic Institute for Social Research, Rome, Italy.

Edouard Glissant, 1993. *Tout-Monde* (Paris: Gallimard), 610 pp.
&
Edouard Glissant, 1997. *Traité du Tout-Monde* (Paris: Gallimard), 261 pp.

English Translation of the Titles: *All-World & Treaty of the All-World.*

Keywords: *Creolization, poetry, relation, technology, media*

Tout-Monde and *Traité du Tout-Monde* problematize the question of difference by showing how the influence of new information technologies renders it increasingly tricky to define one's identity in exclusive terms nowadays. Glissant's thesis about the *Creolization* of the world leads to three fruitful notions about cultural tolerance and social peace that can be sketched briefly here. First, cultural hierarchism is irrelevant. Second, it is through cultural exchange that all cultures survive. Third, the existence of *common-places* between mutually influential but distinct cultures is enough for a society to be integrated. This latter argument is the most decisive in political terms. The actual validity of these conclusions is dependent upon the sharing of some knowledge about the world's totality; the means that Glissant identifies to guarantee this condition are writing and imagination. "The purpose of the *poetics of Relation* [is] to say – the world, the world is totality; to guess how my own place, without moving, ventures out elsewhere, and how it takes me into the immobile movement" (pp. 119, 120).

Edouard Glissant is no social scientist. It is certainly for this reason that his writings, highly literary, have been confined to the fringes of the French academic debate on diversity and multiculturalism. Their heuristic value, nonetheless, is considerable. From an analytical standpoint, first it is upon an analysis of the concrete evolutions of the world that Glissant begs the question of identity and alterity nowadays, thereby breaking, at least in France, with an enduring tradition that still entices thinkers to tackle this issue in absolutes (e.g. Mesure and Renaut in *Alter Ego*, 1999). Second, his normative prescriptions are singular in the sense that they refuse to give a role to the state in the promotion of cultural tolerance. And third, the importance that Glissant attaches to imagination in *Tout-Monde* and *Traité du Tout-Monde* echoes Benedict Anderson's major work *Imagined Communities* (1983). Yet the author's understanding of writing is specific. In his *Traité du Tout-Monde*, he clearly asserts that the purpose of writing is neither to consolidate cultural identities nor to merge cultural identities: it is rather to congeal a framework of self-understanding. The *poet of Relation* certainly explodes the ancient imagining of pure communities by chanting their interconnectedness, but he simultaneously fosters an imagining of Relation that is itself to be constantly re-imagined.

Olivier Rousseau
Interdisciplinary Centre for Comparative Research in the Social Sciences, Paris, France.

Avner Greif, 1994. "Cultural Beliefs and the Organization of Society: Historical and Theoretical Reflection on Collectivist and Individualist Societies", *The Journal of Political Economy* 102, 5: 912–50.

Keywords: *cultural beliefs, institutional structure, societal organization*

Greif's paper shows that cultural beliefs affect the evolution and persistence of diverse societal organizations. This relationship between culture and institutional structure is demonstrated through comparative historical analyses of the Maghribi traders of the eleventh century who were part of the Muslim world, and Genoese traders of the twelfth century who were part of the Latin world. This is a fine economic analysis integrating sociological and mathematically formalized game-theory concepts.

Maghribi and Genoese merchants faced similar environments, employed comparable naval technology and traded in similar goods. Both had to hire overseas agents to handle their merchandise and feared they might embezzle it. An institutional structure needed to be created to require the agents to commit themselves *ex ante* to be honest *ex post* after receiving the merchant's goods. This organizational problem can be captured in a formalized game-theoretical model: the merchant-agent game.

Differing cultural beliefs entail different strategies in the same game-theoretical context and should lead to different economic relations. The Maghribi and Genoese traders were organized with different wages, different enforcement institutions and different ways of acquiring information about the agent's reputation. The historical records show differing cultural beliefs between the Maghribi and the Genoese, as well as evidence for the diversity in economic relations. Maghribi cultural beliefs could be considered as collectivist and Genoese cultural beliefs as individualist. Maghribi agency relations were horizontal: there was neither a merchants' class nor an agents' class. Among the Genoese, by contrast, merchants rarely functioned as agents or agents as merchants. The historical record confirms that these differing beliefs – collectivist and individualist – led to the different forms of organization. Moreover, the paper shows that these cultural beliefs have a lasting impact as they influence the way social organization evolves when "external" conditions (to the game) change. Thus organizations reinforce the cultural beliefs that have led to their adoption.

Neo-classical economics completely ignored institutions. New institutional economics tried to add realism by considering the role of human-made institutions (social and legal norms and rules) in shaping economic behaviour, and by integrating the study of institutions into the neo-classical framework. This paper can be seen as *the* example illustrating what *new institutional economics* is about. New institutional economics focuses on the role of institutions in reducing transaction costs. Each of the two societies responded to the merchant-agent problem, reducing transaction costs in the most efficient way – efficient in terms of its particular cultural beliefs.

The other reason why this paper is such a fine piece of work in economics is its ability to mathematically formalize and demonstrate conceptual insights of sociologists and anthropologists. This strength, however, is at the same time a weakness. Criticisms were levelled at new institutional economics for attempting to reduce institutions to "rational" and "efficient" resolutions to the problem of transaction costs.

Dafne Reymen
IDEA Consult, Brussels, Belgium.

François Grin, 2005. "The economics of language policy implementation: identifying and measuring costs", in Neville Alexander (ed.), *Mother Tongue-based Bilingual Education in Southern Africa: The dynamics of implementation*. Proceedings of a symposium held at the University of Cape Town, 16–19 October 2003 (Cape Town: Volkswagen Foundation & PRAESA), pp. 11–25.

Keywords: *language policy, economics, education, costs, benefits*

François Grin's chapter is one of his many works which explore the economics of language in multilingual settings around the world. One of the difficulties which education policy-makers face in multilingual settings is the issue of affordability. Grin provides an impressive list of linguistically diverse policies and their real rather than imagined costs in order to debunk ill-informed perceptions. The costs in reality are far more modest than policy-makers believe or would have their constituencies believe. Grin is also able to demonstrate that although monolingual education policies appear to be the rational choice, upon closer inspection, such policies often result in a chain reaction of negative factors which drain the system (educational failure, attrition/wastage from the school system, longer-term effect of poor education on health, employment, the fiscal system, etc.). Multilingual policies, however, offer more efficient retention and through-rate in primary and secondary education.

François Grin's pioneering work on the relationship between linguistic diversity and the economy has been of significant value to language policy and planning specialists in many parts of the world for the last fifteen years. This particular chapter arose out of Grin's participation in a symposium held at the University of Cape Town during 2004, at which he was requested to demonstrate a way of modelling the projected costs and benefits of a multilingual approach to education in African countries. This chapter was pivotal to the ADEA-UIE-GTZ Report (Alidou et al., 2006) and continues to influence debates on linguistic diversity in education across the African continent. It offers crucial arguments to debunk the myth that monolingual policies are more cost-efficient and affordable than those which foster linguistic diversity. However, this work needs to be pursued in more finely tuned detail by other scholars and development economists concerned with UNESCO's Education for All goals and frameworks

Kathleen Heugh
University of South Australia, Research Centre for Languages and Cultures, Adelaide, Australia.

Jean-Pierre Gutton, 1971. *La société et les pauvres: L'exemple de la généralité de Lyon, 1534–1789* (Paris: Les Belles Lettres), 504 pp.

English Translation of the Title: *Society and the Poor: The Example of Lyon, 1534–1789.*

Keywords: *misery, marginalization, assistance, disease, repression*

The book is divided into two sections and analyses the relationship between the society of the *ancien régime* and poverty in the specific case of the city of Lyon. In the first part of the work the position of the poor is outlined, characterized by social, economic and cultural aspects. Poverty is unavoidable in France, as well as in every other society of the early modern world. The author sets out the originating causes of indigence – from rural misery to the growth of grain prices – and the different categories of poverty – beggars, vagrants and ashamed poor – showing how these subjects are often victims of illness, old age or solitude. At the same time, Gutton describes the presence of poor people in urban spaces, the origins of wandering, and activities like brigandage and contraband (smuggling) as direct consequences of poverty. These are survival strategies of wretches, forced by need onto the road of delinquency and becoming, in this way, factors of social danger.

The second part of the book is dedicated to the feelings, the attitudes and the social doctrines surrounding poverty. This approach does not cover only the top of the social hierarchy, but also its lower classes, making it possible to understand which social image the poor people have of themselves. The author conveys deep understanding of the needs of the poor and knowledge of the related economic mechanisms. He provides an analysis of the social judgment of poverty and of the institutions created to manage it. There is an evolution from the image of poverty in the low Middle Ages, when the poor are associated with Christ and therefore accepted as such, to the early modern age, when a negative perception emerges, and they are criminalized, becoming a problem of public order.

Gutton describes the ways of organizing assistance and charity in the specific case of Lyon. He lists the institutions deputed to these activities, like hospitals and charitable organizations, and at the same time describes the first attempts to exclude the poor or to deport them to the colonies. The whole of Gutton's essay is centred on the diversity of the poor, on the doctrines elaborated around them and on the policies adopted to control them. It provides a basic contribution, moreover, to understanding how diversity is linked historically to criminality and deviance.

Augusto Ciuffetti
Marche Polytechnic University, Department of Social Sciences, Ancona, Italy.

Paul Haggis (Dir.), 2004. *Crash in L.A.* (United States: Lions Gate; Bob Jari Productions).

Keywords: *racism, cultural sensitivity, cultural bias, irrational prejudice*

Crash tells the story of a series of characters whose lives collapse within thirty-six hours. It takes place in Los Angeles, where their stories intertwine through the common themes of irrational prejudice and racism. The film stresses the harshness of living in the city, emphasizing how easy it is for human beings to succumb to fear of others. *Crash* shows how easily our perception is biased when we choose to emphasize differences over similarities in our relationships with other people. It explores the theme of racism in an emotionally compelling way, exposing the challenges of living in a diverse but insensitive environment.

This lack of sensitivity is best illustrated in one of the opening lines of the movie, narrated by the character Graham Waters, detective for the LA Police Department, son to a drug addict mother and brother to a young criminal: "It's the sense of touch. In any real city, you walk, you know? You brush past people; people bump into you. In LA, nobody touches you. We're always behind this metal and glass. I think we miss that touch so much, that we crash into each other, just so we can feel something."

When using this movie as a reflection tool about our own prejudices, I discovered with my first-year college students that it was a very useful means to open up a theme that is difficult to talk about as a personal experience. It seems natural to talk of prejudice and racism as something alien to us, something that happens out there and hardly ever as something that we can fall into as perpetrators. Among the reflections resulting from this exercise, there was the story of a Spanish white girl who fell in love with a Dutch boy of Moroccan descent (her first inter-ethnic relationship). In her reflection, she realized that she had been conditioned by her upper-class upbringing not to build a romantic relationship with someone of a *lower class* than hers. She acknowledged her own fear of letting her parents and friends know of her romantic involvement with the boy, as she was convinced they would disapprove of her choice. Other reflections pointed out the difficulties that Dutch students had in accepting Chinese students in their working teams, because they believed that they were passive, spoke English poorly, and thus were undesirable in their teams.

In these particular reflections, students realized that they were choosing the comfort of prejudice against the challenge of changing their biased beliefs about the other, therefore becoming more culturally sensitive. In comparing the film with the personal lives of my students, I noticed that the best way to delve into our own prejudices and accept them is to appeal to the irrationality and (in)sensibility of our own emotions: we need to *crash* against and deconstruct our own conviction that we are never prejudiced.

Manuela Hernández-Sanchéz
The Hague University, Academy of European Studies and Communication Management, The Hague, The Netherlands.

Cliff Hague & Paul Jenkins, 2005. *Place Identity, Planning and Participation* (London: Routledge), 249 pp.

Keywords: *place identity, planning, sustainable development, contested identities*

The central concern of this book is place identity, and its representation and manipulation through planning. Place identity is of growing international concern, both in planning practice and in academic work. This publication aims to connect theory and practice. The book is divided into ten chapters. The first three are largely concerned with theory and concepts. The second part of the book applies and develops these ideas in relation to planning practice. The final chapter reflects on the content and process of creating narratives of place identity through planning.

The book draws on collaboration between local governments from four countries in analysing the changes that are happening in places, identities and public engagement in the planning process, such as the emergence of new regional bodies which sidestep the nation-state in their dealings with the EU. This book has emerged out of planning practice. It draws on insights from geography, politics and cultural studies to analyse how those involved in the planning process are addressing the practical questions posed by urban expansion and the loss of traditional place identities. It provides a critical commentary on the way that new practices of *spatial planning* are being driven through the development of the EU. The editors argue that globalization and the politics of neo-liberalism challenge planners everywhere to rethink their assumptions and create a new approach to planning.

The book has been used to inform an understanding of identity in particular reference to Northern Ireland. The book examines concepts of place identity, discourses and imagined communities. Components of regional and local identity are discussed with specific reference to Belfast, alongside concepts of space, place and territory. This text has been used to inform a general understanding of such key terms and ultimately to inform SUS.DIV research from an architectural standing.

Hisham Elkadi & Karen McPhillips
Deakin University, School of Architecture and Building, Victoria, Australia & University of Ulster, School of Architecture and Design, Belfast, UK.

Josiane F. Hamers & Michel H. A. Blanc, 2000. *Bilinguality and Bilingualism* (Cambridge: Cambridge University Press), 468 pp.

Keywords: *bilingualism*

This book was originally published in French in 1983 and the first edition in English was published in 1989. This is the second edition, which is revised and updated. The book is a classic in the study of bilingualism and basic for the study of linguistic diversity. Hamers and Blanc distinguish between *bilinguality*, the use of two linguistic codes by the individual, and *bilingualism*, the use of two linguistic codes at the societal level. These terms are not used by all researchers in the field, but the distinction has been very important in analysing bilingualism at both levels, individual and social.

The volume has eleven chapters, a glossary, a list of references and subject and author indexes. Chapter 1 discusses different definitions of bilingualism and Chapter 2 focuses on the methodological question of measuring bilinguality and bilingualism. Chapters 3 to 7 focus on various aspects of bilinguality such as the relationship between bilinguality and cognition, neurolinguistic aspects of bilinguality and language processing in bilinguals. Chapters 8 to 11 look at bilingualism from a social perspective and are more relevant for research on diversity. Chapters 8 and 9 approach bilingualism from a social psychological perspective and can be considered as a bridge between the individual and the social levels; they deal with culture, identity and intercultural communication as related to bilingualism. Chapter 10 focuses on a more socio-linguistic perspective and Chapter 11 on bilingual education.

The volume emphasizes the psychological and social psychological aspects of bilingualism more than the socio-linguistic and educational. Therefore it is of interest for the study of linguistic diversity, because it provides a theoretical background that shows the complexity of bilingualism. However, this volume is not always easy to read and sometimes lacks examples that could make the different distinctions and proposals easier to follow. In spite of this difficulty, the book provides very useful information on different aspects of bilingualism.

Jasone Cenoz
University of the Basque Country, Donostia-San Sebastián, Spain.

Ulf Hannerz, 1990. "Cosmopolitans and Locals in World Culture", *Theory, Culture and Society* 7: 237–251.

Keywords: *globalism, localism, mobility, network, aesthetics*

Written in the late 1980s, this essay marks the emergence of the notion of transnationalism and of world culture on the academic stage. Ulf Hannerz questions the continuing validity of the contingent relation of the cosmopolitan and the local, whose distinction was a part of the sociological vocabulary for the second half of the twentieth century, since Robert Merton developed it in the late 1950s out of a study of patterns of influence in a small town on the eastern seaboard of the USA.

Observing the shifting of the scale of culture, turning what was cosmopolitan during the 1940s into a moderate form of localism now, Hannerz raises critical issues around the vanishing credentials of cosmopolitanism as a perspective, a state of mind, or a mode of managing meaning in the face of labour migration, mass tourism and a new appeal of extreme localism. For him cosmopolitanism includes a stance towards diversity in that it is built upon an inherent recognition of the coexistence of cultures in the individual experience. It is a stance of openness towards divergent cultural experiences, a search for contrasts rather than uniformity, vested in cultural competence and supported by skills of listening, looking, intuiting and reflecting that navigate across divergent systems of meaning.

Hannerz isolates varieties of mobility, those that do and do not condition cosmopolitan attitudes of mind and that relate to degrees of participation and immersion. His analysis shows that in fact cosmopolitanism does not necessarily flourish in conditions where one would assume to find it, such as among those living in exile or among expatriates, as such experiences tend to condition the self to the past in ways which negate commitment to a place that is perceived as transitional. Neither does cosmopolitanism thrive under conditions of heightened mobility of occupational cultures which command technical or institutional networks. Transnational networks of relationships thrive on specialized but collectively held understandings that, although inhabited by people who are involved with more than one culture and one transnational network, are nevertheless exclusionary.

The culture of intellectuals, which in 1940s New York simulated local knowledge and linked the core of culture to the facts of everyday life in an attempt to master it, yet never to become local. Transnational intellectuals, in turn, form alliances over shared, rather than different, concepts and values. Having established the absence of cosmopolitanism among those predisposed to know what lies beyond the local, Hannerz concludes that to find the cosmopolitan, one has to go local, where it is possible to become a cosmopolitan without going away at all.

The essay's status as a classic piece of writing on diversity lies in its replication of the conditions for an interest in diversity, and of the historical nature of its synonymy with an "ideal type of local", the aspiration of which he singles out as the critical problem of our time.

Susanne Küchler
University College London, Department of Anthropology, London, UK.

Jeremy Harding, 2000. *The Uninvited: Refugees at the Rich Man's Gate* (London: Profile Books), 128 pp.

Keywords: *fortress Europe, trafficking, desperation, enterprise*

This very readable piece of documentary journalism sets out the causes and effects of the phenomenon we know as *Fortress Europe*. Its cast of characters includes all the players – governments, traffickers, refugees, economic migrants, immigration officials. Although reference is made to more than a dozen ethnic groups across Europe, Asia and Africa, the diversity at issue here is of interests and interest groups; Harding does a masterful job spelling out the interrelations among them. His conclusion is controversial: "Western Europe's project of seclusion has many attractions, but it tends to widen the gulf between . . . rich and . . . poor. It is seriously harmful to both – and it should carry a health warning to that effect" (p. 6). The argument is thoroughly researched and plainly stated, much of it illustrated by richly detailed case material.

Part I of the book tells the story of refugees trying to reach wealthy countries, but emphasizes that neither the effort nor the numbers involved are new to the twenty-first century. It finds present "pressures" comparable to those felt in the 1920s and 1930s, when refugees were on the move all over the continent – except that our tradition of moral obligation towards disadvantaged or persecuted people has been eclipsed by new levels of panic and indifference to their plight. Part II extends the scope to include "economic migrants", many of them illegal and without grounds for claiming asylum, but facing hardships in their own countries and in transit which match the refugee experience. Many of these "asylum seekers" are highly skilled; all are potential sources of the economic and social energy which the rich world lacks. Yet this category is vilified in popular and media discourse, carrying too much of the blame for crime and credit crunch.

By spelling out the complexities of modern-day migration, this admirable book brings the inherent contradictions of *diversity management* into focus. First, restriction, far from controlling immigration, simply leads to more trafficking. "To inhibit immigration is . . . to invite a growing disregard for the law" (p. 10). If borders were open, migrants would come and go according to rational economic strategies and free of the hideous implications of indentured status. Second, rich countries have too many elderly people to care for and too few young ones to work and reproduce. In-migration can/could redress the economy and restore the birth rate, but hostility to it seems to increase in tandem with the demographic imbalance. Third, these contradictions create a double-bind for democratically elected governments. They must please voters on the liberal/ethical left who hold the values of asylum and charity, and they must respect the (democratically equally valid) sentiments of the restrictive/xenophobic right. So governments lurch between policy extremes with no resolution of this humanitarian crisis. Finally, and most relevant to diversity studies, note the confusion of labelling which follows these anomalies.

The rights of individuals depend on their allocation to one or other migrant category, just as too-tight boundaries of age, race or ethnicity limit the life chances of even the most affluent.

Sandra Wallman
University College London, Department of Anthropology, London, UK.

Julian Harding, 2007. "Investment Diversity through Equity Index and Passive Funds", *Legal & General Investment Management* (April): 1–4.

Keywords: *investment equity finance, pension fund*

This article embodies the question of how to protect pension schemes in order to be ready to meet the challenge of "deficit repair" as a consequence of a bear market. One solution is to apply a more structured risk framework for managing pension schemes assets. The risk within the pension fund is defined through the so-called Liability Driven Investment (LDI). Related to this approach, the adoption of greater diversity of growth assets in the portfolios has become evident. In effect the clients can choose the best investment alternative for their pension fund scheme. Nevertheless, there are always significant barriers which can hinder this process, such as a lack of immediate market capacity, limited diversification of individual assets and a concentration on managing risk.

The article focuses on diversity assets which cover a range of investments such as real estate, infrastructure and private equity. Three main funds have been created in order to meet the need for diverse assets for pension schemes: Global Real Estate Equity Index Fund (GREEIF), Global Infrastructure Equity Index Fund (GIEIF) and Global Listed Private Equity Passive Fund (GLPEPF). The first one (GREEIF) has the benefit of reducing the impact of the cyclical nature of property values by investing in many countries around the world. The Index is compiled by the Financial Times London Stock Exchange (FTSE International) in cooperation with the European Public Real Estate Association (EPRA) and the National Association of Real Estate Investment Trusts (NAREIT).

The Index represents the performance of real estate companies and real estate investment trusts worldwide. The second (GIEIF) is benchmarked against the FTSE/Macquarie Global 100 Infrastructure Index which provides a representative global coverage of the top listed 120 companies. The Index is market capitalized, free-float adjusted and is fixed at 100, representing a partnership between FTSE International and Macquarie Bank. The third (GLPEPF) aims to provide diversified exposure to the listed private equity market around the world and to provide exposure to a diversified range of companies in a cost-effective manner. The Fund has the advantage of investing in less well established small- and medium-sized companies. The Index captures the performance of a wide range of companies that specialize in private equity investment.

The paper is particularly interesting because it analyses how pension funds use the speculative market in order to avoid risks in the management process of pension schemes with an indicator to rate the degree of risk in the capital market. The three main funds offer a diversified structure of assets, dealing with risk avoidance. The aim is to provide diversified exposure and safety to the diverse range of top companies in the world.

Iskra Christova-Balkanska
Institute of Economics, Bulgarian Academy of Sciences, Sofia, Bulgaria.

David A. Harrison & Katherine J. Klein, 2007. "What's the Difference? Diversity Constructs as Separation, Variety, or Disparity in Organizations", Academy of Management Review 32, 4: 1199–1228.

Keywords: *separation, variety, disparity, group performance*

Since the 1980s, the authors argue, psychological research output on diversity within groups has almost doubled every five years. However, this is not true for scientific insights into the effects of diversity, as research has produced a number of inconsistent results: partly, diversity is described as leveraging group members' individual potentials and increasing group creativity and performance; partly, it is described as leading to miscommunication, conflict and bad group performance. To reconcile these seemingly irreconcilable results, Harrison and Klein suggest a new conceptualization of diversity: "We propose that diversity is not one thing but three things" (p. 1200). Specifically, they differentiate between *separation, variety* and *disparity*. Each of these three different types of diversity is supposed to have markedly different effects within groups. *Separation* denotes differences among group members regarding traits, attitudes and values. These differences reflect oppositions and may spark frictions and disagreements. Thus separation should impact negatively on group processes and group performance. *Variety* denotes categorical differences between group members, such as professional background or knowledge. Combining these differences increases groups' requisite pool of information, allowing adequate reactions to changing demands. Thus it may increase groups' creativity and performance. In contrast to separation, variety should impact positively on processes and group performance. Finally, *disparity* refers to status differences among group members, such as pay or power, which may cause dissatisfaction and conflict within groups. As with separation, it should impact negatively on group processes and group performance.

Harrison and Klein provide a new conceptual approach to diversity. Not only do they define different types of diversity, they also explain how to measure them and reason about the different effects of maximum values of the respective type of diversity. Their reflections give valuable insights into potential pitfalls and make recommendations for how to build diverse work groups.

Myriam N. Bechtoldt
University of Amsterdam, Department of Psychology, Amsterdam, The Netherlands.

Simon Harrison, 1999. "Identity as a Scarce Resource", *Social Anthropology* 7, 3: 239–251.

Keywords: *identity, ethnic conflict, symbolic practices, percpetion*

This article draws from the intuition that the reason for ethnic conflict is often not the perception of difference, but the perception of the ethnic *Other*. In other words, the reason for which a group decides to fight another group is the feeling that their existence is being threatened and they must prevent their own disappearance against the others' subversive intimidations. Harrison investigates the symbolic practices by which social groups and categories represent their identities, which he believes are as vulnerable to being copied and need to be protected against unauthorized replication as much as any material object.

The author illustrates political, religious, ethnic, social and commercial situations where the authenticity of identity symbols is threatened because the group they belong to perceives that they have been imitated, and in all of them he attempts to explain "why social actors, in certain circumstances, view *perceived* resemblances between themselves and others negatively, as a challenge to their identity, and act to safeguard themselves from such threats" (p. 242).

Four possible scenarios that explain the insurgence of ethnic conflicts are identified: (1) when relatively powerless social actors seek to appropriate the symbolism of the powerful; (2) when the privileged group seeks to appropriate the ethnic practices of the subordinate group; (3) when social actors aim at diminishing or eradicating the differences between themselves and other groups, or aim at exacerbating existing differences; (4) when one group claims to be the right and only group entitled to carry certain ethnic symbols and pursues other groups' disappearance and dispossession of such symbols.

Throughout the article, ethnic identity assumes the form of a scarce resource, but I believe the central issue addressed is that difference and resemblance are both based on perception. Ethnic studies have mostly concentrated on the differences that are perceived amongst groups that feed and perpetuate conflicts. What this article suggests is that perception of commonalities as much as of diversities leads to divisive and contentious circumstances, both of which foster boundaries and distinctions. Resemblances and similarities can be equally harmful and powerful in giving people reasons to justify a conflict: we must not imagine threats, and we must not fear either the *Others* or the *Us*.

Rossella Lo Conte
University College London, Department of Anthropology, London, UK.

Einar Haugen, J. Derrick McClure & Derick Thomson (eds.), 1981. *Minority Languages Today* (Edinburgh: Edinburgh University Press), 254 pp.

Keywords: *minority languages, language policy, bilingual education, multilingualism*

This hardcover book contains papers presented at the First International Conference on Minority Languages (1st ICML). It contains all eight plenary papers as well as sixteen selected from the thirty-five other papers presented at the conference. The names of several of the authors reappear many times in later publications on minority languages, bilingual education, multilingualism and linguistic diversity. Central is a discussion on the term *minority language*. The diversity of situations in which minority languages are used makes it hard to arrive at a general acceptable definition.

The book was well received. Some of the papers are still worth reading today. There was a continuous demand for the book, and nine years later, in 1990, a paperback edition appeared with some corrections, updates and additions.

The timing of the first conference was excellent because the attention on minority languages was on the rise, not only in academic circles but also in the political arena. Around that time the European Parliament accepted the now famous Arfé Report and the European Bureau for Lesser Used Languages (EBLUL) and the Mercator-network were established. Also the groundwork was under way for the later European Charter on Regional or Minority Languages (1992). Since 1980 important changes have taken place at the European level, both inside the EU and within the Council of Europe.

The ICML series continues and the next (twelfth) conference will take place in Tartu, Estonia, in 2009. Many other conferences, workshops and meetings have been held around the same theme. In that sense minority languages are still very much an issue today. The conferences offer an opportunity to discuss various disciplinary approaches. Good research practices are transmitted and disseminated. A lot of progress has been made in theorizing about minority languages, in models for comparative studies and in the application of outcomes of research to the revival and protection of these languages. The conferences are always organized in cities where minority groups are present and the participants get a first-hand impression of their daily reality. The ICML series combined have in no small measure been conducive to the development of the field of European minority language studies and linguistic diversity.

This book has strongly influenced the direction and development of my own work, which aims at understanding and comparing the diverse situations of indigenous minority languages in Europe, in particular in an educational context. Attending and being involved in organizing the ICML series, and reading the publications coming out of them, has taught me a lot. They are highly recommended for anyone interested in minority languages, language policy or linguistic diversity.

Durk Gorter
University of the Basque Country, Donostia-San Sebastián, Spain.

Shirley Brice Heath, 1983. *Ways with Words. Language, Life, and Work in Communities and Classrooms* (Cambridge: Cambridge University Press), 421 pp.

Keywords: *language development, social/ethnic group, community/school, interaction, communication*

Ways with Words is a study about children learning to use language at home and school. The study takes place in two communities a few miles apart in southeastern USA and is based on fieldwork, both in classrooms and at children's homes. While one of the communities is composed of white working-class families steeped for four generations in the life of textile mills, the other community is mainly composed of black working-class families whose older generations grew up farming the land but whose recent members work in the mills. The author shows the deep cultural differences between the two communities, whose ways with words differ as remarkably from each other as they do from the patterns of the townspeople. The townspeople are those mainstream blacks and whites who hold power at schools and workplaces in the region. Differences in language use are portrayed in this book as linked to the systemic relations between education and production in the three groups. Of special interest is the way language mediates knowledge about culture.

For me this book was a breakthrough to understanding what culture is really about. The way the author describes the three different groups of actors' habits and norms is very sensitive and makes it easy to grasp the depth of the different cultural meanings imposed by the actors themselves. One of the most striking things shown in this book is how easily people can misunderstand each other. This book is set in schools and shows what can happen to those who are not in control of the dominant norms. It covers class as well as ethnic cultures and it makes it uniquely relevant for European countries where schools have to respond to increasing numbers of immigrant children.

Angela Nilsson
University of Stockholm, Centre for research in international migration and ethnic relations, Stockholm, Sweden.

Nancy Hornberger, 2007. *Encyclopedia of Language and Education* (New York and Berlin: Springer), 10 volumes.

Keywords: *education, bilingualism*

This is a collection of ten volumes, which is a fully revised and updated edition of the eight-volume collection published in 1997 under the general editorship of David Corson. The general editor of this revised edition of the *Encyclopedia of Language and Education* is Nancy Hornberger. The ten volumes cover a wide range of topics in language and education which are of great interest for the study of linguistic, cultural and educational diversity.

The content of the volumes is as follows: Volume 1, *Language Policy and Political Issues in Education* (eds. Stephen May & Nancy H. Hornberger); Volume 2, *Literacy* (eds. Brian Street & Nancy H. Hornberger); Volume 3, *Discourse and Education* (eds. Marilyn Martin-Jones, Anne-Marie de Mejia & Nancy H. Hornberger); Volume 4, *Second and Foreign Language Education* (eds. Nelleke Van Deusen-Scholl & Nancy H. Hornberger); Volume 5, *Bilingual Education* (eds. Jim Cummins & Nancy H. Hornberger); Volume 6, *Knowledge About Language* (eds. Jasone Cenoz & Nancy H. Hornberger); Volume 7, *Language Testing and Assessment* (eds. Elana Shohamy & Nancy H. Hornberger); Volume 8, *Language Socialization* (eds. Patricia Duff & Nancy H. Hornberger); Volume 9, *Ecology of Language* (eds. Angela Creese, Peter Martin & Nancy H. Hornberger); Volume 10, *Research Methods in Language and Education* (eds. Kendall A. King & Nancy H. Hornberger).

This volume has a special emphasis on multicultural and multilingual education and focuses on aspects of diversity in different parts of the world. Moreover, the diversity of this collection is reflected in the fact that it has over two hundred and fifty contributors from forty-one countries. There are a number of contributions from non-Western parts of the world. The collection provides a comprehensive state-of-the-art reference for anybody interested in diversity in education and particularly for language planners who have to develop policies to educate children in a linguistically and culturally diverse world.

Jasone Cenoz
University of the Basque Country, Donostia-San Sebastián, Spain.

Darrell Huff, 1991. *How to Lie with Statistics* (London: Penguin Books), 124 pp. [First published by Victor Gollancz, 1954].

Keywords: *manipulation of numbers, statistical terms, presentation strategies*

Despite its jokey title, a liberal punctuation of original Calman cartoons and chapter titles like "Much Ado about Practically Nothing" (Ch. 4) and "The

Gee-Whiz Graph" (Ch. 5), this is a very serious little book. Its back cover blurb sets the tone: when it was first published this now classic book was hailed as "a splendid piece of blasphemy against the preposterous religion of our time". Today statistics continue to baffle us, and this trenchant book remains an invaluable guide through the maze of facts and figures that is designed to make us believe anything.

How to Lie with Statistics is more than a popular guide to understanding tables and numbers and extrapolations in the popular media. It also works as the necessary and sufficient means to curing any personal fear of numbers, and/or as a background text for anyone designing an introductory course for number-phobic social scientists.

In the context of this bibliography, the book can be recommended as an invaluable aid to understanding the reality behind expert pronouncements about all kinds of diversity and diversity ratios. It demonstrates how the same facts of population mix can be presented in ways to frighten us or to make us feel good: *See how our culture is threatened by the influx of foreign immigrants. Look at the crisis of teenage pregnancy/knife crime/drug addiction.* What we have come to know as *the politics of fear* is built on statements of this kind.

True, awful things do happen, are happening, and they need to be reported. But there are large proportions of immigrants who make creative contributions to the host's economy and civil society; and of teenagers who don't get pregnant, stab each other or take drugs. Presenting *those* numbers would make a very different impression – and, crucially, would support a very different political agenda.

Employment statistics are a good case in point. They can vary hugely, according to the simple matter of who is counted among the unemployed – only those who sign on to claim state benefit; those who do either for more than six months; those who are ineligible, informal, non-legal and invisible because they are not caught in the official lens . . . Different logics of counting can make comparisons between countries or political eras dangerously difficult. Similarly, of course, in the matter of assessing good and bad, greater and less, welcome or scary diversities.

It is important to recognize that, *pace* Huff's title, statistics can mislead without being based on an out-and-out lie. His point is that we must learn to see behind the common but clever strategies of presentation to understand what point is being made, by whom, and with what aim.

Sandra Wallman
University College London, Department of Anthropology, London, UK.

Samuel P. Huntington, 1996. *Lo scontro delle civiltà e il nuovo ordine mondiale*, translated by Sergio Minucci (Milano: Garzanti, 2000), 499 pp.

English Translation of the Title: *The Clash of Civilizations and the Remaking of World Order.*

Keywords: *civilizations, conflicts, multipolarism, conservatism*

A classic of the geopolitical studies of the last decades, Huntington's book sketches the new, post-Cold War equilibrium of international relations. At the base of his analysis he puts the concept of civilization, defined as a long-term, essentially cultural formation. With references to Toynbee, Sprengler, Braudel, Malko and others, Huntington's idea of civilization includes the shared history, religion, traditions and, to a certain extent, institutions, language, etc., of a population, and represents the broadest scope of identification for individuals, wider than a local area, region or nation, and just a step before the common belonging to humankind (p. 48).

The author focuses on some major contemporary areas of civilization – Sinic, Japanese, Hindu, Latin American, Islamic, perhaps sub-Saharan, and Western, subdivided into the Orthodox, the West European and the Neo-European of North America and Oceania. He describes their evolution, their diverging interests and the "fault line conflicts" (p. 304) between one and another – with the related risks of "core state conflicts" (p. 304). Besides its good predictive capacity, the book became famous at the time of the New York Twin Towers attack in 2001, having been published in 1996 and signalled by an article published three years before.

Huntington's hypothesis can be considered an eloquent example of the vision of diversity underlying North American and more generally Western conservative (or neo-conservative) policies in the recent age of globalization. Its basic idea revives the concept of the multipolar concert of the European powers before World War I, transferring it to an intercontinental context and refounding it on an articulated, long-run analysis. It gets back, after the end of the Cold War, to the traditional vision of a variety of different blocks, structurally in contrast for cultural reasons which are deeply rooted in their diverse forms of civilization (see in this regard Thomas Mann's *Reflections of an Unpolitical Man*, 1918). Consequent to these assumptions, the book states the necessity of a political realism which, recognizing that diversity is insuperable, balances conflict and agreement, and manages the contrasts in ways that defend (and impose) the interests of its own civilization.

For his relativism and for his refusal to admit any element of universalism, Huntington's theses are essentially in contrast to the progressive perspectives of Fukuyama's *The End of History* (see reference, p. 70), in opposition to which they were initially published in 1993. Yet universalism is discussed by

Huntington with regard to modern liberal culture, which, together with consumption models or the hegemony in mass communication, is considered by him as an aspect of the specific forms of Western civilization. Fukuyama, by contrast, sees in liberal democracy universal values which promote integration and cohesion without abolishing, but rather enhancing, the diversity of individual and collective identities.

Francesco Chiapparino
Marche Polytechnic University, Department of Social Sciences, Ancona, Italy.

Hasan Azizul Huq, 2006. *Agunpakhi*, 1st edn (Dhaka: Sandhani Prakashani), 158 pp.

English Translation of the Title: *The Firebird.*

Keywords: *religion, identity, Diaspora, home, family*

Agunpakhi, "The Firebird", is an award-winning novel by Hasan Azizul Huq of Bangladesh. Part fiction, part biography of the author's mother, it is an extraordinary story, the life of *Metar-bou*, the wife of the second son. We never get to know her name; her identity is only as her husband's wife. Metar-bou grows from a motherless, somewhat uncared-for child to a woman of deep perception; she questions established norms, but in silence, as per custom. With great insight and sensitivity she describes the world around her, the family and the land, her joy and her pain. Her sadness is almost tactile as she watches the joint family disintegrate into nuclear units, as brothers show insensitivity to the family or as death takes away a few. The description of the 1943 Bengal famine, the dry parched land, hunger, devastation and death and the subsequent floods turning fields to endless rivers is heart-rending. Her exuberance is lyrical when the good harvest finally arrives; long stretches of golden paddy sparkling in the sun; paddy, the real gold, the gold that sustains life. It is all still in silence.

Metar-bou's children leave for Pakistan soon after India's Partition in 1947, but life gets a new rhythm, even if lonely and slow. Suddenly her husband informs her of his decision to migrate to Pakistan, with her. After a lifetime of silence, Metar-bou finds her voice: she says a decisive "No". No, she will not migrate; she will not leave her home, her homeland, the earth around her. Her grit is remarkable. Yes, as a Muslim she is part of a minority, but a minority whose identity is the land around her, not a Muslim homeland. She asks a simple question: Pakistan is created as a home for Muslims and India is the home for Hindus, but if, after all the division, there are still Muslims in India and Hindus in Pakistan, then what kind of Partition is it? If you have an answer to this, she says, I am willing to migrate. There is no answer. Metar-bou stays on in her village all alone, facing the sun, waiting for the bright sunlit day.

The book is a historic document with a wide canvas. It opens up gender issues and issues of politicization and communalization of communities, Hindus and Muslims, who had lived in harmony for generations, even if in their separate individual spaces. It paints most vividly the trauma of division, separation and the forced need to find an alternative home. *Agunpakhi* is a remarkable novel, not only because of the sensitive portrayal of a young girl's journey through life, but also because it asks an eternal question, especially valid in today's world: Why divide a people? Why play with that piece of earth, the ground that gives identity and security? It is a thought-provoking book that raises questions on diversity, multicultural society, harmony, conflict, identity and diasporic pain that form a major part of the reviewer's own work.

Alaknanda Patel
Centre for Development Alternatives, Ahmedabad, India.

Marc Hooghe, Tim Reeskens, Dietlind Stolle and Ann Trappers, 2006. "Ethnic Diversity, Trust and Ethnocentrism and Europe: A Multilevel Analysis of 21 European Countries", paper presented at the 102nd Annual Meeting of the American Political Science Association, August 31–September 3, 2006, Philadelphia.

Keywords: *social cohesion, ethnocentrism, trust, social capital*

This paper investigates the relationship between diversity and social cohesion and expands earlier research on this relationship by combining attitudinal measurements from the European Social Survey (2002) with OECD data on migration patterns to include European countries. The study utilizes the more detailed measurements of both social cohesion (including generalized trust and ethnocentrism) and diversity (including type and rise of diversity over time as well as the legal status of immigrants) in multilevel models. Therefore, the study aims to overcome most of the limitations of earlier work, such as (1) the exclusive concentration on studying the effects of diversity in the USA or other one-country settings; (2) the limited measures of diversity utilized; (3) the sole concentration on trust; (4) insufficient controls; and (5) modelling errors, by creating a variety of measurements of diversity and two attitudes that capture social cohesion – generalized trust and feelings of ethnocentrism, and combining with a cross-national research using multilevel modelling.

The results of the study on the impact of ethnic diversity on social cohesion in European countries show that at the individual level most of the familiar relations between individual characteristics and trust and ethnocentrism were confirmed across Europe: men, older people, the less-educated and the unemployed are more ethnocentric and less trusting, while at the country level hardly any indicators for migration or diversity proved to be significantly related to social cohesion. According to the results of this study, the more static diversity variables do not affect generalized trust in Europe in any significant way: whereas citizens of ethnically heterogeneous countries are less trustful than those in homogeneous places, this difference is statistically insignificant. Contrary to earlier studies, the results of this study cannot conclude that (increasing) ethnic diversity has a negative impact on generalized trust. On the other hand, the analysis of the diversity indicators on ethnocentrism revealed diverse results: the effects of ethnic diversity on feelings towards immigrants are not uniform. There is no trend that ethnic diversity affects outsider hostility. Only the recent increase in asylum seekers is significant, as it tends to boost ethnocentrism. Overall, though, the analysis of the diversity indicators on ethnocentrism revealed the same conclusion as for generalized trust: it is difficult to sustain the theory that ethnic diversity affects social cohesion negatively, at least within Europe.

Despite several such findings for USA society, in Europe it was not confirmed that rising ethnic diversity, or even the rate of influx of foreign citizens, had any significant detrimental effects on social cohesion. To the contrary, the higher the share of immigrants, the less ethnocentrism the paper found in European societies, although not significantly so. At least with regard to European countries, therefore, the pessimistic notion that (increasing levels of) diversity threatens social cohesion could not be confirmed in this analysis. While some indicators of (increasing) diversity seem to have some effects, the overall conclusion of the study has to be that for Europe ethnic diversity cannot be considered as a threat for the maintenance of social cohesion.

Tüzin Baycan-Levent
Istanbul Technical University, Department of Urban and Regional Planning, Istanbul, Turkey.

Jane Jacobs, 1961. *The Death and Life of Great American Cities* (New York: Vintage Books Random House), 458 pp.

Keywords: *planning, infrastructure, regeneration, decline*

Since its first publication in 1961 this inspiring book has been reprinted many times and translated into many languages. It was written as a polemic against the anti-diversity planning fashions of the post-World War II period, but remains a classic must-read for anyone – of any discipline – concerned with the dynamics of big cities. Following an introductory overview, the volume is divided into four chapter sets: The Peculiar Nature of Cities; The Conditions for City Diversity; Forces of Decline and Regeneration; and Different Tactics. The twenty-two chapters cover "all" aspects of city life – except that racial/ethnic/religious diversities are never mentioned. In the present era their absence is striking: fifty years ago our concerns were different. But the insight into cultural diversity provided by this account of urban structures and opportunities is remarkable.

Jacobs makes a persuasive case for diversity as essential to urban vitality and sustainability and identifies the factors generating it. "Diversity . . . rests on the fact that so many people are so close together, and among them contain so many different tastes, skills, needs, supplies and bees in their bonnets" (p. 240). Concentrations of population are not enough: the infrastructure needs to echo and enable the mixture and interaction of people – specifically with mixed economic uses, small city blocks, and aged buildings along with the new. "We need all kinds of diversity, intricately mingled in mutual support" (p. 141). Each element has a chapter devoted to it; each is shown to increase variety and sustainability, interaction and creativity; and, significantly in the 1960s, all of them went against the ideals of order, tidiness, uniformity and control – objectives which Jacobs knew then, and most planners know now, would lead only to monotony and decline.

Jacobs' insights into the process of diversity and the connectedness of urban variables are most crucial to our concerns here. *The self-destruction of diversity* (Ch. 13) describes the process: truly diverse settings are attractive places to live and work. People are drawn to them and compete for space in them. Property values rise and small investors/entrepreneurs/homeowners are priced out, taking the vibrancy of mixture with them. Diversity becomes a victim of its own success. *The kind of problem a city is* (Ch.22) explains the connectedness. Commonly, urban problems are approached as simple, dependent/ independent two-variable duos, or as disorganized complex systems which only statistical methods can unravel. In fact, they are neither: cities constitute systems of organized complexity to which the key is not the number of variables – more than two, less than two million – but their interrelatedness. To understand cities, diversities, the reasons for planning failure or urban success, we must know how the variables interact. This book destroys the assumption that intervention made without reference to systematic connections among them can solve anything, but there are wonderful compensations: it makes the chaos of city life intelligible – and it's a very good read.

Sandra Wallman
University College London, Department of Anthropology, London, UK.

Martin Jay, 2002. "Cultural Relativism and the Cultural Turn", *Journal of Visual Culture* 1: 267–278.

Keywords: *cultural determinism, visual experience, technology*

This essay throws critical light on assumptions which have been driving the analysis and even arguably the staging of experiences of the visual in culture over the last decade. These assumptions are steeped in a perceptual paradigm which took distinct 'scopic regimes' or visual practices to be relative to the cultures out of which they emerge. The visual turn of cultural critique has given way to theories of cultural determinism and incommensurability which embrace the concept of diversity as basic to the concept of culture.

Founded on the earlier work of art historians such as Erwin Panofsky and Michael Baxandall, as well as cultural critics like John Berger, philosophers like Richard Rorty and literary critics like W. J. T. Mitchell, is the idea that visual experience is 'culture all the way down'. This became an academic juggernaut during the 1990s, following a well-attended conference staged at the Dia Art Foundation in New York in April 1988. Journals were launched to publish the flood of work being done on visuality in all corners of the humanities and social sciences. Critically at stake appeared the very possibility of translation of what was seen to be determined by "intellectual worldviews" and by partial perspectives on the reality which the visual purports to describe and to evaluate. Under the strain of the discursive analysis of images, the Platonic idea that images can be understood as analogic signs with universal capacities to communicate gave way to a theory of technologically mediated conventions which govern the global flow of images. Drawing on the work of theorists such as Bruno Latour, David McDougall and Régis Debray, Martin Jay offers an enlightening summation of a decade of visual theory and a stinging critique of its displacements. Jay offers no clear theoretical foundation for an alternative explanation of the materiality of images, evoking merely the ghost of phenomenology and the takeover of the humanities by science. Yet despite his reticence to set out clearly the terms and conditions of a post-visual theory of images which is engaged in the crafting of cultural dialogue, the essay has acted as a powerful reminder of what is at stake in understanding and managing diversity.

We can take away from this essay the importance of working towards a theoretical foundation and perhaps a new methodology which is capable of explaining what enables images to be exchanged across cultural boundaries. These images Merleau-Ponty famously called "the flesh of the world". In years to come, this essay will be seen as marking the moment when a decisive shift occurred in academia and public policy towards a new interpretation of cultural dialogue, shifting attention away from culture-bound meaning to the vehicles of culture-transcending flows.

Susanne Küchler
University College London, Department of Anthropology, London, UK.

Patty Jenkins (Dir.), 2004. *Monster* (Los Angeles, CA: Media 8 Entertainment)

Keywords: *prostitution, serial killer, death penalty, mental illness, poverty*

Gender has been and continues to be a largely neglected issue in criminological research. Theories and research tend to focus on the male offender, whereas female offenders, when considered, have traditionally been seen as disturbed rather than criminal. It is only in the last thirty years, with the rise of feminist criminology, that this image – both in criminological theory and in popular conceptions of the female criminal – has been critically questioned and reconsidered in light of apparently new forms of female offending and a changing social structure in Western countries. Despite this, much of the mainstream work being done remains male-centric.

Monster, a biographical film portraying the life of Aileen Wuornoss prior to her conviction to death by the state of Florida, tackles some of the most difficult and sensitive issues related to female criminality. The film depicts Wuornoss, an impoverished prostitute of questionable mental stability, as she takes in a young female lover and then tries to leave the world of prostitution and enter the job market. Repeated failures bring Wuornoss back to prostitution and an encounter with an abusive client who brutally rapes and beats her, leading Wuornoss to commit her first murder. Wuornoss's actions from then on are portrayed as the desperate acts of a woman striving to maintain her lover while killing her clients in increasingly brutal ways.

The film can be criticized for its portrayal of female criminals and for its very title, in that it recalls traditional theory and notions in which women who commit acts of violence are aberrations of nature, monsters. This, however, can also be seen as a powerful social commentary on the harsh world in which destitute women with limited resources may turn to prostitution with its inherent risks of abuse and violence committed by clients.

The film encourages one to think critically about the circumstances in which Wuornoss lived, the trappings of poverty and lack of marketable skills that may keep individuals at the margins of society. Above all, it shows the interconnections between victim and victimizer and the part that women may play in both roles. The film leaves the watcher questioning whether justice was done and the part which Wuornoss's gender and profession played in her sentencing, raising questions about bias and failed justice that neglected to consider factors such as a history of abuse and mental instability.

Taken in its totality, *Monster* can be seen as presenting a critique and social commentary of multiple aspects of society in which not only gender, but also poverty, violence and abuse, mental health, substance abuse, and other factors that contribute to marginalization may influence the way individuals are treated within the criminal justice system and in society at large.

Vanja M. K. Stenius Psychoanalytic Institute for Social Research, Rome, Italy.

Frank Kalter & Nadia Granato, 2002. "Ethnic Minorities' Education and Occupational Attainment: the German Case", Arbeitspapiere – Mannheimer Zentrum für Europäische Sozialforschung, No. 58: 1–28.

Keywords: *ethnic inequalities, labour market*

This article was produced in the frame of an international project aiming to investigate the labour market performance of immigrants relative to natives in the USA and several European countries, focusing on Germany. While there is an increasing amount of literature devoted to the disadvantages of ethnic groups in the labour market of single societies, comparative studies are generally scarce. Looking at the German situation, there is no doubt that most interest and research focuses on the so-called *guest-workers* stemming from Greece, Italy, ex-Yugoslavia, Portugal, Spain and Turkey. These *classical labour migrants*, as they are referred to in the analysis, were recruited to fill a gap of low-qualified labour in a specific historical situation. The existence of ethnic stratification in the German labour market was not really surprising in the 1960s and 1970s. However, most empirical studies agree to the general conclusion that ethnic inequalities in the labour market have persisted until today. Although the situation has noticeably improved over the last decades, it is nevertheless very clear that immigrants still occupy lower positions and that this holds true, even for the descendants of the former migrants (second generation). This article is an attempt to conduct empirical analyses for different contexts in order to examine whether and why the amount of ethnic disadvantage differs.

This paper is an effort by the authors to further enhance knowledge about the major paths of ethnic inequality in the German labour market, setting it in the context of an international comparative project. The article provides an overview of the general theoretical arguments and the relevant specific contextual conditions in Germany. The study uses the German *Mikrozensus* data for the analysis, and it bases its theoretical background on a number of hypotheses. The general finding is that ethnic inequality in the German labour market seems to be mainly a matter of human capital, i.e. of educational qualifications and factors directly related to the migration experience (country-specific capital), rather than a matter of discrimination in the labour market. This holds true, at least, for most of the classical labour migrant groups. This is backed up with statistical evidence, estimating the impact of ethnicity, generation and education on occupational attainment. The authors run logistic regression models when analysing the odds of being a salaried employee versus being a worker, and use the multinomial logic model when addressing different access to social classes.

Tonia Damvakeraki
National and Kapodistrian University of Athens, Athens, Greece.

Annette Kamp & Peter Hagedorn-Rasmussen, 2004. "Diversity Management in a Danish Context: Towards a Multicultural or Segregated Working Life?", *Economic and Industrial Democracy* 25, 4: 525–554.

Keywords: *diversity, equality, ethnic minorities, multicultural organizations*

Using critical discourse analysis and neo-institutionalism as their theoretical framework, the authors critically scrutinize the existing literature on diversity management, and argue for a dynamic perspective to understand how diversity management may bring change in a specific context.

The existing literature draws on the following discourses. *Human capital* is a discourse on efficiency and how to achieve it at an individual level. People are the same and what is at the core is to judge the merits of individuals, disregarding other differences between them. In order to improve effectiveness, organizations must recruit disadvantaged groups. Discrimination and differential treatment are seen as inducing failures in the functioning of meritocracy. The ideal is differentiation. Derived from the debate on globalization, in the *cultural capital* perspective, people with a transcultural background are expected to make a special contribution. In the *learning and synergy* perspective, linked to the concept of the *learning organization*, diversity refers to the diversity of every single individual, but unique individuals should be brought together. The dynamic learning organization thus becomes a context in which people constantly challenge each other to release the potentials for synergy, innovation and creativity. People are viewed as unique and valued assets which can be developed. Merits cannot easily be identified, implying that managing creativity allows for experimentations and improvizations. Finally, *social justice* deals with ethics and fairness.

Diversity makes sense only if both individual and institutionalized (structural) discrimination is abolished. It implies a focus on group identities, especially of minorities who have formerly been discriminated against. These discourses have different implications for the position of ethnic minorities in organizations. They lead to ambiguities and contradictory meanings of diversity management. Often a shift occurs from moral discourses (of justice and tolerance) to market discourses where diversity turns to the business case. However, when diversity is taken up in a specific context, it is reinterpreted under the influence of established institutions which imply that certain of the four discourses are pushed to the forefront or modified, while others are suppressed.

A Danish case study is analysed to understand how one of the four discourses is appropriated in a specific context, emphasizing the sameness of people and thus leading to assimilation, while the existing Danish discourse on social responsibility tends to position *the other* in an inferior position in relation to the normal Danish worker. The authors conclude that diversity management draws on several discourses, most of them related to globalization, but focusing on different aspects. But, also, discourses of justice survive within the diversity management discourse. Diversity management does not only prescribe the way to business success; as a result of its historical roots, it also delivers a story of how to obtain equality as well as depicting a win-win situation where the first and the fourth perspectives – human capital and social justice – are united.

Kiflemariam Hamde & Nils Wåhlin
Umeå University, Umeå School of Business, Umeå, Sweden.

James G. Kellas, 1993. **Nazionalismi ed etnie**, translated by Marta Innocenti (Bologna: Il Mulino), 240 pp.

English Translation of the Title: *The Politics of Nationalism and Ethnicity.*

Keywords: *nationalism, political history, nation, ethnicity, religion*

Nationalism is known for the decisive role it has played in the often conflicting and tragic dynamics of the single states and of the whole international scene in the twentieth century. Kellas investigates it as a social and cultural phenomenon, rather than a political one. Although he does not neglect a historical approach, his analysis is focused mainly on the present, in particular on the nationalistic movements of the post-World War II period. In this regard, it is interesting now, in the light of what these movements produced in the decades around the turn of the century, to read the last part of the book, where the author reviews the principal theses of the experts from the 1960s onwards, proposing a set of hypotheses on the future evolution of nationalistic trends.

More generally, Kellas compares various case studies of nationalism in what he defines the First, the Second and the Third World, each in a different chapter of his work. Nationalism is distinguished in three typologies: official, ethnic and social. The first pertains to state and has juridical characteristics: all the people, who are recognized legally as citizens, are members of the nation, apart from their ethnic identity or their cultural matrix. Official nationalism – Kellas says – is therefore fundamentally inclusive, or at least it seems sufficiently unselective to allow a large plurality of subjects to enter the national community.

Social and ethnic nationalisms are different: actually they are framed in different and, importantly, competing perspectives. Social nationalism is founded in the social links and in the cultural elements of a national community. Its degree of exclusivity is, however, relatively low, because it is sufficient that a subject – individual or group – adapts himself to the social rules and the cultural traditions of the community in order to be accepted in it. Ethnic nationalism, on the contrary, has its roots in history, namely in a supposed common descent of the member of a community. Fundamentally it has no exceptions, and can represent an insuperable obstacle for those who have different origins. Thus, in Kellas's approach, social and ethnic-cultural diversity figures as the basic criteria of selection and the inclusion/exclusion of a subject in/from a national community.

Roberto Giulianelli
Marche Polytechnic University, Department of Social Sciences, Ancona, Italy.

Mondher Kilani, 1994. *Antropologia: una introduzione* (Bari: Dedalo), 352 pp.

English Translation of the Title: *Anthropology: An Introduction.*

Keywords: *social anthropology, diversity, culture, geography, history*

The book provides a broad introduction to anthropology: it goes beyond the Western tradition as it covers the contributions in history, geography and ethnology from the Arab and Muslim world. Of particular interest is Kilani's focus on three key concepts: human geography, travel geography and global history.

The concept of *human geography*, as developed by Arab scholars (starting around 205 according to the Islamic calendar, or AD 820), conceives geography in its broadest sense, including human beings and the world in which they live, as affected by climate and characteristics of territory. In modern terms, human geography can be seen as a precursor to ethnology. *Travel geography* represents another Arab tradition that was developed during the ninth and tenth centuries. This went beyond literature and poetry as seamen, merchants and Islamic pilgrims reported on what they had seen during their travels. The writing was in accordance with the concept of *iyān* (visual and direct evidence), which initially focuses on other cultures and leads them to view their internal diversity in the light of newly acquired perspectives. This led to the development of the tradition of *masālik wa l-mamālik*, or *itineraries and states*. Finally, Ibn Haldūn, in writing *Kitāb al-'Ibār* (in the fourteenth century), laid the foundations for historical and sociological studies in his development of the concept of *global history*.

Mondher Kilani is professor and director of the Institute of Anthropology and Sociology in Lausanne, Switzerland. With this book he shows that it is possible to go beyond the Eurocentric way of understanding and thinking about anthropological theory and research. The work presents a comparative history of ideas and cultures, introducing *the anthropology of others*, and the history of how diverse cultural traditions (in particular, in the Arab and Islamic world) have developed their own ideas of diversity. Diversity is no longer about *primitive people living far away*, as in classical Western anthropology, but may be seen in a wider perspective. This may entail, for example, the social capital linked to the economic value and symbolic meaning, with a basis in tradition, of a particular breed of cow in the Swiss Alps.

The key contribution of the text is to provide the reader with an introduction to anthropology that reflects theory and evidence from around the world, including the influence of non-Western thought on Western scholars, encouraging one to think about *the local* in the light of perspective from elsewhere, in accordance with *iyān*.

Maria Alessia Montuori
Psychoanalytic Institute for Social Research, Rome, Italy.

Irena Kogan, 2003. "A Study of Employment Careers of Immigrants in Germany", *Universität Mannheim* Working Paper No. 66: 1–32.

Keywords: *ethnic inequalities, labour market*

This study examines immigrants' employment careers and their similarity/dissimilarity with the standard career sequence of native Germans. Applying sequence analysis techniques, the study shows that career patterns of ethnic Germans and EU immigrants are closer to the employment patterns of the native-born than is the case for other immigrant groups. Career paths of guest-workers from Turkey remain, for example, extremely dissimilar, even when differences in the age structure and the educational level are taken into account. Long and frequent unemployment seems to be behind this dissimilarity. Immigrants, and particularly Turks, not only have a higher propensity to be unemployed, but they are also pushed into the unskilled occupations. The second generation, although displaying the closest degree of similarity to the employment career patterns of native-born Germans, largely fail when it comes to occupational assimilation, even though they seem to escape labour market segmentation, pronounced among their parents, often entering occupations in which unprivileged first-generation immigrants are rarely found.

The current study is based on the employment history data from the German Socio-Economic Panel (GSOEP), a representative panel survey of the resident population, thus providing important information from a rich database on labour market, employment and job dynamics for the five most important immigrant groups residing in Germany: Italians, Turks, Yugoslavs, Spaniards and Greeks. Some of the most interesting and useful results indicate that none of the immigrant groups has an employment pattern identical to that of the native-born Germans. Moreover, the most dissimilar group remains guest-workers from Turkey. They are substantially remote from native-born Germans of the older cohort with regard to both zero and non-zero distances, and have the highest proportion of those with particularly distant employment patterns.

Tonia Damvakeraki
National and Kapodistrian University of Athens, Athens, Greece.

Takeshi Koyama & Stephen Golub, 2006. "OECD's FDI Regulatory Restrictiveness Index: Revision and Extension to More Economies", *Organisation for Economic Co-operation and Development (OECD) Working Papers on International Investment No. 2006/4:* 1–17.

Keywords: *Foreign direct investment (FDI), foreign restrictions, foreign ownership*

This article provides measures of the FDI Regulatory Restrictiveness Index for OECD countries and extends the approach to ten non-member countries (NMCs). FDI is defined by the OECD as an investment for the purpose of establishing lasting economic relations, with an undertaking in a particular investment, offering the possibility of exercising an effective influence on management. Attached to the OECD Declaration, the index covers nine sectors and eleven subsectors, with analysis based on the work of the Investment Committee. Among these sectors the most restricted are electricity and transport, and the most open are tourism, construction and manufacturing.

In order to obtain more accurate results, when measuring the FDI Regulatory Restrictiveness Index, the OECD and NMCs adhere to the National Treatment Instrument. The indicators measure deviations from discrimination against foreign investment. These restrictions on national treatment can be on entry and post-entry operations. Entry restrictions can be treated as limitations of foreign ownership and post-entry restrictions represent special procedures applied specifically to foreign investors.

Although the EU is still not completely unified in terms of policies towards inward FDI, substantial harmonization and intra-EU liberalization means that FDI flows are almost unrestricted in the EU.

OECD countries with the highest levels of overall regulatory restrictiveness are Iceland, Mexico, Australia and Canada. Among the non-OECD countries, the most restricted sectors are electricity, transport, telecommunications and finance and the least restricted are manufacturing, tourism and construction due to the reduced FDI regulatory restrictiveness.

Regulatory restrictions on foreign ownership are the most obvious barriers to inward FDI. They usually take the form of limiting the share of companies' equity to less than 50 percent, or even prohibiting any foreign ownership. Other limits to inward FDI or activities which will discourage FDI inflows include constraints on the ability of foreign nationals either to manage or to work in affiliates of foreign companies and other operational controls on these businesses.

Foreign ownership is a necessary and essential condition for FDI. The idea is to capture non-linearity in ownership restrictions as well as the inverse relationship between permissible foreign equity and restrictiveness. Restrictiveness is calculated at an industry level and then weighted: the national average is obtained using FDI and trade weights.

What is interesting in the paper is the emphasis on the regulation of restrictions on FDI, which have been estimated for OECD countries, but the methodology is extended to ten NMCs. The FDI Regulatory Restrictiveness Index for OECD countries in fact evaluates the degree of openness of the national economy, especially in some very strategic sectors of the economy such as telecommunications and electricity. It shows also in which sectors FDI may penetrate easily, but nevertheless the strategic sectors remain of great interest for foreign investors.

Evgenia Vladimirova-Krasteva
Economic and Investment Bank (part of KBC Group), Sofia, Bulgaria.

Will Kymlicka, 2001. *Politics in the Vernacular: Nationalism, Multiculturalism and Citizenship* (New York: Oxford University Press), 392 pp.

Keywords: *multiculturalism, nationalism, liberalism, civil rights, indigenous peoples*

The book is a collection of eighteen essays, published in 2001, which exemplifies Will Kymlicka's ongoing work on ethno-cultural diversity within liberal democracies. His theory of multicultural citizenship was discussed extensively during the 1990s, due to the pioneering nature of his engagement with issues of diversity in the context of liberal political philosophy. Although the book was widely celebrated for its innovation, broad compatibility and relevance, it refers back to an earlier model on ethno-cultural diversity within liberal democracies which was criticized for its exclusive Canadian context and lack of cross-regional transferability.

Kymlicka's new volume considers these critiques and reformulates a flexible array of good practices sensitive to the contingencies of different regional contexts. This is made apparent by the broad temporal and spatial scope of his analysis. Examples span from the French Revolution through to contemporary land-rights and language-policy struggles, and originate from globally diverse regions, from Australia and the USA to Bangladesh.

The essays in this volume share a common trajectory which is threefold in its concerns: first, the dialectic between minority rights and nation-state building; second, the encouraging tendency of multinational federalism; and third, the gap between the theory and practice of liberal democracies. All three concerns should have repercussions for those interested in political and social issues of diversity. The first allows Kymlicka to reconsider the liberal myth of the state as ethno-culturally neutral, against which he posits that states necessarily participate in a process of nation-building in which one culture dominates. Central to ensuring the normative desirability of the state, therefore, is its ability to rectify its lack of ethno-cultural neutrality by entering into a dialectical relation with minority rights. Regarding the second concern, Kymlicka's account provides a series of encouraging precedents from which he critiques other post-Westphalian narratives of the nation-state (post-nationalism, multicultural cosmopolitanism, etc.), proffering an alternative account of modern nationhood. Finally, Kymlicka presents an ethical discussion of the gap between the theory and practice of liberal democracies. According to the author, minority rights practice emerged in a theoretical vacuum – a fact entailing both positive and negative consequences. In order to close the gap between theory and practice, new orientations for research and action must be developed and investigated. Kymlicka both rises to this challenge and carries it forward to others.

By virtue of Kymlicka's admirably clear and reflective style of argumentation, this volume should be useful to those approaching the issue of diversity both from within and from without the intramural sphere of debates over minority rights. His *mid-level theory* is usefully balanced between abstract theorizations of pure political philosophy (whose practical utility is brought into question) and context-specific case study analyses (whose broader applicability is uncertain). Nations who institutionally support the concerns of minorities better protect against monocultural hegemony and thereby foster their own diversity. Accordingly, a volume so attuned to the political, philosophical, juridical and social context of minority rights – and the challenges and opportunities that reside there – is indispensable for those to whom diversity is an empirically pressing concern.

Jasper Jack Cooper
Interdisciplinary Centre for Comparative Research in the Social Sciences, Paris, France.

Ronald D. Laing, 1959. *The Divided Self* (London: Tavistock Publications), pp. 218.

Keywords: *identity, sanity, anti-psychiatry, madness*

Diversity and alterity provoke a multiplicity of emotions: fascination and curiosity, amazement, annoyance. Diversity challenges our daily experience of the world and offers a different perspective of it. An experience with alien people is by definition an experience with a provocative diversity. Our assumptions, our beliefs, our interpretations of words, gestures, emotions, are profoundly challenged when we talk about mental illness. This diverse world – intrinsically meaningless for those who are not psychotic – rises suddenly in our group, our family, perhaps inside us. It is like an aggression by an internal enemy. This is the reason why the history of insanity, or better the history of psychotic people, is one of progressive segregation and isolation from the mainstream society.

As changes in the production system moved towards a capitalistic system, with stricter social organization, more capable of satisfying the new demand for labour, the strangeness brought about by mental disease has been interpreted as an impediment to right performance as a social and economic actor. The result of this progressive social repulse of madness was an increasing difficulty in capturing the meaning of this strangeness and a dehumanization of mad people. How can we show the general human meaning of the patient status, when the words we have to use have been invented just to isolate them?

The parallel with the view that Western society had on *non-civilized* culture is impressive and has been deeply analysed. It took time to develop a different regard on the behaviour and language of psychosis – to state that it is absolutely possible to understand the psychotic patient. In a way, we can state that it took time to consider that the internal experience of a psychotic person is not radically different from the internal experience of a *normal* person. It took time to understand that the sense of desperation of a psychotic person is nurtured by the same existential food that nurtures our daily anxiety, though with a different level of intensity. It took time and we had to wait until the end of the 1950s to witness a radical – and I would say poetical – movement, ready to fight for the dignity and respect of psychiatric patients. It is not by chance that the civil rights movement claimed the need for the same respect for any kind of diversity: gay, lesbian, black people, psychotics, all of those who were oppressed, humiliated, segregated by the mainstream majority.

This book is illuminating for two reasons. First, it is a brilliant and plain introduction to the behaviour and language of psychotic patients, full of respect and understanding. Second, it is a wonderful image of the initial stage of revolt against society and the ideology of a one-dimensional human being, against the poverty of the sense of conformity and adoption brought about by capitalistic society. However, in this book the diversity we experience in a psychotic patient is anything but exotic: psychosis is one of the most painful conditions. To use Laing's words, a schizophrenic is a hopeless man. It was, and we think it still is, a touching lesson on the care we should use in interpreting and pretending to understand any kind of diversity.

Raffaele Bracalenti
Psychoanalytic Institute for Social Research, Rome, Italy.

Ethan G. Lewis, 2005. "Immigration, Skill Mix, and the Choice of Technique", *Federal Reserve Bank of Philadelphia* Working Paper No. 05/8 (May): 1–61.

Keywords: *technological change, immigration, local labour market*

The market response to the inflows of immigrants can vary greatly, as it includes not only wage and employment variation, but can also encompass change in firms' adoption of technology. A puzzling fact is how the USA markets, facing large immigration, have succeeded in productively employing such large flows of unskilled labour, despite the overall higher demand for skilled labour. The USA labour market has experienced advances in technology that have raised the skill requirements. At the same time the country is in the midst of an immigration boom, which has increased the supply of low-skilled workers.

The hypothesis of the paper is that the economy was able to absorb the inflow of less-skilled workers by using less of a skill-intensive technique. Rather than treating technology differences across plants or industries as given, this paper introduces potential adaptation of technologies to local inputs. This extensively constrains the effect of immigration on relative wages in local labour markets. The hypothesis of the paper is tested by analysing the impact of the relative supply of less-skilled labour on the use and adoption of automation technologies in manufacturing in USA cities. The less-skilled labour supply is measured by high-school dropouts per high-school equivalent, after the author controls for reverse causality, given that the less-skilled workers might seek out low-technology markets, where the relative demand for less-skilled labour is higher. The main instrument selected for this purpose is the share of dropouts among predicted recent immigration, which proves to be highly correlated with overall less-skilled labour supply. This high correlation is indicative of the strong influence that immigration has on local supply and of the strengths of immigrant enclaves in settling the location of newly arrived migrants.

The results indicate that, *ceteris paribus*, a higher local relative supply of less-skilled labour is associated with lower use of manufacturing automation technologies. The effect is larger when using historical patterns of immigration as relative skill supply. This last finding can indicate that less-skilled immigrants have a larger impact on technology choice than overall less-skilled labour supply. This paper finally raises doubts about the direction of the causality between adoption of technology and demand for skills. The author claims that the skill supply drives the diffusion of skill-complementary technologies, rather than new technologies being responsible for the demand of high skills.

Cristina Cattaneo
Eni Enrico Mattei Foundation (Milan, Italy) and University of Sussex (UK).

René Leicht, Andreas Humpert, Markus Leiß, Michael Zimmer-Müller, Maria Lauxen-Ulbrich & Silke Fahrenbach, April 2005. "Die Bedeutung der Ethnischen Ökonomie in Deutschland", Institut für Mittelstandsforschung, Universität Mannheim, pp. 1–30.

English Translation of the Title: *The Contribution of the Ethnic Economy in Germany.*

Keywords: *ethnic identity, migrant assimilation, migrant integration, entrepreneurship*

This study explores the propensity of immigrants in Germany to start up their own businesses. The Federal Ministry of the Economy and Labour has sponsored this study with the aim of identifying independent migrant workers, and in particular their creation of new businesses and the actual and potential contribution of these firms to the German economy. In 2003 there were 286,000 independent migrants in Germany, half of them from other EU member states, the majority being Italians, followed by Turks and Greeks. Female entrepreneurship was highest among the Greeks (24 percent), followed by the Italians and then Turks. Greeks and Italians have quite a substantial share of independent entrepreneurs within the whole migrant population (16 percent and 13 percent respectively), a higher share than German natives.

Overall fluctuations in entries and exits are higher in the migrant population, conditioned partly by unemployment. The characteristics of migrant entrepreneurs are that their enterprises are full-time occupations, while a higher share of Germans are part-time independent. One quarter of migrant entrepreneurs acquire existing businesses from German owners. They are much less active in ethnic niches than in the past, meaning that they are not only operating in the ethnic food chain. Greeks and Turks are in bigger cities than Italians; Turks go less into knowledge-intensive activities. Ethnic minorities are more entrepreneurial when they have German citizenship. They often operate ethnic restaurants, which are visited both by ethnic minorities and by Germans.

Migrant enterprises contribute 3–4 percent of total German employment, although their businesses have an average employment of four people. Turks have the largest average employment, followed by Italians. What is more important is that while German entrepreneurship is diminishing, that of migrants is increasing. However, their contribution to skills is lower as they offer less training than corresponding German companies, but when they do the training, size and quality is comparable. Finally, migrants have a much stronger family spirit, employing their own ethnicities more than others, employing family members and themselves working often more than sixty hours per week. At the same time they often expect family members to help without formal rewards. The determining factors for becoming entrepreneurs are the same among migrants as among natives: social improvement, family background and skill level.

Lena Tsipouri
National and Kapodistrian University of Athens, Athens, Greece.

Thomas Liebig, 2007. "The Labour Market Integration of Immigrants in Germany", *Organisation for Economic Co-operation and Development* (OECD) Social, Employment and Migration Working Paper 47: 1–66.

Keywords: *migration, integration, labour markets*

This paper focuses on the labour market integration process of immigrants in Germany, a country which has received, after the USA, the largest inflows of immigrants in the OECD area over the past fifteen years. The paper begins with a general description of the methodology that was used for the country review, including the definition of integration, the target population and the labour force characteristics examined. This is followed by an outline of the main migration groups, their history in Germany, and the development of the labour market situation of immigrants, to identify the key issues. Then, the institutional framework for integration and the important changes it has experienced with the new law on immigration that came into force in 2005 is presented and explained. This is followed by an assessment of some key issues that affect the labour market outcomes of natives and immigrants.

Particular focus was placed on two groups: ethnic Germans – who are the single largest migrant group in Germany; and the second generation – who are now entering the labour market in larger numbers. The paper ends with an overall summary including recommendations.

This study is mostly useful for scholars interested in studying the labour market integration of immigrants and how this has evolved since the post-war economic boom and the recruitment of low-skilled workers (until 1973), up until today. What is most interesting and useful about this paper is the fact that, apart from the analysis regarding the evolution of the labour market situation of people with a migration background, there is also an analysis of the integration policy framework, including the legal framework and the role of subnational governments and non-governmental actors. Additionally, the author includes a number of policy recommendations with regard to improving migrant integration in the labour market and in the sub-society.

Lena Tsipouri
National and Kapodistrian University of Athens, Athens, Greece..

Sonia Liff & Judy Wajcman, 1996. "'Sameness' and 'Difference' Revisited: Which way forward for equal opportunity initiatives?", *Journal of Management Studies* 33, 1: 79–94.

Keywords: *workplace equality, diversity management, sameness, difference*

The authors debate different organizational approaches to workplace equality between women and men within an analytical framework based on sameness and difference. Using this distinction, they point to the underlying reasoning of specific policies and tools and present critiques that address the fundamental weaknesses of both approaches. First, they discuss the dominant approach of *equal treatment/sameness* which is reflected in policies and techniques that aim to ensure that women are assessed in the same way as men, such as bias-free selection techniques or explicit examination of job requirements. Second, the authors introduce and discuss the (at that time) recent notion of *managing diversity* as another approach which is about a more positive valuing of difference. They argue that the initiatives of diversity management or *equality based on difference* are more individualistic and line-manager-based, resembling more a human resource management approach than the traditional industrial relations approach which is collective in nature.

The authors then move on to discuss the possibility that both approaches have something to offer. They point to the perspective that it is possible that sometimes women are disadvantaged by being treated differently when in fact they are the same, and at other times are disadvantaged by being treated the same when their difference needs to be taken into account. However, given the limitations of both sameness- and difference-based initiatives, the authors argue that there is a growing interest in moving beyond these divisions. They propose to redefine the norm in terms of women's needs and interests and to develop parallel policy frameworks around other interest groups, so that the workplace can be transformed into something more generally inclusive of diversity.

This article has strongly influenced my own thinking about organizational initiatives on diversity. This distinction of *equality based on sameness* versus *equality based on difference* helped me in identifying the underlying assumption of an organization's approach to managing a diverse workforce and its strengths and weaknesses. For instance, the dominant approach of *equal treatment/sameness* is limited, as the goal of achieving sameness is being judged against a norm of male characteristics and behaviours. Policies based on equal treatment/sameness require women to deny, or attempt to minimize, differences between themselves and men as the price of equality. The second *diversity* approach recognizes differences within the workforce and sees it as the responsibility of the individual to grasp opportunities assisted by an empowering organization. However, such an approach to gender equality may lead to resentment among men, as the differential treatment may be conceived as receiving extra benefits. It may also lead to an overemphasis on difference through which women may be seen as less attractive employees because their different needs are stressed. Finally, and maybe most importantly, their suggestion to look for new bases of equality, e.g. equality based on needs of employees, is in my opinion a fruitful way to think about changing and enlarging the norms themselves and consequently creating an inclusive workplace for all.

Maddy Janssens
Katholieke Universiteit Leuven, Faculty of Business and Economics, Research Centre for Organisation Studies, Leuven, Belgium.

Ping Lin & Kamal Saggi, 2005. "Multinational Firms, Exclusivity, and the Degree of Backward Linkages", *Deutsche Bundesbank*, Discussion Paper Series 1: Economic Studies, No. 10/2005: 1–48.

Keywords: *multinational firms, exclusivity, backward linkages*

The paper develops a model in which the entry of a multinational firm (MNF) results in a technology transfer to its local suppliers and also impacts the degree of backward linkages in the local industry. There is a connection between the technology transfer from an MNF to its local suppliers and the degree of equilibrium of backward linkages to the local industry. The latter is the objective of this article and reveals a new kind of effect, the so-called "de-linking effect" (p. 10), which is implied between local final goods firms and their suppliers. Such de-linking makes the goods market less competitive due to foreclosure of competition and can cause total output of the final goods to shrink.

The paper focuses on effects on the supply side of the MNF. Backward linkages may not be so important, especially when under contracts where multinationals transfer technologies to their local suppliers. This feature explains exclusivity, which discourages local suppliers from serving a MNF, but also has the strategic incentive to protect MNFs from their local suppliers. In fact, it helps prospective suppliers to set up production capacities, provide technical assistance, provide training and help in management and organization.

Exclusivity occurs in equilibrium if, and only if, it is more profitable for the MNF relative to market interaction. Exclusivity protects the MNFs from local rivals who might benefit from technology transfer and limits the number of competing suppliers that serve the local rivals. MNFs depend on how many other suppliers accept their offer, on the extent of technology transfer, and on the intermediate demand generated by local producers. The MNFs can have an important and lasting effect on backward linkages, if such entry impacts on the structure of imperfectly competitive markets linked by their local suppliers.

MNFs choose either to participate through market interaction, as an anonymous buyer, or to set up contractual relationships to their suppliers. Exclusive contractual relationships separate the suppliers into two groups: those who supply MNFs only, and those who supply local producers only. Suppliers have two options, either to become an exclusive supplier to the MNF, or only to serve home producers. Local suppliers usually benefit from technology transfer, which tends to raise the level of backward linkages.

The paper is valuable and informative because it focuses on the supply side of the MNF's entry into the local industry of the host country. This article provides new evidence for the relationship between MNFs and local industries through backward linkages. All the processes have been econometrically tested. Some results have been obtained in order to underline the role of MNFs in the transfer of technology in the local market. Exclusivity is one of the factors explaining the incentive of MNFs to move outside and to have a real impact on the host economy.

Evgenia Vladimirova-Krasteva
Economic and Investment Bank (part of KBC Group), Sofia, Bulgaria.

Deborah R. Litvin, 1997. "The Discourse of Diversity: From Biology to Management", *Organization* 4, 2: 187–209.

Keywords: *diversity management, diversity discourse, discourse analysis, essentialism*

In this article, the discourse on diversity in the workplace is based on the analysis of mainstream organizational behaviour textbooks, on the exploration of its origins in philosophy and natural sciences and on the comparison with two other contemporary discourses on diversity. Litvin argues that these three discourses on diversity (workplace diversity, biodiversity, and the Human Genome Diversity Project) all share essentialist underpinnings and resemble taxonomy and classification schemes used in pre-Darwinian biology to group animals, plants and even people in species based on observable similarities.

Focusing on the workplace diversity discourse, we see that in mainstream textbooks, diversity is mainly based on certain demographic characteristics (such as age, ethnicity, gender, physical abilities, race and sexual orientation), which are considered as immutable and as defining people's essences. The author argues that through such definitions, groups are constructed, which are considered both natural and obvious, while being internally homogeneous and essentially and exotically different from each other. Litvin states that such an approach to diversity is divisive as it stresses differences, overlooks common-alities and teaches us to treat individuals based on their category membership. As such, the deeper complexities of a person's motivations and actions are ignored, just like the influence of the wider context, power relations and other elements not acknowledged in the diversity discourse (e.g. class). In response,

Litvin promotes a process-oriented approach that treats people as complex, evolving and multidimensional and that acknowledges that experiences, differences, categories and their meanings are continually constructed in social interactions and in particular contexts with specific power relations.

In my opinion, this article is fascinating for several reasons.

First, it is both interesting and alarming to see how there are similarities between different discourses on diversity and approaches from the seventeenth and eighteenth centuries to describe and classify the world's flora and fauna, including humankind, based on generalizations, stereotypes and *typical* or *average* examples. Such comparisons show us how closely the mainstream diversity discourse, attributing specific characteristics to certain demographic groups, sometimes resembles lines of reasoning that also underlay forms of *scientific racism*. As such, the article can be read as a strong warning for diversity scholars and practitioners, telling them (us) that if we simply keep reproducing the dominant, mainstream diversity discourse, we are on dangerous territory. This is a warning that is, in my opinion, hard to ignore as a reader, and it has influenced my understanding of diversity ever since.

Second, this article offers a strong and in-depth analysis of the diversity discourse and its consequences. Moreover, it avoids simply limiting itself to critiquing existing views, by arguing for an approach that acknowledges the context and power relations in which specific categories are constructed, realities are created and differences become meaningful.

Koen Van Laer
Katholieke Universiteit Leuven, Faculty of Business and Economics, Research Centre for Organisation Studies, Leuven, Belgium.

Luis Enrique López, 2005. *De resquicios a boquerones: La educación intercultural bilingüe en Bolivia* (Cochabamba: PROEIB–Andes), 648 pp.

English Translation of the Title: *From Crevices to Big Gaps: Intercultural Bilingual Education in Bolivia.*

Keywords: *intercultural bilingual education, bilingualism, educational reform, social exclusion, indigenous people*

This book makes an inventory of the itinerary followed by intercultural bilingual education (EIB by its acronym in Spanish) in Bolivia. With abundant details, it analyses the historical antecedents of EIB emergence as part of the process of ethnic self-affirmation and the defence of their social rights by indigenous and peasant sectors. It also describes different pilot initiatives and experiences of EIB within specific indigenous groups (Aymara, Quechua and Guarani) in the 1980s, and the later transformation of EIB into a state public policy with the Educational Reform Law in 1994. Then it focuses on the description of a number of EIB training initiatives of human resources implemented in the 1990s, after the educational reform, and the impacts of EIB in schools and society. Finally, it discusses the strategic tasks and challenges of EIB in Bolivia and compares it with similar experiences in other Latin American countries.

In comparative perspective, the uniqueness of the Bolivian EIB experience is that it has been promoted by indigenous and peasant sectors, which gave it vitality and sustainability, rather than by academics as in the case of Peru, or by the state as in the case of Mexico. With abundant data the book points out the lights and shadows of the EIB experience in Bolivia. On its positive side it suggests how EIB allowed indigenous people to take a hegemonic position in the production of educational knowledge and pedagogical proposals with respect to teachers' unions, the state and the universities (p. 489). And on the negative side it shows how the adoption of EIB as a public policy, though it widened and legitimized it at a national level, had the unwanted consequence of depoliticizing it as a social movement (p. 279). Overall the book expresses an optimistic view of the advances of EIB and its future prospects in Bolivia. However, the current context (2005–8), characterized by a deep state crisis and a political process led by a pro-indigenous/peasant government, has put EIB on standby and centred attention on the issue of the decolonization of education and culture, thus putting the continuity of the EIB process at risk.

The book's descriptions of the rise and development of EIB provide abundant information for drawing two intercultural models in Bolivia: a liberal model promoted during the 1990s by the state and based on an individual logic of action, and a modern indigenous model, promoted by indigenous and peasant organizations and based on a communitarian logic of action. Although not explicit in the analysis, the book provides good descriptions of the advances and limitations of the encounter between these two intercultural models. Nevertheless, in the last few years (2005–8) Bolivia has evolved from a context combining these two models to one in which they are polarized.

José Fernando Galindo-Cespedes
Centre for Research and Promotion of Peasantry, Cochabamba, Bolivia.

Anna Lorbiecki & Gavin Jack, 2000. "Critical Turns in the Evolution of Diversity Management", *British Journal of Management* 11: S17–S31.

Keywords: *diversity management, critical approach, difference, discrimination*

The principal aim of this article is to contribute to the critical debates about diversity management and its basic assumptions. These debates emerged when it became clear that diversity management does not seem to be able to fulfil its promises in practice.

Lorbiecki and Jack reflexively explore and extend some of these critiques, based on perspectives from outside the (diversity) management literature. They first of all argue that diversity management can be said to perpetuate, rather than end, structural inequalities in the workplace. Its general aim is, after all, to make a profit, and in trying to do so, it draws clear boundaries between the *managed diverse* and the *managers of diversity*, whose point of view is dominant in this matter. Second, they point to the fact that diversity approaches, often based on the idea that everybody is different, sidestep, or make it harder to fight, racism and discrimination against specific groups. Third, they examine how difference is looked at in the traditional diversity management approaches, and argue that it tends to classify people in seemingly objective groups, based on essentialist interpretations of identity. In this, diversity management often ignores more important elements, such as power differences. Lastly, they argue that diversity management offers problematic dualisms for pursuing social change, and that it should deal with, rather than ignore, historical, discriminatory and hierarchical assumptions. The authors promote the idea that post-colonial theories can help diversity management to be more critical, reflexive and historically sensitive.

This article is, I believe, valuable to anybody who is working on diversity from a more critical angle. It clearly describes some of the critical debates on the management of diversity, and does so by drawing on diverse perspectives, such as linguistics, radical feminism and ethnic and racial studies. In this way, they manage to infuse these critical debates with some new arguments. Therefore this article has been a very helpful basis and inspiration for my own critical writing. One interesting point is the fact that diversity management separates the *managers of diversity*, who apparently have a stable, fixed and singular identity, and the *managed diverse*, who are seen as liabilities and possess low-status multiple identities (e.g. a female employee of Chinese descent).

Another point that I appreciated about this article is the political purpose that seems to underlie it. As becomes clear in the introduction, in which the authors describe a racist murder in the UK and its poor investigation due to institutionalized racism within the police force, the authors want to play their part in rethinking diversity management approaches that fail to tackle such important and unacceptable issues. I believe such attempts can only be applauded. Moreover, and in line with their idea of reflexivity, they promote the idea that post-colonial perspectives can be an asset to thinking about diversity management. I believe they are correct in assuming that this body of literature can help us tackle some of the problems in diversity management approaches.

Koen Van Laer
Katholieke Universiteit Leuven, Faculty of Business and Economics, Research Centre for Organisation Studies, Leuven, Belgium.

Setha M. Low (ed.), 2005. *Theorising the City: The New Urban Anthropology Reader* (New Brunswick, New Jersey and London: Rutgers University Press), 433 pp.

Keywords: *the city, culture, diversity, space, urban policy*

Theorizing the City presents a significant contribution to urban anthropology at the turn of the millennium. The introductory chapter leads us from a brief history and theoretical milestones in urban anthropology to twelve case studies of major cities in the Americas, Asia, Africa and Europe. On the basis of rich comparative ethnographic material, the essays in the volume bring fresh perspectives on the development of urban forms and spaces in contemporary cities. The studies are divided into five sections according to a framework of five city images: the divided city, the contested city, the global city, the modernist city and the postmodern city. All urban ethnographies in the book theorize the city from different perspectives and concepts which the editor sees as the dominant research trends in current urban anthropology: post-structural studies of race, class and gender in the urban context; political economic studies of transnational culture; and studies of the symbolic and social production of urban space and planning (p. 21).

The book is a fascinating reader in urban anthropology and an inspiration for all scholars who wish to better understand the city and its diverse forms. In the subdiscipline of anthropology which has developed in the shadow of urban sociology, human ecology, geography, history and urban planning, this volume fills the gap in an undertheorized field and is an excellent edition to the urban anthropology literature.

The collection of essays provides a broad range of contemporary theoretical and methodological approaches towards studying and understanding the diverse city in the national, transnational and global context. In addition, the book is not only a valuable resource to spark new ideas and provoke new questions in urban anthropology, but also a relevant inspiration for other social scientists, urban policy-makers, planners, civic activists and everyone who is interested and actively involved in creating and managing an inclusive and sustainable city.

Alexandra Bitusikova
Matej Bel University, Research Institute, Banska Bystrica, Slovakia.

Roger Lowenstein, 2008. "Long-Term Capital Management: It's a short-term memory", *International Herald Tribune*.

Keywords: *long-term capital management, hedge funds, mortgage crisis, derivatives*

The article analyses the financial development and consequently the fall of one of the most powerful hedge funds in the USA: Long-Term Capital

Management (LTCM). LTCM had two crises; the second was fatal. The first time the fortune's fund took a significant downturn, bond markets turned skittish and all the fund's gambits ran into trouble with terrifying abruptness. This time the fund was rescued by one of the giants in banking, Bear Stearns Bank, who invested around 4 billion US dollars. Ironically, it was the same Bear Stearns Bank that sounded the first shot in the current mortgage crisis. The second time, two hedge funds in high-rated mortgage securities in which Bear had invested imploded. As foreclosures kept rising, other institutions suffered losses and the crisis spread. After LTCM's fall, many commentators blamed a lack of liquidity, claiming that panic selling in thin markets pushed its assets below their economic value. That is why leverage is dangerous: if you operate with borrowed money, you lack the luxury of waiting until prices adjust themselves. However, major mistakes were to believe that randomness in pricing can ensure a diverse performance, or to believe that diversity guarantees safety. The second mistake was grounded in this and in particular in the notion that markets could be modelled.

Risk can be neatly calculated or quantified, but financial markets are subject to uncertainty, which is far less precise. Markets have less information about where risk lies, which results in periodic market shocks. LTCM's tragedy comes mainly from the fact that they were playing on the market with the most potent tinder of modern finance: derivatives. However, markets were stunned to discover that LTCM owned outsized portions of obscure derivatives and subsequently panicked. In other words, derivatives, which allow individual firms to manage risk, may accentuate risk for the group. The theory of option pricing, or the so-called Black-Scholes formula, is the cornerstone of modern finance and was devised by two LTCM partners, Robert Merton and Myron Scholes. It is based on the idea that each new price is random.

The article gives us a very clear example of the unpredictability of risk undertaken in the world financial market; and of how a financial giant like LTCM, or any other hedge fund, is never really protected from financial collapse, even when effective financial option pricing models are applied by their management. It becomes obvious that financial institutions must be cautious of their financial actions, their safety is never guaranteed and their behaviour is defined by the financial market situation – i.e., there is always a possibility of bankruptcy, which can lead to serious shocks in economic and financial policy of a certain country. To some extent rash actions to gain profit might turn out to be fatal and could set off a full-scale market meltdown.

Iskra Christova-Balkanska
Institute of Economics, Bulgarian Academy of Sciences, Sofia, Bulgaria.

Michael Lyons, 2007. *Place Shaping: A Shared Ambition for the Future of Local Government* (London: HMSO), 391 pp.

Keywords: *place-shaping, policy development*

In July 2004, Sir Michael Lyons was asked by the Deputy Prime Minister and Chancellor of the Exchequer to look at changes to the English local government system and to make recommendations on how to develop a new, stronger relationship between central and local government, founded on a shared interest in the prosperity and well-being of the UK and its citizens. *Place-shaping* was a key component of this review.

Place-shaping is identified as capturing the central role and purpose of local government, defining it as the creative use of powers and influence to promote the general well-being of a community and its citizens. The challenges for local governments were presented and Sir Michael Lyons stated that shifting the relationship between central and local government by reducing central control and prescription will enable local government to respond better to local need and to manage pressures and expectations of public services more effectively. He also identified a clear need for local government to step up to the place-shaping challenge and develop its style, skills and behaviours in order to make the role a reality.

Effective place-shaping is as much about the confidence and behaviours of local government as it is about statutory powers or responsibilities. The report concludes that place-shaping requires local government to be more consistent in raising its sights beyond the immediate delivery of services, the short-term political cycle and the timetables of funding and performance management. Vision for the future therefore requires: (1) having a sense of where place should be in five, ten, twenty and even thirty years' time; (2) awareness of long-term trends locally as well as in the world beyond their geographic boundaries; (3) a sense of how the local area can be prepared and well placed to respond to these challenges; (4) an ability to be responsive; (5) development of strategies to achieve this. This text has been used to supplement an understanding of place-making and its influence on architecture, cultural identity and diversity.

Hisham Elkadi & Karen McPhillips
Deakin University, School of Architecture and Building, Victoria, Australia & University of Ulster, School of Architecture and Design, Belfast, UK.

Emmanuel Ma Mung & Michelle Guillon, 1986. "Les commerçants étrangers dans l'agglomération parisienne", Revue Européenne des Migrations Internationales 2, 3: 105–134.

English Translation of the Title: *Foreign Traders in the Paris Agglomeration.*

Keywords: *location, immigrant trade, diversity, adaptation*

The paper provides a systematic and detailed analysis of immigrant trade in the Paris conurbation, where this phenomenon is very relevant. Ma Mung offers an exhaustive description of the issue. First of all, he underlines the variety and heterogeneity of immigrant trade, which is differentiated by the character, sector and provenance of the traders. Special attention is given to spatial location of the phenomenon, which seems very concentrated in certain areas, while another *arrondissement* has only a small presence of immigrant shops. There is a further analysis of the origin of traders which represents a crucial element in the birth and development of activity: membership of an ethnic group influences admittance to financial resources, layout of point of sale, sectors of activity and the trade typologies.

Ma Mung underlines the way any commercial activity results from a match between an immigrant person and the opportunities presented in the territory; different aspects of this *match* explain speed and strategies of insertion in the market. The use of a perspective that jointly considers demand and supply elements explores firm heterogeneity, and for instance separates *new* shops, directed to immigrant needs, from activities already existent but now left by French people. This perspective, moreover, allows the creation of a typology of firms (banal, exotic, of community). Ma Mung also notes the importance of capabilities to adapt that some groups, for cultural reasons or territorial root-edness, have more than others.

For my work the paper represents a fundamental reference: it is a good example of a pioneer study, very articulated and methodologically correct, on entrepreneurship and immigrant trade. It presents an analysis that integrates quantitative elements with qualitative reflections on single communities. It also offers many suggestions: the idea of immigration as a diversified phenomenon, segmented both by subjects and by territory; and the advantages of using a perspective that joins demand and supply side factors; the way that each specific shop is born of the match between people who can use the ethnic capital of their groups, and the opportunities offered by the territory. This match is based on diversity, because "diversity characterises the commerce of foreigners: diversity of origin, despite larger presence of some nationalities, diversity of activities, with preference for some commercial sectors, and finally diversity of localities" (p. 129).

Gabriele Morettini
Marche Polytechnic University, Department of Social Sciences, Ancona, Italy.

Becky Mansfield, 2003. "'Imitation Crab' and the Material Culture of Commodity Production", *Cultural Geographies* 10: 176–195.

Keywords: material culture, commodity production, material aesthetics, social geography

Commodity forms are generally taken for granted and are rarely brought into the discussion of diversity and its management. This essay is a case study of the Euro-American imitation crab industry, which orchestrates the de- and re-contextualization of a globally traded product both materially and symbolically throughout production processes. This essay will be of interest to those attuned to the construction of the local and the global through cultures of consumption. Emerging from the cultural economic analysis of material production, it highlights key moments in the social geography of *things*, which delineates frontiers drawn by the familiar, the foreign and the forgotten. Surimi, or imitation crab, is a fish paste, first developed in Japan several hundred years ago, made of mixing fish protein with starches. Surimi is a flexible food that can be used in a variety of ways, of which the imitation crab form has been the most globally successful export since its invention in the late 1970s. Imitation crab is a mass-produced, low-cost source of fish protein designed to imitate high-cost, luxury goods, including not only crab, but also lobster, shrimp and scallops.

The essay highlights specific interrelationships between cultural and economic practices to explain the material-symbolic transformation of the ubiquitous paste, which is given decidedly different forms, from irregular pieces to precise geometric shapes, in the different locales of production. By tracing the significance of material production in the fashioning of business cultures and identities, the essay goes beyond existing studies of individual commodities and brands that have depicted the multiple ways in which commodities are involved in cultural processes, giving credit to consumers' choices and uses of goods as cultural forms that reflect and create individual and group identities, while paying little attention to the actual things being produced, or the significance of materiality.

By focusing on Surimi production, Mansfield aims to shed light on the synonymy of economic and cultural sites and activities, rediscovering cultural signification as a constitutive moment of production itself. She shows how, in the process of making and selling imitation crab, lobster and scallops, seafood firms are not just creating products to compete in the marketplace, but are creating new and yet familiar cultural forms that are entangled with associations of both nationality and exoticness.

The essay is uniquely valuable in showing us a new approach to the material aesthetics of things that feature in our daily lives and capture our sense of the familiar and the foreign. The stories of things and how they come to be tell us much, as Mansfield puts it, about the material-symbolic geographies of these distances and connections from which notions of identity and difference are constructed. Cultural processes of meaning construction are shown not to be limited to consumption, but to be integral throughout material production and trade. To ignore material production is to miss key moments in the social geography of things, and the importance of these things for both daily life and social relations stretched over time and space.

Susanne Küchler
University College London, Department of Anthropology, London, UK.

Gustavo Marquez, Alberto E. Chong, Suzanne Duryea, Hugo Ñopo & Jaqueline Mazza (eds.), 2007. *Outsiders? The Changing Patterns of Exclusion in Latin America and the Caribbean* (Cambridge, MA: Harvard University Press), 286 pp.

Keywords: *social class, social exclusion, inclusion*

Implicit in the title of this book is the question of how individuals or groups with historic connections to a place can be regarded as outsiders. The question is answered and discussed by examining the ways in which individuals and groups are discriminated against in a local setting. Such discrimination affects employment, job opportunities, education, health and every aspect of well-being. Above all, it condemns a significant majority of the population to poverty. A combination of factors which maintain inequality and access to jobs also prevent both social and economic mobility. The result is various forms of social exclusion.

The authors believe that the matter of social exclusion in Latin America and the Caribbean is such an important issue that it constitutes the most dangerous threat to democracy and democratic institutions in the region. Social exclusion also prevents participation in the economic and social activity essential to development. The authors make a key observation that social exclusion is now mainly urban and therefore visible, ensuring that the effects can no longer be hidden or ignored. What are illuminating are examples of this exclusion which illustrate the inability of individuals or groups to cope with a market economy. Banks require guarantees, guarantors, a permanent address and proof of regular sources of income before opening an account. Meeting these requirements without assistance can be insuperable.

Similar impediments exist when interacting with institutions which could provide legal protection from discriminatory practices. It is claimed that discrimination is widespread in Latin America and the Caribbean. The research work to establish the basis of such discrimination or the ways in which it operates is one of the interesting and intriguing aspects of this work. Most respondents do not believe that there is discrimination against indigenous peoples, Afro-descendants or women. They do agree, however, that there is discrimination against the poor and the uneducated. Research to determine the ways in which social factors, economics, racial or other visible factors operate to affect social exclusion is largely inconclusive at present. The problem is multidimensional and it appears that poverty and lack of education are the principal factors in preventing access to jobs, education and other resources. Considering these factors, it is clear that social exclusion is a formidable barrier to economic development.

To sum up: social exclusion is not the consequence of some specific event, material deprivation or particular forms of discrimination. Policies directed at remedial action must consider measures for engaging with politics and social and economic institutions. The alleviation of poverty should be part of a total programme. The suggestions for social inclusion are encouraging, optimistic and visionary. The authors stress that social inclusion is not measurable; there are no *outcomes* or end points. Social inclusion is a process that is both central and necessary to democracy. There are many examples in both Latin America and the Caribbean showing that the processes of social inclusion can be assisted by organizations both inside and outside the region. These offer useful lessons concerning the definition and management of diversities in other parts of the world.

Walter V. Baker
Holborn Community Association, Bedford House, London, UK.

Linda Martin-Alcoff, 2006. *Visible Identities: Race, Gender and the Self* (Oxford: Oxford University Press), 326 pp.

Keywords: *identity, race, gender, ethnicity*

The discussion of identity in this book relies on observations and examples in the USA, but the arguments and conclusions can apply elsewhere. The author quotes from personal experience, which gives the book an impressive authenticity.

Discussions relating to *identity* are often confused and confusing. It is therefore useful to have an indication of the various contexts in which the term is used. Identities are multiple and naturally lead to some selection by the observer. For example, one might be identified racially and/or by gender, but not by occupation, education or profession. The author gives many examples of situations where an identity is *imposed* from the outside or even imagined by an observer. One result of such externally defined identity is that the person labelled by it conforms to the stereotype. Hence the visible identity remains unchallenged and the stereotype is reinforced.

There are situations in which the visible is challenged, particularly when there is some ambiguity due to gender, skin colour or other physical feature. Where economic or social advantage is to be gained, the visible features can be manipulated to conform to the advantageous characteristics. The author asserts that any ambiguity is confusing and socially uncomfortable for the observer. The philosophical discussion of self-identity is lucid and comprehensive. Self-identity is often in conflict with the visible, that is, the way in which one is *classified* by others or even the way in which one classifies oneself in order to conform to a social stereotype. The visible identity defined as *race* is socially constructed and as such leads to the classification of an individual or groups of individuals which allows them to be treated in some particular manner. Where such treatment is discriminatory, the connection between race and racism becomes evident and negative values are projected onto a group of individuals who can be visibly identified.

The discussion of identities is both impressive and illuminating. The author observes that in the USA race and identity are fused, such fusion is worldwide and racial identity – wherever and however defined – could give rise to the racism and the economic and social discrimination suffered by individuals and groups as a result. The suggestion that the term *race* should be used and understood in its biological context and *ethnicity* used to include the historical, cultural and other invisible aspects that make up an identity is helpful. This suggestion is worthy of consideration even though at the present time the terms are used interchangeably, and are therefore confused.

I found two questions to be of the utmost importance, since they focused the arguments about race, gender and identity. First, how can the visibility of difference be recognized and discounted? Second, can people of colour be de-racialized? No discreet answers are given to these questions. Human behaviour is not immutable. Observations and experiments suggest that racial/colour awareness in children is acquired as part of their social upbringing. If such is the case, it is possible to envisage a future in which the visible aspects of colour and gender are not the only defining features of individual identity. This book strikes a hopeful note.

Walter V. Baker
Holborn Community Association, Bedford House, London, UK.

Doreen Massey, 2004. "Geographies of Responsibility", *Geografiska Annaler*, 88 B (1): 5–18.

Keywords: *space, identity, politics of place*

Starting from the view that identities are mutable and relational, Massey addresses the issue of spatial identities and the meaning of space and considers the challenges of a redefinition of space and local/global boundary as "an emotionally charged issue" (p. 6). How is the identity of space relationally constructed and how is it connected with political responsibility? Taking London as a case study, Massey argues that the redefinition of identity can lead to two possible scenarios: in the first, London assumes an identity which is precisely around *mixity* rather than coherence derived from common roots; in the second, London reflects the *globality* of the constructive process which has led to its constitution.

London remains the city of which Massey analyses the politics and decision-making of the last decades (from Thatcher's to Livingstone's interventions), but references to other authors' accounts are given throughout the text. In fact, by comparing other authors' perspectives on the dichotomy of space/place, local/global, Massey suggests a politics of place which does not deny the meaning of connections, relationship and practices that construct space, but goes beyond it, and which accounts for the vital role of local heterogeneity for the sustainability of space. As more of the complexities of our cities are understood, the demand arises for responsibility for those relationships through which identity is constructed.

This long paper reflects the complexity not only of the society and the place/space in which we all live, but also the slipperiness of the term *politics of place*: the definition of what is local/global changes constantly and relationships on which space is built up mutate as fast. Massey is asking for more responsible political discourse, which puts Londoners in the position to enjoy their high differentiation, as well as responding to the necessity of handling the wider global relations on which they depend.

This is an extremely relevant paper, which stresses the idea that "diversity is out here and now in every society" (p. 10). It offers a very vivid and mature consideration of how local and global politics affect and are affected by definitions and classification processes, which might in some cases undermine the outcome of the policies themselves. It does not pinpoint a particular type of diversity, but assumes diversity as an intangible phenomenon, which everyone is part of and to which everyone is asked to respond. It is not an entirely positive paper, but suggests interesting points for further research into the politics of place and geography.

Rossella Lo Conte
University College London, Department of Anthropology, London, UK.

Marcel Mauss, 1990. *The Gift: The Form and Reason for Exchange in Archaic Societies*, translated by W.D. Halls (London: Routledge), 199 pp.

English Translation of the Title: *The Gift: The Form and Reason for Exchange in Archaic Societies.*

Keywords: *exchange, gift, reciprocity, social cohesion*

The central idea of *The Gift* is that exchange is constitutive of social life and social order. In a sense, gifts transform parties into partners. They are the earliest solution to the Hobbesian war of all against all. Gifts and relations are thus inextricably linked. The essence of giving is reflected in three kinds of obligations: in certain situations one is obliged to give, the other party is obliged to receive and to reciprocate. To shy away from these obligations is tantamount to a declaration of war on the community of which one is part. Even though this type of exchange is not determined by impersonal and purely business-like considerations, but by the principle of reciprocity, there is always some element of personal interest involved.

According to Mauss, every gift is basically given with the conscious or unconscious expectation of getting something in return. However, a gift does carry its own reward through the *do-ut-des* principle: somehow, some day, one will get something in return. According to Mauss, the fabric of any type of community can be analysed as a complex intertwining of exchange activities taking place at many levels: gifts, goods, services, favours, insults, etc. This exchange forges or consolidates ties between relatives, neighbours, colleagues, strangers, business associates, heads of state, but also between people and spirits, ancestors, etc. As such, the character of gifts is that of a *fait social total* or a *prestation totale*, in which personal, legal, economic and religious obligations are inextricably bound up together. In other words, the social order is also and probably foremost a moral order. In the final chapter, Mauss points out that this social order is under pressure in modern capitalist society. Here, the gift as a structuring principle has been replaced by the contract, giving the individualistic and utilitarian *homo economicus* free rein to pursue his personal interests, a development that socialist Mauss views with regret.

The Gift is a lasting source of inspiration to anthropologists, philosophers, theologians, ethicists, sociologists, psychologists, economists, cultural and literary scholars. Mauss shows us that differences can be reconciled and coordinated through the exchange of gifts. With differences being maintained, which after all is a basic condition for people living together as a community, gifts can lead to partnerships in which differences in views, interest and practices are tuned in such a way that they remain durable and stable, provided that – paradoxically – a certain measure of imbalance continues to exist. With perfectly balanced gift-sheets there are no more social obligations. Thus a certain deficit or surplus is necessary. Even though Mauss stresses the positive, binding and conciliatory aspect of gift exchange, he is not blind to the fact that gifts can also be used as weapons: gifts can be used to humiliate others and to acquire power and status. What Mauss does fail to pay (enough) attention to is the use of the gift as a ruse (think of the Trojan Horse, for example), or as an instrument of revenge for injustices suffered.

Selma M. van Londen & Arie de Ruijter
Tilburg University, Faculty of Social and Behavioural Sciences, Tilburg, The Netherlands.

Chris McVittie, Andy McKinlay & Sue Widdicombe, 2008. "Organizational Knowledge and Discourse in Employment", *Journal of Organizational Change Management* 21, 3: 348–366.

Keywords: *diversification, organizations, older workers*

The authors argue that diversity management in employment has failed to meet expectations of increased inclusion and organizational competitiveness in an ever-changing globalizing context. Data is collected using semi-structured interviews with human resources managers and personnel managers. A focus on language as action in its own right shows how diversity as used in employment accomplished outcomes that are totally divergent from the usual assumed benefits of diversity. The authors encourage research on how diversity is described in practice, and the related language or discourses.

The article is inspired by ideas from discursive psychology, which emphasizes the action orientation of language in use. Language is treated not as representative of other phenomena; rather, the focus becomes what language in everyday use accomplishes in its own right. Accordingly, the authors look more deeply into language in organizational contexts where organizations are viewed as ongoing and ever-changing patterns of human interactions, meanings, negotiations, conflicts and ambiguities. "It is the ways in which those within the organisation make sense, both to themselves and to others, of the organisation's practices that constitute the organisational culture and processes" (p. 353).

Based on this perspective, the author studied how older job seekers from many sectors in the UK have been treated in employment encounters. The findings point out that the use of language by practitioners in descriptions of diversity does not make reference to the employment of members of social groups and equity in practice; that diversity management has not led to the inclusion of disadvantaged groups in the workplace; that diversity can be used to describe assimilation of individuals into existing practices and that the language of diversity is little more than "hype" or "rhetoric" (p. 361); that diversity functions to render differences in group memberships invisible without the need for explicit challenge or reformulation. Thus language, in describing diversity management, should not be taken unquestionably as knowledge of optimal employment practice, nor of organizational commitment to change (p. 361).

The article uses critical discourse analyses to discuss the extent to which language can be used as if it was neutral, and the extent to which older job seekers are camouflaged in a language that conceals inequality rather than ensuring equal treatment.

Kiflemariam Hamde & Nils Wåhlin
Umeå University, Umeå School of Business, Umeå, Sweden.

Tomasz Marek Mickiewicz, Slavo Radosevic & Urmas Varblane, 2000. "The Value of Diversity: Foreign Direct Investment and Employment in Central Europe during Economic Recovery", *Economic and Social Research Council* (ESRC) Working Paper 05/00: 1–31.

Keywords: *Foreign direct investment (FDI), employment in transition economies, job generation, job preservation*

The article examines the role of FDI in job creation and job preservation in transition economies from CEE countries, in particular the Czech Republic, Slovakia, Estonia and Hungary, during the period 1993–6. The FDI has a strong influence on domestic employment through types of jobs created, and on regional distribution of new employment, but mostly on aggregate employment. The main task is to examine whether FDI is contributing to the preservation and generation of new employment in CEE countries. Markets can be diversified through both horizontal and vertical types of FDI. In transition economies FDI is mainly export-oriented and is concentrated in three main branches, technology, electrical machinery and the car industry, becoming an important mechanism for integration with the EU. With higher levels of penetration of FDI inflows we would expect the structure of FDI types to become more diversified, meaning a higher share of exporters compared to distributors and local suppliers. More diversified structures of FDI types will have more beneficial effects through direct and indirect links to the domestic labour force, thus diversity of FDI is seen as favourable to the economy. Indeed, the increasing differences in FDI employment across countries is seen as closely related to FDI inflows per capita.

The role of FDI in employment creation/preservation has been most successful in Hungary and Estonia. These two countries have chosen the direct sales method, giving equal access to all bidders, including foreign investors.

The analysis follows the progress of transition in these four countries, where it seems that only Hungary represents the switch from a period of rapid downsizing and restructuring to one of job creation and preservation. This is due mainly to the fact that Hungary already has an employment structure similar to those of other developed European countries.

The discussion informs my own work in three major directions. The first is connected to the penetration of MNFs through FDI in the CEE countries, and especially in the real sector, which enables the restructuring of some old industries and the creation of new technological entities, generating the possibility of job creation and diversification of the industrial branches and production. The second is the analysis of the impact that diversified FDI has on the internal market and its spillovers throughout the CEE region. The third is connected with the evaluation of the role of FDI as a powerful instrument of development and integration of CEE economies into the European market.

Iskra Christova-Balkanska
Institute of Economics, Bulgarian Academy of Sciences, Sofia, Bulgaria.

James Clyde Mitchell, 1956. *The Kalela Dance: Aspects of Social Relationships among Urban Africans in Northern Rhodesia* (Manchester: Manchester University Press), 52 pp.

Keywords: *social anthropology, sociology, ethnicity, situational analysis, Africa*

The study is an inspiring example of situational analysis and illustrative research into ethnic diversity. It shows us that many important social relations are observable in social ceremonies.

The objects of Mitchell's interest are urban Africans from the Copper Belt. During 1951 he watched Kalela dances performed by a Bisa team in Luanshya, assembled information about dancers and also observed their relations and social behaviour during various everyday social situations. Mitchell noticed the stable hierarchical structure of the dancing teams. He compared the positions of dancers in the dancing team with their social positions in work, their marital status, kin relations, their ethnic provenance and place of residence in Luanshya, and found the transfer of social structure from everyday life to the dancing team structure. Then Mitchell analysed the texts of songs and indicated frequent topic recognition of the ethnic diversity of the urban population. This takes two forms. The first is that the dancers emphasize the beauties of their own land or origin and extol their own virtues. The second form is the obverse of this, in that the distinctiveness of other languages and customs are emphasized and lampooned. Kalela and its songs emphasize the unity of Bisa against all other ethnic groups on the Copper Belt. Mitchell identified, with the help of the texts, a *tribal* dance in which tribal differences are emphasized, but, unlike the tribal dances in the countryside, the language and the idiom of the songs and the dress of the dancers of Kalela are drawn from an urban existence which tends to submerge tribal differences.

Mitchell alluded to very important aspect of (ethnically) diversified society. The Bisa adopted from Europeans what they found prestigious and also encapsulated a lot of manners important for successful urban life, including specific forms of communication. At the same time, however, they kept the notion of their former social structure and power relations. They only amended some positions within their structure derived from their experience with Europeans and urban situations. Moreover, they projected their ethnic affiliation onto socio-economic class divisions and, consonantly with their non-urban experience, created coalitions with other ethnic groups living in an urban milieu.

Not only dance teams but also, for instance, burial societies expressed the unity of former ethnic groups in cities during Mitchell's observations and resulted in his statement about the transformation of former tribal social relations to political attitudes and loyalties in the diversified urban environment. The new ethnicity of urban Africans in European clothes was considered *not* to be entirely new. Nevertheless, in a transient diversified society it is impossible to generalize about the operation of ethnic principles without reference to the specific social situation in which the interaction takes place. Mitchell wrote his study in 1956. This is apparent in his language, arguments and references; later on his study was criticized as well as praised. Nevertheless, it shows us how a diversified urban environment transforms former indigenous ethnic relationships to symbolic ethnicity, to political attitudes, to class relationships and forms of identity that emerge differently in various social situations.

Zdenek Uherek
Institute of Ethnology of the Academy of Sciences of the Czech Republic, Prague, Czech Republic.

Ajit Mohanty, Minati Panda, Robert Phillipson & Tove Skutnabb-Kangas (eds.), 2009. *Multilingual Education for Social Justice: Globalising the Local* (New Delhi: Orient Blackswan), 774 pp.

Keywords: *multilingualism, literacy, mother-tongue education, indigenous peoples, social justice*

This volume comprises a set of seventeen chapters which were originally presented at the International Conference on Multilingual Education: Challenges, Perspectives and Opportunities, New Delhi, India, 5–8 February 2008. The focus of the volume is on linguistic diversity as an issue for social justice in all parts of the world, but most particularly in remote geographic settings and where minority and endangered languages exist. It draws attention to developments in mother-tongue, bilingual and multilingual education in a number of case studies amongst indigenous peoples of India, Nepal, Peru, Canada and the Nordic countries. It also includes analyses from the global stage which show contemporary research evidence and trends arising from macro-analyses of language education developments in linguistically diverse settings. A significant emphasis of this volume is that the authors' evaluation and assessment of interventions in smaller local and diverse regions are able to contribute powerful evidence of the feasibility and efficacy of multilingual education on the larger global platform.

This remarkable collection of papers is exceptionally diverse in terms of material, geographic and scholarly terrain. What makes the volume different from others on multilingual education is that many of the authors are directly involved in multilingual educational programmes in remote regions of the world and therefore they are able to bring to the text immediate first-hand insights about challenges and successes. The implication is that if multilingual education is viable in such often under-resourced contexts, then it should be much easier to implement in other better-resourced locations as well. The argument for linguistic diversity for reasons of social justice and educational success is reinforced by the unusual and diverse linguistic and scholarly backgrounds of the contributors to the volume, and the title suggests that it is no accident that the volume is published in India. This volume offers both theory and practice and would be a useful text for policy-makers, educational planners, teacher educators and development agencies.

Kathleen Heugh
University of South Australia, Research Centre for Languages and Cultures, Adelaide, Australia.

Mira Nair (Dir.), 1991. *Mississippi Masala*, USA.

Keywords: *diversity, social and cultural relationships*

The film *Mississippi Masala* addresses the social and cultural complexity of relations between ethnic groups. In the early twentieth century, the English government moved people from India to Uganda to build the railroad. Some of the Indians stayed and became lawyers, physicians, etc. When Idi Amin Dada came to power with a military coup in January 1971, he established a terrible dictatorship in terms of human rights abuse and ethnic persecution, and he expelled all non-black Africans, mainly Asians. Some of the Indians moved to Mississippi and began running motels and shops.

Mississippi Masala is about one of these families: Mina (Sarita Choudhury) is the daughter of an Indian family who fled Uganda for Mississippi. She falls in love with Demetrius (Denzel Washington), a local self-employed man. Her family does not approve of her dating a black man, and Demetrius's friends do not like him dating an Indian woman. The movie shows how both the blacks and the Indians were displaced from their lands and harbour racist attitudes towards each other. *Masala* is an Indian word for "mix", usually referring to spices for curry, but in this case it refers to the mixing of people and traditions, linked to the building of one's identity.

The film provides an opportunity to think about the relationships between different minority groups in an emigration country, but also to reflect on colonial exploitation and the *rooting out* of people. The film encourages one to consider the meaning of roots, and the fact that they are not necessarily embedded in one's original culture or ethnic group as attributed by others. The portrayal of Mina's father demonstrates the conflict between self-identity and labels imposed from outside: he does not think of himself as an Indian, but as an African, trusting more the place in which he spent an important part of his life, rather than his supposed ethnic identity. He will try for the rest of his life to win a case in the Uganda courts to be authorized to go back and regain his properties. The point of the film is to show how racism and undemocratic governments are spread all over the world, and how social diversity can be more important than cultural or ethnic difference.

Maria Alessia Montuori
Psychoanalytic Institute for Social Research, Rome, Italy.

William V. J. Neil & Hanns-Uve Schedler (eds.), 2001. *Urban Planning and Cultural Inclusion: Lessons from Belfast and Berlin* (Palgrave Macmillan), 249 pp.

Keywords: *urban design terms, inclusive city, cultural inclusion, city marketing*

The book has been used to inform several SUS.DIV-related projects which have focused on the city of Belfast. These include: (1) the Belfast festival project which examines festivals as a tool for cultural integration; (2) the religious architecture project which examines cultural identity in relation to religious architecture; (3) the Belfast initiative which combines several key projects aiming to examine cultural diversity from a number of diverse disciplines.

The book provides an in-depth examination of urban planning and the relationship between cultural identity and diversity. Through a selection of interesting papers the book demonstrates the difficulties of planning with an ethic of cultural inclusion. The book is divided into three key parts, focusing on spatial planning and urban design, cultural diversity, and finally promoting the cities in terms of cultural diversity. This book has presented the challenges facing Belfast and emphasized the role in which planning can stimulate cultural inclusion and spatial equality. The literature assists in the understanding of urban segregation in tensioned societies such as Belfast. Belfast is a city which is clearly divided by ethnic and cultural conflict. As a result the city has a strong need to identify, create and maintain some kind of shared identity among its inhabitants. Urban planning and city management can take these identifiers on board constructively and can assist them without allowing the city to deteriorate into a disconnected and hostile conglomeration.

The potential of Belfast is explored through the examination of differences between ethnic, neutral, transcendent and shared cultural space. The conclusions of the book provide key lessons for planning with an ethic of cultural pluralism. These include the importance of creating a civic culture of inclusiveness, respecting the need for spatial equality, enabling cultural difference to exist where it is desired, facilitating cultural integration and contact where it is desired, openness to the introduction of new and novel differences within the city, and lastly recognizing the unavoidability of marketing the difference in place promotion.

Hisham Elkadi & Karen McPhillips
Deakin University, School of Architecture and Building, Victoria, Australia & University of Ulster, School of Architecture and Design, Belfast, UK.

Daniel Nettle, 1999. *Linguistic Diversity* (Oxford: Oxford University Press), 168 pp.

Keywords: *linguistic diversity, geographic distribution, languages, typological differences*

This book addresses the central question, "Why does linguistic diversity exist?" The 6,500 human languages are unevenly distributed across the globe. Most of the world's languages are found in a broad belt around the equator. Language diversity decreases as one moves towards the poles and is low in arid environments. The highest density of languages exists in Central and West Africa, in South and South-East Asia and in the Pacific.

According to Nettle, the reasons for the diversity of languages have not been the subject of adequate attention. He suggests that a multidisciplinary approach is necessary to answer the questions about linguistic diversity. He first investigates a neutral model of linguistic divergence, in which geographically isolated groups innovate randomly. But there are problems with this model, thus Nettle develops a simulation that incorporates the processes of (1) migration, for contact between groups; (2) social selection; and (3) functional selection, in terms of chain-shift in a vowel system. Of these factors, social selection is the most important.

This book is an investigation of the types of diversity in human language. Questions are asked such as: Why is there diversity at all? Why is there as much diversity as there is? Why is it distributed in a very uneven way? It pursues the issue of diversity back to its ultimate causes.

Nettle introduces the concepts of *linguistic pool* (analogous to the human gene pool) and *linguistic item* (the atomic elements of language). After the theoretical introductory chapters he devotes one chapter to each of the different aspects of language diversity: patterns in space or geographical distribution, with emphasis on the numbers of languages per country; changes in time, including an overview of linguistic prehistory; philo-genetic diversity, or the lineages and stocks per continent; and structural diversity, where he deals with typological differences, their distribution and possible causes.

This is a basic text if one wants to understand linguistic diversity and the way it comes about, and at the same time the concern about the disappearance of languages in our modern world. About the latter issue the author Daniel Nettle has written another important book, together with Suzanne Romaine, with the telling title *Vanishing Voices: The Extinction of the World's Languages* (Oxford University Press, 2000).

Durk Gorter
University of the Basque Country, Donostia-San Sebastián, Spain.

Stella M. Nkomo & Taylor Cox, 1996. "Diverse identities in organizations" in Stewart R. Clegg, Cynthia Hardy & Walter R. Nord (eds.), *Handbook of Organization Studies* (London: Sage), pp. 338–356.

Keywords: *diversity, identity, social construction, research implications*

This essay discusses the concept of diversity itself and presents a literature review of how diversity is defined in different theoretical approaches within the field of management and organization studies. Starting from both narrow and broad definitions of diversity, Nkomo and Cox first argue that the concept of identity appears to be at the core of understanding diversity in organizations. They then indicate that, despite the newness of the notion, a number of bodies of work already exist that are relevant to understanding diversity in identities. In order to advance the theory on diversity, they critically review these major theoretical orientations: social identity theory embedded in inter-group theory, racial-ethnicity and gender research, organizational demography and ethnology. For each theoretical approach, they focus on six dimensions of the treatment of identity: (1) explicitly versus implicitly defined; (2) physically versus culturally defined; (3) proposed measurement; (4) self versus other defined; (5) levels of analysis; and (6) effects of diversity. Additionally, they review three meta-theoretical diversity frameworks that combine and translate the information of several of these research streams into a more complex, conceptual model of diversity. Nkomo and Cox end their review with prescriptions for how identity might be reframed and explore the methodological and research implications of these prescriptions.

This chapter has been very important to me and other diversity scholars in the field of organization studies, as it points to the lack of specificity in the concept of diversity itself. Nkomo and Cox argue that diversity is underdeveloped as a scientific construct because it has largely drawn from the meaning that organizational practitioners gave it. They raise awareness that the concept of diversity lacks rigour, theoretical development and historical specificity. The authors further offer a reframing of identity based on different research streams, proposing that identity should be understood as a complex, multifaceted and transient construct, and formulating research implications. The most important implications that I took away were that the study of one identity necessarily involves attending to its interactions with other identities and that the content could not be excluded in doing so. If one were to focus only on universal processes regardless of the basis for identity, one would equate socio-historical identity categories (race, gender) with less socially marked categories (organization function), which means that the significance of racism, sexism and other forms of domination in organizations and the broader society would be overlooked. Overall, this chapter contributed to my understanding of diversity as a relational construct which needs to be situated in the socio-historical and cultural context, taking into consideration the unequal power relations between different identity groups.

Maddy Janssens
Katholieke Universiteit Leuven, Faculty of Business and Economics, Research Centre for Organisation Studies, Leuven, Belgium.

Bart Nooteboom, 2000. "Learning by Interaction, Absorptive Capacity, Cognitive Distance and Governance", *Journal of Management and Governance* 4: 69–90.

Keywords: *interactive learning, absorptive capacity, cognitive distance, governance*

Much of the literature on innovation claims that it derives from an interactive exchange of information or knowledge between actors (firms, research institutes, etc.). However, all new information will be perceived, interpreted and processed by actors in the context of their existing body of knowledge, shaped by the social and physical environment in which they have developed. This context determines their *absorptive capacity*, which can be considered as the domain of the *cognition function*: the extent to which one can make sense of things, i.e. perceive, interpret and evaluate. Learning then entails an extension of this function. The difference in this cognitive function between actors or individuals is the *cognitive distance*. Interactive learning is achieved by bridging or even reducing this distance. Bridging cognitive distance is communication, through which one makes sense of what another thinks. The next step is to understand, which enables one to make sense of the way by which another reasons and thinks. Understanding is stimulated by explanation, and requires more intensive interaction. For interactive learning to occur, the cognitive distance should not be too small, otherwise no learning will be achieved, as no new information is exchanged. On the other hand, if the cognitive distance is too big, understanding each other becomes too difficult. Furthermore, each interaction involves transaction costs. These costs are higher if the cognitive distance is large. In order to reduce the transaction costs, governance via a third intermediary institution is necessary, e.g. an (inter)national authority, that can serve to regulate the interaction.

The paper provides a very simple but elaborate outline of how and under what conditions interaction can lead to learning, and subsequently to innovation. It argues the advantages of diversity, as it is a condition for interactive learning. However, it also mentions the limitations of diversity, as too much of it leads to misunderstanding and holds the danger of becoming uncontrollable. The beautiful thing about this line of reasoning is that it can actually be applied to every scale on which interaction takes place: firms, countries and individuals.

Steven Knotter
IDEA Consult, Brussels, Belgium.

Barack H. Obama, 1995 (Re-released 2004). *Dreams from My Father: A Story of Race and Inheritance* (USA: Three Rivers Press), 442 pp.

Keywords: *identity, diversity, race*

This book was written before Barack Obama had any public profile or political status. Reading it in the year of his inauguration as 44th president of the USA has been surreal. He reports that as a community activist in Chicago he struggled to get more than ten people into a hall to discuss important issues; now his constituency is global.

In any era this book will be an essential guide to racism, diversity and, most importantly, roots in our complicated multiracial societies. It is a very honest book, some – including Obama in his introduction to the 1995 edition – are embarrassed by parts of it. The writing is simple, clear and rather innocent. Its themes: Who am I? Where have I come from? What can I contribute? These are important questions for us all. A recent survey found that one out of ten UK children is born into a multiracial family; identity, community and culture are all more complex than they used to be.

Obama had a quintessentially diverse youth. He spent years in Honolulu, where he was born in 1961 of a white American mother and black African father, and in Indonesia, where he lived in relative poverty, also suffering his mother's ambitions: when he fell back in his studies she would rouse him at 4 a.m. to do five hours' work before going to school. He acknowledges the enormous support of his mother and her parents throughout.

On the other side, his father once wrote him a letter saying that the important thing is to know your people and where you belong. Obama observes that he made it sound so simple, like calling directory enquiries: "Information. What city please?" "Oh I'm not sure. I was hoping you could tell me. The name's Obama. Where do I belong?" (p. 114).

He was teenage before he came up against the real anger of the black struggle in America that was aimed at the white community. Since the drama of Little Rock happened only thirty-eight years before this book was written, the anger makes sense – but so does the dilemma in which it put the half-white Obama. Given his background, he fits in neither category. The dilemma, though painful, fascinated him and throughout his twenties he pursued dialogue with angry fellow students; his own lack of anger has contributed to his recent electoral success.

In so far as anybody arrives at a destination in the search for identity, it is after a trip to his father's people in Kenya that Obama is finally comfortable enough with his ambiguities to develop the confidence which we have recently seen.

The lessons of this autobiography are that multiple identities are neither rare nor fixed; and that sustainable diversity and integration can only come about if people are secure in their own identity before engaging with others.

Anthony N. Kendall
Social Action Radio, London, UK.

Gianmarco I.P. Ottaviano, Giovanni Peri, 2006. "The Economic Value of Cultural Diversity: Evidence from US Cities", *Journal of Economic Geography* 6, 1: 9–44.

Keywords: *cultural diversity, immigrants, productivity, local amenities, urban economics*

The paper considers a multi-city model of production and consumption to assess the economic value of diversity brought by foreign-born people into each city. The foreign-born own different sets of skills and abilities from the USA-born, and could bring valuable resources for the production of differentiated goods and services. The positive effect of cultural diversity may arise through a productivity channel, because of complementarities of skills among natives and immigrants, and/or a utility channel, through taste for variety.

However, these gains can be questionable, as natives may not enjoy living in a multicultural environment, where their own cultural values can be endangered. Moreover, the risk of job losses among natives due to the inflow of immigrants can create intercultural frictions that eventually reduce productivity.

To provide some hints on this relationship, an open city model is developed where the variations in wages and rents of USA-born workers are observable and allow the identification of production and consumption gains associated with cultural diversity. The paper also empirically investigates the effect of cultural diversity, measured with an index of fractionalization, on the average wage received and the average rent paid by USA workers. The authors control for potential endogenous bias, which arises because any increase in wage from a positive economic shock may attract immigrants and may thus increase diversity. If this is the case, the measured effect of diversity on wages and rents would be biased upward.

The empirical findings indicate that US-born workers living in cities with higher cultural diversity are paid, on average, higher wages and pay higher rents than their counterparts living in more culturally homogenous cities. This joint positive effect of diversity on wages and rent is crucial as it indicates that the positive productivity effect dominates any utility effect. A more multicultural urban environment makes USA-born citizens more productive.

An open question of the paper that merits attention regards the channels through which the effect works. A candidate answer is the existence of complementarities of skills between native and foreign-born workers. Even at the same level of education, skills such as problem solving, creativity and adaptability may differ between natives and immigrants, so that reciprocal learning can take place.

Cristina Cattaneo
Eni Enrico Mattei Foundation (Milan, Italy) and University of Sussex (Sussex, UK).

Gianmarco I.P. Ottaviano & Giovanni Peri, 2008. "Immigration and National Wages: Clarifying the Theory and the Empirics", *National Bureau of Economic Research* (NBER) Working Paper 14188 (July): 1–67.

Keywords: *immigration, economic performance, low-skilled wages*

This paper estimates the effects of immigration on wages of native workers at the national level using USA Census data. It applies the methodology outlined by Borjas (2003), focusing on national labour markets for workers of different skills, and it enriches it by refining previous estimates.

The paper emphasizes that a production function framework is needed to combine workers of different skills in order to evaluate the competition as well as cross-skill complementary effects of immigrants on wages. It also emphasizes the importance (and estimates the value) of the elasticity of substitution between workers with at most a high-school degree and those with none. Since the two groups turn out to be close substitutes, this strongly dilutes the effects of competition between immigrants and workers with no degree. An estimate of the substitutability between natives and immigrants is also provided: there is a small but significant degree of imperfect substitution that further decreases the competitive effect of immigrants. Finally, the paper accounts for the short-run and long-run adjustment of capital in response to immigration.

Using their own estimates, the authors find that immigration in the period 1990–2006 had small negative effects on native workers with no high-school degree (-0.7 percent) and on average wages (-0.4 percent) in the short run, while it had small positive effects on native workers with no high-school degree (+0.3 percent) and on average native wages (+0.6 percent) in the long run. These results are perfectly in line with the estimated aggregate elasticities in the labour literature. The authors also find a wage effect of new immigrants on previous immigrants in the order of -6 percent.

Ottaviano and Peri's article is innovative for three reasons: (1) it produces and uses an elasticity of substitution between workers with a high-school degree and workers with none in line with the practice of the rest of the labour literature; (2) it identifies a small but significant degree of imperfect substitutability between native and immigrant workers within the same education-experience group; (3) and most importantly, it emphasizes the need for a general equilibrium approach based on a production function that accounts for direct and cross-skill effects of supply (immigration) on wages, as well as for capital adjustment.

This paper is important as it reconciles the estimates and the findings of the national approach to the effects of immigration on wages with most of the estimates of the substitutability across workers of different skills produced by the labour literature in the last fifteen years. It also reconciles the aggregate evidence on the wage effects of immigrants with the evidence from the local area approach which has always found small effects across USA cities. The modelling strategy proposed in this paper as well as the estimates and simulations provided can be seen as a unified reference point for the current and future debate on the wage-effects of immigration in the USA.

Carlo Fiorio
Eni Enrico Mattei Foundation and University of Milan, Milan, Italy.

Robert Paine, 1992. "The Marabar Caves, 1920–2020" in Sandra Wallman (ed.), *Contemporary Futures: Perspectives from Social Anthropology,* Association of Social Anthropologists Monograph No. 30 (London and New York: Routledge), pp. 190–207.

Keywords: *migration, cultural compression, participant observation, Forster, Rushdie*

This paper was first presented at a conference of the Association of Social Anthropologists (of the UK and the Commonwealth) on the topic *The Future.* It is one of four presentations speculating on the future of the discipline, but can claim non-specialist relevance: images of the future necessarily reflect preoccupations of the present, which the disciplines tend to share; and the global changes which Paine claims will challenge the business of anthropology are the new forms of diversity, boundary and identity which affect all kinds of people and which form the rubric of this bibliography.

In E. M. Forster's *A Passage to India,* the Marabar Caves of the title are the site of a climax of the culture shock felt by British "migrants" to the subcontinent. The book is set in the 1920s when cultures were distinct and the movement of population and influence was outward from Europe, west to east (and north to south). Paine contrasts this with the 1989 world of Salman Rushdie's *The Satanic Verses,* described by its author as "[a celebration] of hybridity, impurity, intermingling, the transformation that comes of new and unexpected combinations of human beings, cultures, ideas, politics, movies, songs" (p. 190). Paine extends the time trajectory to 2020 with some inspired speculation about the effects of these trends on anthropological fieldwork and, more to the point here, on ethnicity, population mix and the very nature of diversity in our inner cities. He conveys the process with the term "cultural compression", which represents the shifting complexities of the migration experience and provides a means to understanding it.

Paine describes cultural compression as an outcome of the movement of people and ideas from monocultural peripheries into multicultural urban centres, and anticipates both the redundancy of the bounded culture as we know it, and a recasting of the authorial eye inward towards the Euro-American centre instead of outward from it. It refers to the effects of cultures-up-against-each-other, as others have done, but brings the subtleties and fluidities of cultural mixing into better focus. Cultures no longer *clash.* They may *borrow from each other,* and members of the same cultural/ethnic group may *borrow different elements.* Cultures can interrelate – i.e. the actors assigned to various cultures may affect one another – without the originals *withering on the vine.*

Nor do they need to be in the same physical space: in the modern era culture contact, cultural dialogue, cultural compression can take place at a distance, in virtual space or by long-distance media. As separate observations, none of these is extraordinary, but Paine's compression metaphor has alerted this fieldworker to their interrelation. And his exploration of two global trends – the direction of migration reversed and the boundedness of cultures lost – makes sense of the new complexities of diversity in our local arenas of inner-city research.

Sandra Wallman
University College London, Department of Anthropology, London, UK.

Robert Ezra Park, Roderick McKenzie & Ernest Burgess, 1925. *The City: Suggestions for the Study of Human Nature in the Urban Environment* (Chicago: University of Chicago Press), 239 pp.

Keywords: *urban sociology, immigration, social control, social policy, human ecology*

The City contains nine essays written by the authors and a bibliography compiled by Louis Wirth. This collection of papers influenced urban theory and research in sociology as well as anthropology for many years. It is a foundational book dealing with diversity research.

The two most inspiring texts are at the beginning of the book. The first one, Robert Ezra Park's "The City: Suggestions for the Investigation of Human Behaviour in the Urban Environment", is a brilliant introduction and a research plan at the same time. Park posed in it substantial statements which still dominate the thinking of urban anthropologists. For diversity purposes the crucial point is the doctrine that diversified city society creates an entire specific environment that influences the feeling and behaviour of every single city person. This environment is a part of the research topic and an inseparable part of human city life. People come to the city with different customs, beliefs, traditions, but only the city creates the diversity. At the same time diversified society creates the city as a geographical, ecological and economic unit. Such units could be studied by anthropological methods applied to traditional societies.

Park's emphasis on the simultaneous research of the physical structure of the city and its moral order found its expression in the second most important text of the book, "The Growth of the City: an Introduction to the Research Project", written by Ernest W. Burgess. Burgess thinks of urban growth as a result of organization and disorganization processes. These processes are seen to be a metabolism of the city. Diversified people create specific zones and spaces that are most sufficient for their status and personal situation. Their possibility to expand elsewhere depends on the state of mutability of the person, and the number and kind of contacts or stimulations in his/her environment. In this text Ernest Burgess thinks of how to measure mutability and contacts. In following texts he suggests how to increase them.

Beside the chapters mentioned, we can find in this book contributions on making ties among immigrant groups, on the needs and wishes of city newcomers, and early scientific contributions trying to grasp the problem of social work among socially excluded people. The publication shows us that city diversity is not chaos, but a system. It is a system based on common physical environment, social cooperation and competition of single persons and diversified groups bonded by social contacts and mechanisms of social control. The notion that diversity creates in the cities a kind of systemic unity and that people can discover and influence its inner logic is strong. But a lot of questions remained unanswered. Are all the city dwellers included in the system? Do all the city diversities create systemic unity? There are also a lot of questions that the Chicago sociologists failed to pose. Two crucial ones are as follows: Do all city dwellers have the same needs and goals? Do they all perceive the city the same way?

Zdenek Uherek
Institute of Ethnology of the Academy of Sciences of the Czech Republic, Prague, Czech Republic.

Robert Pearce, 2006. "Globalization and Development: an International Business Strategy Approach", *Transnational Corporations* 15, 1: 1–36.

Keywords: *Foreign direct investment (FDI), transnational corporations, efficiency, growth and development*

Central to the analysis of FDI is its diversity, because it highlights the way investments are connected to separate areas such as job generation, employment conditions and industry structure. The publication considers the effect of FDI in developed countries and analyses the character of transnational corporations as agents that carry out FDI.

Transnational corporations (TNCs) are represented by four main characteristics, and are described as a general instrument for free use of international transfers and as a participant in the processes of globalization. The role of TNCs is to enrich the expansion of work in the areas of science and technology. Transnational corporations apply different strategies in order to attract FDI more successfully, of which export promotion trade strategy is the one which has most favourable results for them.

The article seeks to investigate the use of TNCs in a *globalized* economy. In this matter, institutions of globalization have motivated the opening of national economies. Furthermore, the processes of globalization have increased the likelihood of national economies adopting characteristics that respond to external challenges and opportunities. Efficiency improves the way in which productive resources are used and consequently improves TNCs' performance. This efficiency is influenced by two global changes: the so-called *globalized* competition for TNCs, and the *free-trade* environment. The first is connected with the rise of major internationally operating firms in many industries. The second embodies all the important multilateral negotiations and regional-integration schemes such as GATT and the EU. After all, growth and development are necessary to a TNC's globalization.

These processes complete the evaluation framework with the issue of how the expansion of productive resources (capacities) can support growth and development specifically. Distribution of gains between TNCs and host countries affects the pricing of products and technologies. This element is influenced by explicit bargaining processes between TNCs and the host countries. Economic sovereignty is an issue, since it concerns the opening up of global markets for capital, technology, skilled labour, intermediate goods and final products. In this way, TNCs can be seen as distinctive contributors to such sovereignty.

It is important to note that TNCs are characterized by different tasks; the most significant are market seeking, efficiency seeking (which can support countries' moves towards outward-oriented industrialization) and knowledge seeking (which can enhance the technological and skill-related sources of sustainable growth in these countries).

What is interesting from my work is how TNCs have influenced the globalized economy. TNCs lead to the acceleration of capital flows and FDI. They cooperate in increasing the freedom of international transfer of capital, which is useful for the enlargement of their business. The most striking aspect in the article is the influence of FDI on diversity in the real sector and employment.

Evgenia Vladimirova-Krasteva
Economic and Investment Bank (part of KBC Group), Sofia, Bulgaria.

Giovanni Peri & Chad Sparber, 2008. "Task Specialisation, Comparative Advantages, and the Effects of Immigration on Wages", *Centre for Research and Analysis of Migration* (CReAM) Discussion Paper No. 02/08: 1–57.

Keywords: *immigration, less-educated labour, manual tasks, communication skills, comparative advantage*

This paper offers a promising explanation for the modest wage and employment consequences of immigration for less-educated natives across USA states. If workers' skills differ solely by their level of educational attainment, then any flow of less-skilled immigrants should reduce wages paid to less-educated workers, while increasing wages paid to highly educated natives. This statement assumes that production technology and productivity of each type of labour are given. However, this is not the case as natives and foreign-born within the same educational group might not be perfect substitutes. The unique skills possessed by the two groups induce them to specialize in different occupations and mitigate the natives' wage losses from immigration.

This paper demonstrates why it is the case that natives and foreign-born workers with little formal education are imperfect substitutes in production. Given that immigrants are endowed with few language skills but possess physical skills, they have a comparative advantage in occupations requiring manual labour tasks. Less-educated native workers, on the contrary, have a comparative advantage in jobs demanding communication skills. The effect of immigration is to encourage workers to specialize in occupations where they own a comparative advantage. The existence of null or even positive effect of immigration on natives' wages indicates that natives reallocate towards communication tasks, and that the returns in language-intensive tasks can be enhanced by the increased supply of manual-intensive tasks that complement them. The complementary nature of the two skills and the occupational upgrading of natives may favour wages paid to native workers.

The empirical findings give support to these ideas. The share of foreign-born in low-skill jobs decreases the relative supply of manual versus communication tasks by less-educated natives. Native-born react to immigration by specializing in occupations which require less physical and more language skills. A second finding is that the immigrants more than compensate for the change in skill supply among natives, as indicated by the positive impact of immigration on total relative supply of manual versus communication tasks. In other words, states with large inflows of less-educated migrants experience significant increase in physical production skills relative to language skills, despite the shift of natives towards communication-intensive occupations. Finally, simulations show that the wage loss of less-educated natives in states with large immigration is significantly smaller than in cases of perfect substitution and no occupational upgrading.

Cristina Cattaneo
Eni Enrico Mattei Foundation (Milan, Italy) and University of Sussex (Sussex, UK).

Katherine W. Phillips & Denise L. Loyd, 2006. "When Surface and Deep-level Diversity Collide: The Effects on Dissenting Group Members", *Organizational Behaviour and Human Decision Processes* 99, 2: 143–160.

Keywords: *surface-level diversity, deep-level diversity, social categorization, dissent, expectations of similarity*

Psychological researchers have distinguished between surface-level (e.g. social categories) and deep-level (e.g. attitudes, opinions, information) diversity.

Whereas surface-level characteristics are immediately visible, group members need time to become aware of deep-level diversity. In this paper, Phillips and Loyd explore the conjoint effects of surface-level and deep-level diversity in groups. The authors analyse how the relationship between surface-level and deep-level diversity affects emotional and behavioural reactions of dissenting group members, as well as how it impacts on the effectiveness of group decision-making.

The authors compare three-person surface-level homogeneous groups including all similar individuals to surface-level heterogeneous groups including two similar and one dissimilar individual: MBA students from a USA university had to imagine themselves as members of three-person student teams who were asked to develop a business plan. In one of two experimental conditions, their instructions read that their team consisted of two other MBA students (surface-level homogeneous groups). In the other conditions, students read that their team included one other MBA student and a medical student. As part of their business plan, they had to decide which of two markets would be preferable to invest in. The focal MBA student per group was instructed to hold a different opinion compared to the other two group members, i.e., he or she preferred to invest in market X whereas both other students voted for market Y.

The results showed that group members expected greater deep-level similarity, i.e., congruent opinions on which market to choose, with those who shared their surface-level characteristics than with those who did not. Dissenting group members also reported more surprise and irritation when disagreeing with those group members who shared their surface-level characteristics than when disagreeing with those who did not. Additionally, group members perceived the group climate as less accepting and open to divergent opinions, i.e., to deep-level diversity, if the group was surface-level homogeneous. Accordingly, dissenting group members were more willing, persistent and confident to voice their divergent opinions in surface-level diverse groups.

In contrast to common reasoning in the psychological literature on diversity, this study shows that surface-level diversity may be beneficial for groups. Dissenting group members, even when they are part of the surface-level majority, will be more likely to voice their divergent viewpoints when groups are surface-level diverse. Thus, having surface-level diversity in groups may indeed be more beneficial for group functioning than surface-level homogeneity.

Myriam N. Bechtoldt
University of Amsterdam, Department of Psychology, Amsterdam, The Netherlands.

Jan Nederveen Pieterse, 1994. "Globalisation as Hybridisation", *International Sociology* 9, 2: 161–184.
Keywords: *culture, hybridity, globalization*

In this article, Nederveen Pieterse argues that globalization is best understood as a process of hybridization, in which phenomena held to be different become mixed, categories are crossed and new options of identification and modes of organization emerge. Focusing on cultural hybridization, he claims that theories of globalization that stress cultural uniformity, homogenization or Westernization ignore elements such as the way Western culture is received locally, or how non-Western cultures influence each other. Moreover, they overlook the heterogeneity of Western culture and centuries of non-Western influence on the West. Therefore, he argues to acknowledge the hybridity, fuzziness, boundary-crossing and *mélange* effects of globalization and cultural contact. In the past, such mixtures were often concealed by religious or national chauvinism, or considered as negative and undermining some perceived purity. However, if we acknowledge their existence, this can show us that perceived differences and boundaries are relative, and can point to similarities beyond these constructed boundaries. Of course, if we follow the hybridity logic to the extreme, hybridization becomes a tautology, because if cultures have been hybrid (rather than pure) all along, then what we are seeing now is the hybridization of hybrid cultures. Nederveen Pieterse argues that hybridity is mainly important as a critical tool, challenging boundaries, essentialism and inward-looking notions of culture, often underlying nationalism, chauvinism and (cultural) racism.

As a researcher, this article influenced me, not because of its focus on globalization, but because of its discussion of the idea of hybridization. At present, it is clear that culture is a central aspect in debates on diversity in Europe: immigrants and their descendants are often accused of being unwilling to adapt to our culture, and questions about whether Islamic culture can be reconciled with Western culture often emerge.

Based on an article such as this, one can of course wonder how useful it is to think in binary terms, of *their culture* and *our culture*, as both are heterogeneous and have been influencing each other throughout history. Moreover, many people can be said to have developed mixed identities, or identifications with groups, cultures or ideas which are normally held to be different. One example is the convinced Muslim who feels both Belgian and Moroccan and who pursues a "traditional" career in an American corporation.

On the whole, this article was important to me because it made me realize even more that boundary-crossing experiences are probably more natural than boundaries themselves. As such, it taught me to be more critical and reflexive about approaches based on clear boundaries and cultural essentialism, to challenge (or at least avoid) such simplifications in my own research, and to try to capture the world in all (or at least more) of its complexities.

Koen Van Laer
Katholieke Universiteit Leuven, Faculty of Business and Economics, Research Centre for Organisation Studies, Leuven, Belgium.

Karl Polanyi, 1974. *La grande trasformazione: Le origini economiche e politiche della nostra epoca*, translated by Roberto Vigevani (Torino: Einaudi), 383 pp.

English Translation of the Title: *The Great Transformation. Economic and Political Origins of Our Ttime.*

Keywords: *market economy, traditional societies, merchandizing, welfare state, social sustainability*

Written during exile in Istanbul in 1944, this book is probably the most comprehensive presentation of the broad vision of the Hungarian political economist. At the centre of its structure is the market economy and the changes that it introduced into modern European society. Market relations and their presumed self-regulating capacity become the main principle of organization in Western societies through the late eighteenth and nineteenth centuries. Before the sixteenth century, when they were embedded in social relations and even economic life was organized largely through other mechanisms (e.g. shared householding, reciprocity or redistribution structures).

The new mechanized way of large-scale production requires the full merchandizing of the production factors – labour, land and money – which are transformed in fictitious commodities like any other market ware. This produces big economic gains in the new capitalistic system of production, but involves the risk of destroying social relations, wasting the environment and creating ravaging crises of instability in the circulation of the means of payment. After a century of growth of the market economy, the outcome of this process is the generalized crisis of the first half of the twentieth century, when all the pillars of the liberal world (nation-state, gold standard, liberal insti-tutions, even the economic field itself) crashed under the destructive impact of market forces and their social and political effects. Connected largely to Marx's analyses, Polanyi's vision stresses also the parallel emergence of society's forms of self-defence against these forces, predicting developments of a socialist type, which are not far from the modern welfare state.

With regard to the theme of sustainable diversity, Polanyi's relevance consists first of all in focusing on the issue of *social* sustainability (in addition to environmental sustainability) – and the risk that social constructions, such as the mechanisms of the market economy, could represent a danger to society itself. Second, but no less important, Polanyi's analysis shows how the socio-economic diversity deriving from these mechanisms represented a major factor of conflict in the twentieth century and, indeed, the risk of potential self-destruction of developed societies. At the same time, however, the central position given to the concept of a self-regulating market in the analysis of these destructive trends pushes Polanyi to undervalue other, not strictly economic factors – as later studies on nationalism showed. (*Contributor details overleaf.*)

Francesco Chiapparino
Marche Polytechnic University, Department of Social Sciences, Ancona, Italy.

Mario Polèse & Richard Stren (eds.), 2000. *The Social Sustainability of Cities: Diversity and the Management of Change* (Toronto, Buffalo and London: University of Toronto Press), 334 pp.

Keywords: *diversity, sustainability, city, inclusion, integration*

The Social Sustainability of Cities. Diversity and the Management of Change looks at urban policies, institutions, planning and social processes that have an impact on integrating diverse groups of urban population. It was initiated by the UNESCO–MOST project on cities and their management in the 1990s. The editors have put together case studies and essays from ten different cities (Montreal, Toronto, Miami, Baltimore, Geneva, Rotterdam, São Paolo, San Salvador, Nairobi and Cape Town) that are analysed in terms of social sustainability. In the introductory chapter, Polèse and Stren offer an overview of a new approach to local policies addressing the management of ethnic and cultural diversity in the large cities of today.

The crucial point of departure in the book is the authors' definition of social sustainability in the city, described as "development (and/or growth) that is compatible with the harmonious evolution of civil society, fostering an environment conductive to the compatible cohabitation of culturally and socially diverse groups while at the same time encouraging social integration, with improvements in the quality of life for all segments of the population" (pp. 15, 16). Polèse and Stren identify six policy areas that are important for understanding and managing social sustainability in the city: governance; social and cultural policy; infrastructure and public services; urban land and housing; urban transport; and employment and economic revitalization.

The book is a source of inspiration for all who study, but also for those who govern social and cultural diversity in an urban environment, and who want to know how to build an inclusive and sustainable city. The theoretical chapter that offers a definition of social sustainability and identifies policy areas related to it is a good starting point for any scholar studying diversity and sustainability in an urban setting. The collection of case studies from ten diverse cities explores municipal policies in different parts of the world that aim at removing spatial segregation and social segmentation and at building inclusive cities.

As Polèse observes in the final chapter, it seems that differences between different world cities are not explainable by fundamental differences in economic systems, levels of development or the impact of de-industrialization or globalization, but often by policy choices and different governance systems (p. 310). And that is what is important to remember when studying sustainable diversity. We can easily be trapped in looking for the global perspectives or for Western vs. Eastern differences and forget about the importance of local practices and local decision-making. Polèse's and Stren's volume teaches us to understand local diversity and sustainability policies in the global context.

Alexandra Bitusikova
Matej Bel University, Research Institute, Banska Bystrica, Slovakia.

Robert D. Putnam, 2007. "E Pluribus Unum: Diversity and Community in the Twenty-first Century: The 2006 Johan Skytte Prize Lecture", *Scandinavian Political Studies* 30, 2: 137–174.

Keywords: *ethnic diversity, social solidarity, social capital, trust.*

This article uses the Social Capital Community Benchmark Survey, carried out in 2000, with a total sample size of roughly 30,000 and 41 sample communities across the USA, to investigate the implications for social capital of immigration and ethnic diversity.

Putnam addresses two opposite perspectives, *contact hypothesis* and *conflict theory*, which address the relationship between diversity and social capital: "Contact theory suggests that diversity erodes the in-group/out-group distinction and enhances out-group solidarity or bridging social capital, thus lowering ethnocentrism", and "conflict theory suggests that diversity enhances the in-group/out-group distinction and strengthens in-group solidarity or bonding social capital, thus increasing ethnocentrism" (p. 144). He then suggests *constrict theory*, considering that diversity might actually reduce both in-group and out-group solidarity – that is, both bonding and bridging social capital.

The results of the survey support this: (1) in more diverse communities, people trust their neighbours less; (2) in more diverse settings, Americans distrust not merely people who do not look like them, but even people who do; (3) ethnocentric trust is uncorrelated with ethnic diversity; neither conflict theory nor contact theory correspond to social reality in contemporary USA; (4) diversity does not trigger in-group/out-group division, but anomie or social isolation; (5) people in ethnically diverse settings appear to "hunker down" – to pull in like a turtle.

Areas of greater diversity show also: (1) lower confidence in local government, local leaders and local news media; (2) lower political efficacy – less confidence in their own influence; (3) lower rates of voter registration, but more knowledge about politics and more participation in protest marches and social reform groups; (4) less expectation that others will cooperate to solve dilemmas of collective action; (5) less likelihood of working on a community project; (6) lower likelihood of giving to charity or volunteering; (7) fewer close friends and confidants; (8) less happiness and lower perceived quality of life; (9) more time spent watching television and more agreement that "television is my most important form of entertainment".

This new evidence suggests that in ethnically diverse neighbourhoods residents of all races tend to "hunker down". Trust (even of one's own race) is lower, altruism and community cooperation rarer, and friends fewer. Diversity does not produce "bad race relations", rather inhabitants of diverse communities tend to withdraw from collective life. Diversity, at least in the short run, seems to bring out the turtle in all of us.

Putnam evaluates the implications of immigration and ethnic diversity for social capital in three broad points (pp. 138–9). (1) Ethnic diversity will increase in virtually all modern societies over the next decades, in part because of immigration. Increased immigration and diversity are not only inevitable; over the long run they are also desirable. (2) In the short to medium run, however, immigration and ethnic diversity challenge social solidarity and inhibit social capital. (3) In the medium to long run, on the other hand, successful immigrant societies create new forms of social solidarity and dampen the negative effects of diversity by constructing new, more encompassing identities.

Tüzin Baycan-Levent
Istanbul Technical University, Department of Urban and Regional Planning, Istanbul, Turkey.

Assaf Razin & Chi-Wa Yuen, 1999. "Understanding the 'Problem of Economic Development': The Role of Factor Mobility and International Taxation", *National Bureau of Economic Research* (NBER) Working Paper 7115 (May): 1–36.

Keywords: *capital mobility, labour mobility, factor mobility, international income taxation*

The article observes diversity through levels and rates of growth of per capita income across countries and across time. The study focuses on conditions under which capital mobility and labour mobility may interact with cross-country differences in income tax rates and income tax principles to generate such diversity. On the one hand, this suggests that labour mobility facilitates either knowledge spillovers (an optimal structure of taxes on labour income changes) or the harmonization of income tax rates (to ensure growth rate convergence irrespective of the international tax principle). Nevertheless, the latter does not actually happen because there is no balance in either growth rates or income levels. Factor (capital and labour) mobility is found to be a driving force that will equalize aggregate income growth rates due to cross-country differences in income tax rates.

Two common principles of international income taxation are valid. The residence or worldwide tax principle is widely adopted by most industrial countries for the taxation of capital income and is applied to deal with capital mobility. The popularity of this principle is due to its production efficiency and illustrates the possibility of growth rate convergence even when countries adopt different tax principles and different tax rates. One conclusion is that capital taxes are a plausible explanation for the diversity of growth rates, because they are related to income and population. In other words, tax diversity in growth can also be preserved when different countries adopt different international tax principles, or when different international tax principles are applied separately to capital incomes. The source (territorial) principle is implied when capital tax rates under the international income taxation are a source of growth disparity. This principle is applied to determine whether the international income growth rates will be equalized by labour mobility. Unlike capital mobility, labour mobility can serve as an income equalizing force by providing a channel for the transmission of external effects across countries. Tax diversity in this principle can be preserved when labour is mobile.

The article is interesting for its approach to accounting in the field of the evaluation of economic development. It pays particular attention to income per capita amongst countries. The two factors that can equalize income are capital and labour mobility, which can be directly related to cross-country differences in income taxes and with other principles that create diversity. Indeed, capital and labour mobility can equalize aggregate income growth rates, but not necessarily per capita growth rates in the long term. The latter differences persist due to cross-country variation in income tax rates. In discussing the problem of economic development, we must establish under what conditions diversity in income levels and growth rates may vanish completely, or find out why capital does not flow from rich to poor countries. This issue can be better observed through social activity involving groups of people than through the activity of individuals.

Evgenia Vladimirova-Krasteva
Economic and Investment Bank (part of KBC Group), Sofia, Bulgaria.

Edward Relph, 1976. *Place and Placelessness* (London: Pion), 156 pp.

Keywords: *place-shaping, policy development*

This publication offers a good illustration of the trend related to critical protest against theory-building, objectivism, quantification and other goals. This book has been used within SUS.DIV research to inform an understanding of place and placelessness.

The text stands as a counterpoint to many textbooks on spatial organization and systems which appeared during the 1960s. Relph focuses on place as an old pivotal concern for the geographer. To substantiate the view that the nature and identity of places should be an important concern for geographers today, he rallies support from a variety of disciplines, particularly architecture, sociology and literature. Through a series of carefully chosen illustrations, Relph points to relationships between place and space, and to varieties in the human experience of place.

The book offers a useful benchmark summary of the state of the arts within a growing literature on the question of place. It allows the reader to become more aware of the human and environmental significance of locality, uniqueness and rootedness. Treating the genesis of a sense of place and its opposite *placelessness*, Relph leans heavily on the existentialist notion of authenticity. The traditional chorographical definition of place, which promised a framework within which human and physical geographers could hopefully integrate their studies, is not the definition implied in this book.

Place does not connote aerial boundedness in a *map* sense, nor is it defined by the visual, aesthetic or functional criteria of external observers. Rather it appears to connote centredness, as experienced either by residents of a place or by the sensitive visitor who has become attuned intersubjectively to the lives of residents. Focus rests on a humanly defined sense of place or centredness. There is a strong case for letting places speak for them. Examples are discussed in the book which epitomize *sense of place*. The analytical focus in the book is predominately on architectural, technologically-created landscapes and environments.

Hisham Elkadi & Karen McPhillips
Deakin University, School of Architecture and Building, Victoria, Australia & University of Ulster, School of Architecture and Design, Belfast, UK.

Floor Rink & Naomi Ellemers, 2007. "Diversity as a Source of Common Identity: Towards a Social Identity Framework for Studying the Effects of Diversity in Organisations", *British Journal of Management* 18, 1: 17–27.

Keywords: *diversity-based identity, diversity norm, functional diversity, social identity theory, self-categorization theory*

People feel attracted by similarity. They prefer individuals they perceive as similar to themselves, as similarity reaffirms their own identity. When others share the same characteristics, individuals conclude that having these characteristics is a sign of being *right*. Perceiving others as dissimilar, however, may pose a potential threat to people's identity. Therefore, to preserve a positive self-identity, people tend to derogate those they categorize as different (Tajfel, 1972; Tajfel & Turner, 1986; Turner, 1985). Within multidisciplinary teams, these categorization processes may even diminish the potentially positive effects of functional diversity: by stereotyping dissimilar others, team members fail to collaborate and use the potential advantages of multidisciplinarity in terms of increased knowledge and higher flexibility.

While this reasoning is in line with social identity theory, Rink and Ellemers argue differently: they reason that people do not have to share the same features to perceive themselves as part of the same group. Besides feeling attracted by similarity, people also strive to confirm their expectations. Thus, provided that people in multidisciplinary teams *expect* their fellow team members to be different, confirmation of this expectation may even positively influence group identity.

Organizations therefore need to install *norms of diversity*, signalling that group members share the similarity of being different. People will more easily build a common identity if the differences they perceive between themselves and their fellow team members pertain to task-related differences (= functional diversity). The reason is that functional diversity, more clearly than socio-demographic diversity, offers resources from which groups may benefit. To support the building of a common group identity based on the perception of functional differences between/within workgroups, group members should even differ from each other on multiple task-related aspects. In this case they are more likely to recognize these differences and detect their potential value.

To summarize, "within organisations, members of multidisciplinary teams can develop a common identity on the basis of their task-related differences when these differences are expected prior to their collaboration or when these differences are so evident from the outset that they cannot remain hidden or be ignored" (p. 22). This paper introduces the seemingly paradoxical concept of a diversity-based identity: the idea that team members can develop a common identity the more they perceive each other to be different. Thus it offers an inspiring approach to the management of multidisciplinary teams.

Myriam N. Bechtoldt
University of Amsterdam, Department of Psychology, Amsterdam, The Netherlands.

Andrés Rodriguez-Pose & Ugo Fratesi (2004). "Between Development and Social Policies: The Impact of European Structural Funds in Objective I Regions", *Regional Studies* 38, 1: 97–113.

Keywords: *structural funds, convergence, cohesion, Objective I regions, European Union*

European regional support has grown in parallel with European integration. The funds targeted at achieving greater economic and social cohesion and reducing disparities within the EU have more than doubled in relative terms since the end of the 1980s, making development policies the second most important policy area in the EU. The majority of the development funds have been earmarked for Objective 1 regions, i.e. regions whose GDP per capita is below the 75 percent threshold of the EU average. However, the European development policies have come under increasing criticism based on two facts: the lack of upward mobility of assisted regions and the absence of regional convergence.

This paper assesses, using cross-sectional and panel data analyses, the failure so far of European development policies to fulfil their objective of delivering greater economic and social cohesion by examining how European Structural Fund support is allocated among different development axes in Objective 1 regions. The paper finds that, despite the concentration of development funds on infrastructure and, to a lesser extent, on business support, the returns to commitments on these axes are not significant. Support to agriculture has short-term positive effects on growth, but these wane quickly, and only investment in education and human capital – which only represents about one eighth of the total commitments – has medium-term positive and significant returns. The paper gives insight on the drivers of regional convergence (what works and what does not work). The classification of the Objective 1 support intervention into four categories makes it easy to understand and to read. The data analysis is sound and re-usable for similar exercises.

Rob De Lobel
IDEA Consult, Brussels, Belgium.

Blair A. Ruble, 2005. *Creating Diversity Capital: Transnational Migrants in Montreal, Washington, and Kyiv* (Woodrow Wilson Centre Press; Baltimore: Johns Hopkins University Press), 267 pp.

Keywords: *diversity, transnational migration, urban sustainability*

This publication explores the impact of transnational migrant communities in three cities: Montreal, Washington and Kyiv (Kiev). The author examines how the cities adjust to new challenges of massive migrations and fast-changing concepts of place and community. He looks at the cities' capacity for social urban sustainability, which he defines as diversity capital. The three selected cities have only recently experienced a dramatic and rapid increase in the number of transnational migrants moving in to live and work, and therefore are ideal sites for studying how diversity capital is created. They all have something in common. Montreal, Washington and Kyiv used to be cities divided by language, race, ethnicity or religion. The latest waves of transnational migration contributed to the expansion of the cities into massive metropolitan regions. The author looks at social and economic transformations of the cities and observes how the arrival of large numbers of new immigrants has transformed urban neighbourhoods into intercultural communities. He also studies the worlds of work and school as important venues for the accumulation of diversity capital. As he describes it in the case of Montreal, the daily dance of language at work and at school has become accompanied by the dance of culture which has led to an increase in the city's capacity to adapt to diversity (p. 68).

For a social anthropologist from a post-socialist country, which has not experienced much diversity in the past, but starts to witness it more and more every year, reading about the growth and management of diversity in the city is fascinating food for thought. The most interesting part from this point of view concerns the transformation of post-socialist Kyiv described by a Western scholar. It shows that personal experience of having lived in a socialist country can sometimes be a burden in seeing post-socialist transition with open eyes and mind. The author's approach to the study of diversity in three different cities with different historic and political backgrounds is therefore inspiring and educational.

The major part of the book is dedicated to the complex developments of municipal diversity and integration policies. Local strategies and policies as well as public and media attitudes towards migrants may differ significantly in Montreal, Washington and Kyiv; however, all cities have enhanced their capacity for urban social sustainability, leading to the integration of diverse groups in recent years. The book may be a lesson for a social scientist as well as an urban planner or policy-maker – and not a boring one.

Alexandra Bitusikova
Matej Bel University, Research Institute, Banska Bystrica, Slovakia.

Edward W. Said, 1978. *Orientalism* (London: Routledge and Kegan Paul), 384 pp.

Keywords: *diversity, colonialism, post-colonial studies*

This classical work by the distinguished Palestinian-American scholar Edward Said is the basis for much present post-colonial study. What Said identifies as *the Orient* is a system of representations framed by political forces that brought the Orient into Western learning, Western consciousness and the Western empire. What is considered the Orient is a vast region, one that spreads across myriad cultures and countries, to include most of Asia as well as the Middle East.

The depiction of this single *Orient* which can be studied as a cohesive whole is an arbitrary act, but one of the most powerful accomplishments of Orientalist scholars. It gives an essential image of a prototypical Oriental – a biological inferior who is culturally backward, lazy, weak and unchanging, to be depicted in dominating and sexual terms. The discourse and visual imagery of Orientalism is laced with notions of power and superiority, formulated initially to facilitate a colonizing mission on the part of the West and perpetuated through a wide variety of discourses and policies. One can affirm that this applies not only to the colonial past, but to present times: the same cultural process leading to the invention of the *Orient* and *Orientalism* can be found in the effort to support the so-called *war on terror* and the *clash of civilizations* with cultural arguments.

Orientalism is a pivotal work in terms of recognizing diversity and considering the mirror image of the Orient that exists for the West and is constructed by and in relation to the West. In this case, Said makes us aware of the cultural processes (both at an academic – well educated – level and at the level of the man in the street) that operate when building the image of the *Other* in a context of hierarchies and stigmatization. This happened in the past when the colonial status quo had to be justified with the fact that this colonized Other was inferior and alien, or at the present time, when the tremendous inequality of resource distribution can be seen by some nostalgic Orientalists as a result of one people's own cultural failings. This way of conceiving cultural diversity is not sustainable, because its ultimate effort is to deny the other's dignity and right to exist.

Maria Alessia Montuori
Psychoanalytic Institute for Social Research, Rome, Italy.

Albert Saiz, 2007. "Immigration and Housing Rents in American Cities", *Journal of Urban Economics* 61, 2: 345–371.

Keywords: *immigration, housing prices*

This paper considers an alternative way by which immigrants have a local economic impact. Rather than directly assessing the effect of migration on the labour market, it analyses the effects of the inflow of immigrants on the housing market.

The effect of immigration on housing rent is not obvious. Immigrants may be less sensitive to housing rents, because they greatly value local immigrant-specific amenities and migration networks. On the contrary, natives may be more sensitive to local rents and they may suffer from competition in the local labour market. Therefore, natives may choose to move out or avoid areas where immigrants settle. A positive local effect of immigration on rents would indicate that natives are not extremely sensitive to changes in housing costs and they are not displaced one-for-one in the labour market. Conversely, if the outflow of natives is one-for-one with respect to immigrants, then there would not be any increase in the local demand for housing.

An interesting implication of this paper is that the impact of immigration on rents is smaller, the more negative the impact of immigration on the wages of the marginal city-dweller. If the marginal native's wage goes down because of immigration, the native will move out of the city and rents will not increase by so much.

The authors empirically analyse the impact of the annual inflow of immigrants on the annual change in rents and prices. The findings show that immigration pushes up the demand for housing, rents increase in the short run, and the housing prices catch up. This arises because the inflow of foreign-born induces a marginal relocation of natives, even if it seems that immigrants do not displace natives one-for-one. In areas with inelastic housing supply, the inflow of foreign-born affects the migration decision of a certain number of natives. This paper demonstrates that housing rents and prices are important explanatory variables in analyses of the interplay of immigrants, labour markets and the mobility of natives.

Cristina Cattaneo
Eni Enrico Mattei Foundation (Milan, Italy) and University of Sussex (Sussex, UK).

Sandra R. Schecter & Jim Cummins (eds), 2003. *Multilingual Education in Practice: Using Diversity as a Resource* (Portsmouth, NH: Heinemann), 113 pp.

Keywords: *multilingualism, teaching practice, immigration, multiculturalism*

This book looks at diversity in the school context by focusing on multilingualism and multiculturalism. It approaches diversity by combining information provided by teachers and children with academic research. It is an edited book and it has six chapters. The book shows how linguistic and cultural diversity can be used as a resource in the case of a collaborative project where schoolchildren who are speakers of languages other than English can achieve academic success.

The volume provides interesting insights for researchers and can also be used as a guide for teachers and language planners in schools with students with a diversity of languages and cultures. The book emphasizes the importance of attitudes towards new immigrant students as a key element in their multilingual and academic development. Another key element is that teachers should value the cultural knowledge children already have, so that they can build on that knowledge. Some of the chapters in the book are very informative for teacher education (e.g., Chapter 1 by Cummins & Schecter and

Chapter 5 by S6checter, Solomon & Kittmer). Other chapters focus on the feelings immigrant children have when they experience a new situation going to school in another country (see, e.g, Chapter 2 by Sale, Sliz & Pacini-Ketchabaw and Chapter 4 by Solomon & Ippolito). The book also includes chapters that give a more general idea of the educational project developed in the schools and general directions for its further application (Chapter 3 by Chow & Cummins and Chapter 6 by Shaw).

This volume documents a specific project to use linguistic and cultural diversity as a resource and gives suggestions for developing this type of project in other contexts. Even though the book is based on a specific project, it clearly shows the importance of sustainable diversity in the school context. In my opinion, it is extremely useful because it provides specific examples of the way researchers, teachers, parents and children can collaborate to be successful in a context that is diverse both linguistically and culturally.

Jasone Cenoz
University of the Basque Country, Donostia-San Sebastián, Spain.

Dagmar Schiek, Lisa Weddington & Mark Bell, 2007. *Material, Cases and Text on National, Supranational and International Non-Discrimination* (Oxford: Hart Publishing), 998 pp.

Keywords: *discrimination, cases, law, case law*

This casebook focuses on anti-discrimination law in a comparative perspective. It is the result of cooperation among eminent European experts in the field of anti-discrimination law. It provides knowledge on the legislation of the EU, the Council of Europe and EU member states. Since 1997 anti-discrimination law has been developing a lot thanks to a number of EU directives stimulating the implementation of new sets of legislation in each of the twenty-seven EU states. Even if the book deals with the EU legislation, a mention has been made of US law which may serve in many cases as an interpretative tool.

The book illustrates reciprocal influences between international, European and national legislation in the field of non-discrimination law and it takes into account cases, legislation and other relevant sources (research reports and articles), providing the readers with an up-to-date overview of the implementation of the directives and the state of the law. The content covers the main innovations of the anti-discrimination law, such as discrimination grounds covered by Article 13 EC, direct and indirect discrimination, harassment, victimization, reasonable accommodation, positive action, reversal of the burden of proof, and equality bodies. Each chapter includes a comparative overview, which stresses general principles and divergences in the legal systems within Europe.

Thanks to the variety of material and its structure, the book can be suitable for a wide range of readers: law students, researchers, teachers, lawyers, NGO practitioners and the judiciary. It is also a valuable basis for ongoing research on non-discrimination law, inclusion and social cohesion, and for increasing awareness of best practice. This book can be read in many different ways: from the first page to the last, or starting from specific topics in which an individual is interested. For those who are involved in diversity management in the workplace or in the access to services and goods, this is an easy-to-read resource.

Barbara Giovanna Bello
State University of Milan, Cesare Beccaria Department of Law, Milan, Italy.

Jean-Claude Schmitt, 1998. "La storia dei marginali" in Jacques Le Goff (ed.), *La nuova storia*, translated by Tukery Capra (Milano: Mondadori Editore), pp. 257–287.

English Translation of the Title: *The History of Marginal People.*

Keywords: *marginal, integration, exclusion, reclusion, criminality*

Schmitt's essay provides a historical analysis of poverty and a definition of marginality in medieval and early modern European society. The author reviews the various ways used by society to reject marginal people, and focuses on the subjects included in this definition: poor people, criminals, wanderers, as well as those who belong to ethnic and religious minorities, such as heretics, Jews and gypsies. This work also describes the integration processes brought about by labour and the institutional activities of church and state in periods characterized by persecutions, and when inclusive trends prevailed. Finally, Schmitt shows how poverty, as a mass condition in Europe's Middle Ages and early modern times, promotes the parallel diffusion of criminality and deviance.

From the seventeenth century onwards, the attempt to help the poor, distinguishing them from criminals, and to defend the social order led to the practices of indiscriminate incarceration of marginal people in special institutes. For this reason the early modern age is also defined as the age of segregation. Furthermore, the author outlines the social mechanisms which, inside separate communities, are put into action in order to prevent and suppress marginality before it evolves into poverty and criminality. He shows how marginality can also concern heterogeneous but well-organized groups, like brigand companies, for instance, which have their own rules, cultures, languages and ways of life.

Generally speaking, outlawry has negative connotations, but it can also assume positive meanings when it involves the expression of social redemption and the fight against inequality. Another point stressed by Schmitt regards the scarcity of sources – few, contradictory, and in most cases produced by the dominant classes – and the related problems that historians have to face when they try to analyse this universe. Studying the poor, on the other hand, means reconstructing European history *from below*, from the original and unedited perspective. This is substantially new in comparison with the accounts based on the evolution of the top levels of society.

The book provides a useful contribution to the understanding of social diversity, analysing in detail the world of marginal people and their condition of life in pre-industrial Europe. It traces the boundary, not always easy to recognize and often intrinsically uncertain, between the leading classes and marginality. Institutions are considered to have a dual role, supporting coexistence with the poor, wanderers and outlaws, and at the same time circumscribing the social, political and economic consequences of marginality in order to make it sustainable.

Augusto Ciuffetti
Marche Polytechnic University, Department of Social Sciences, Ancona, Italy.

Mihir Sengupta, 2004. *Bishad Brikhho*, 1st edn (Kolkata: Subarnorekha), 320 pp.

English Translation of the Title: *Tree of Sadness.*

Keywords: *village, harvest, transformation, language, oral tradition*

An autobiographical novel has unique appeal; rather than relating a simple chronicle, it paints real portraits, places and events. The reality of it hits intellect and emotion; there is no escape. *Bishaad-Brikho* recounts the tale of turmoil, transformation and decay of a village in East Pakistan, as experienced by the author, while growing up in Kaora, East Bengal. The author was born into a joint family that had once been landed gentry, aristocratic and powerful, but by 1947 its only visible legacy was a discoloured mansion and the lazy feudal temperament of its male members. Weighed down by multiple yokes of poverty, an unreal ambition of education and the changing matrix of his village society, the boy grew up roaming around villages, observing people, their relationships, hearing local myths, stories and songs, even breaking pollution taboos to satisfy pangs of hunger. The rural flavour is unmistakable as he describes the fragrance of newly harvested rice or the taste of tiny shrimps from ponds next door. Harvest was the binding force of rural people, rich or poor.

Through the eyes of the protagonist, the reader observes the dynamics of the village society and, to the extent that the village is a microcosm of a larger world, gets a view of rural Bengal in the immediate aftermath of the partition of India. Despite their spatial separation, Kaora's mixed population of Hindus and Muslims had a stable relationship, with distinct pockets of syncretic culture. The stability collapsed soon after Partition, however, as the balance between the two communities changed. Muslims were no longer subservient to the Hindus, nor did they have to suffer the Hindus' disdain. Unfortunately, the criminal element took over and the scenario altered to one of violence, rape, lawlessness, corruption and fear. As old friends and neighbours acquiesced in the reign of terror, most of the Hindu population left. The village became silent, empty; it lost its soul. Even those who had wanted the Hindus to leave felt the near-tactile vacuum. Economically, the village never recovered. The Hindu middle class left, but no Muslim middle class took its place to fill the gap. In all the turmoil the only constants that remained were *pichharar khhal*, the little stream by the village, the author's lifeline, and the *Bishaad-Brikhho*, the tree of sadness, the mute witness.

The mix of urban Bengali and local dialects used in the book will be of interest to researchers in this field, as will be the local myths, tales, poems and songs for documenting rural lore in the oral tradition. For anyone studying the history of post-Partition Bengal or the effects of mass migration and diaspora, the book will be of immense value. To this reviewer, apart from the pathos of a crumbled society, the socio-economic explanation of the decay and demise of a society that had taken centuries to evolve was of great interest. The tragedy of the common people is an oft-researched subject; this is an analysis of the tragedy of a village, of a culture, of a once-happy place.

Alaknanda Patel
Centre for Development Alternatives, Ahmedabad, India.

Annick Sjögren, 1992. "Moulding a community in Botkyrka" in Åke Daun, Billy Ehn & Barbro Klein (eds.), *To Make the World Safe for Diversity: Towards an understanding of multi-cultural societies* (Helsingborg: Schmidts Boktryckeri AB), pp. 23–50.

Keywords: *neighbourhood, ethnicity, local policies, multiculturalism*

Sjögren describes the process through which an old Swedish neighbourhood on the outskirts of Stockholm matures into a multi-ethnic, multicultural and multifaith community during the 1970s, and examines the way the policy of the local authorities contributes to the development of a real community. After short descriptions of the history and the demographic and economic processes which have led to Botkyrka being perceived as the most multi-ethnic area in Sweden today, the author meticulously examines the combination of factors and resources (space, people, spirit) that have made the area what it is today in every Swedish person's imagination.

Botkyrka is a young and multi-ethnic borough, and one of the strategies used to foster a sense of community was to stimulate innovation and to create a pioneer spirit of improvisation in response to the newcomers' needs. Policies regarding public performances, education and culture were progressive in the sense that they encouraged the strengthening of ethnic identity as much as an a-ethnic sense of community. Outcomes were not always successful, but eventually people from both sides learned from each other. Everybody, regardless of ethnic background, was made to participate in the local initiatives, in so doing having a say and actively contributing to the image of Botkyrka. Most importantly, the author points out that the image that non-residents get of the area differs from the one perceived by the residents.

As in other settings, and as we often find in the literature, it is evident in Botkyrka that what the insiders *perceive* is different from what the outsiders *see*. Ultimately, the product of this multi-ethnic community life, either a child of non-Swedish parents or a Swedish child who has grown accustomed to the multi-ethnicity of his friends, is a person who does not regard ethnicity as a means of defining who is one of us and who is not. This new type of person is problematic and malleable at the same time, someone who is living and building up a "blended world", where solidarity plays the primary role in social relationships.

This essay focuses on the struggles and the successes of a fast-growing neighbourhood responding to the demographic changes following an unexpected wave of immigration and diversity. Sjögren makes examples of daily life situations speak for those changes. Thanks to the combined potential of existing residents and newcomers, and to the improvised but tailored local measures, Botkyrka is transformed from an old Swedish neighbourhood into the multicultural showcase of Stockholm. The book in which this essay is a chapter offers an extremely useful set of ethnographic accounts focused on community and ethnic studies in Sweden, which anyone interested in the field would find of invaluable use.

Rossella Lo Conte
University College London, Department of Anthropology, London, UK.

Georg Simmel, 1908. "The Stranger" in Donald Levine (ed.), 1971. *Georg Simmel: On Individuality and Social Forms, Selected Writings* (Chicago: The University of Chicago Press), pp. 143–149.

Keywords: *stranger, closeness, remoteness*

This 3,000-word essay was written a hundred years ago, yet it is innovative and contemporary. Simmel describes the figure of the stranger who is not a simple wanderer who comes today and goes tomorrow, but rather is "the man who comes today and stays tomorrow . . . who is fixed within a certain spatial circle but his position within it is fundamentally affected by the fact that he does not belong to it initially and that he brings qualities into it that are not, and cannot be, indigenous to it" (p. 143). Simmel mentions mobility and objectivity as main characteristics of the figure of the stranger. The former, described as the connubial of nearness and remoteness (p. 143), gives him the advantage of being in contact with every element of the society he happens to live in, but also the freedom not to feel organically bound to it. The latter, described as the connubial of "indifference and involvement" (p. 143), gives him the advantage of being the man of confidence for many of the people he comes into contact with, as well as the free man whose decisions are taken following no pre-established law of conduct but his own. More importantly, the stranger is the one to whom everybody is generally similar, but from whom he is specifically different, to the extent that he is first of all a person owning a different background to the locals, i.e. ethnic, religious, social, etc., and only later someone bringing new skills and potential to the community. A stigma is unavoidable as much as it is unnecessary, but it clarifies the condition of nearness and remoteness on which Simmel focuses so much.

I thought of mentioning this essay because *diverse* is a category to which anybody can be attached in virtue of the most various criteria of classification. This essay does not choose a particular category. What it does is to illustrate how human beings instinctively find in the classification the way to identify and understand the new, i.e. the stranger.

This essay is of significant interest to anyone keen to investigate the relationship between people and places. It provides an initial statement on how to explore the undercover dynamics that so much dictate people's reactions to the newcomer. It is an easy and extremely lucid essay to read for any anthropologist or social scientist, who will find it useful in understanding what it means to be an outsider, as well as being an objective instrument of investigation and enquiry when conducting fieldwork. As Simmel also indicates, "spatial relations not only are determining conditions of relationships among men, but are also symbolic of those relationships" (p. 143).

Rossella Lo Conte
University College London, Department of Anthropology, London, UK.

Anthony D. Smith, 1992. *Le origini etniche delle nazioni, translated by Umberto Livini* (Bologna: Il Mulino), 510 pp.

English Translation of the Title: *The Ethnic Origin of Nations.*

Keywords: *nation, nationalism, political sociology, ethnicity*

The book deals with the issue of nationalism, the origins of which, in Smith's vision, are to be investigated in pre-modern societies. Nationalism is the basic principle of legitimating political action and the construction of the modern state. Nevertheless, few states appear today homogeneous from the point of view of their ethnic composition, i.e. not including populations that aspire to create their own autonomous nation-state. The problem for the scholar of contemporary history is represented by singling out the border line between nation and ethnicity.

The birth of the modern nation passed through three main, essential changes: in the field of labour organization, in the managing of the *res publica*, and in the field of cultural integration. The revolutions in these three contexts originated two basic concepts of nation: the territorial nation and the ethnic one. The first is identified with a physical space, with the culture and the laws of the people who live in it. The ethnic nation, on the contrary, has no physical borders, being based rather on the most ancient roots of a community, which uses history to motivate its aspiration to become a nation – an entity that does not often coincide with the political and territorial delimitations of the state in which it lies.

Up to the eighteenth century these two concepts were rather distinct. But with the French Revolution many differences faded: the *third state*, the bourgeoisie, identified its own origins with the Gallic age, extended then to the Roman republic, in order to legitimate its aspirations of leading the new nation. Since then, the largest part of European nationalism has been influenced by the *ethnic model* of nation, using more and more a unifying ethnical mythology, with the result that all the nations are based today on both ethnic and territorial principles. Recent history shows how easily the coexistence of various ethnically defined national communities inside the same territorial state becomes a source of conflict.

Smith's essay is a contribution to the comprehension of the mechanisms at the basis of these dynamics. It analyses how ethnic conflicts are developed by a presumed cultural and social diversity, used by ethnic groups as self-definition; and how nationalistic movements exalt these identities with the aim of feeding and justifying the ambitions of independence of their own ethnic communities.

Roberto Giulianelli
Marche Polytechnic University, Department of Social Sciences,
Ancona, Italy.

David A. Thomas, Robin J. Ely, 1996. "Making differences matter: A new paradigm for managing diversity", *Harvard Business Review*, September/October 74, 5: 79–90.
&
Robin J. Ely, David A. Thomas, 2001. "Cultural diversity at work: The effects of diversity perspectives on work group processes and outcomes", *Administrative Science Quarterly* 46, 2: 229–273.

Keywords: *workforce diversity, diversity perspectives, group functioning, sustained effects*

Both articles discuss three different perspectives on workforce diversity: the discrimination-and-fairness perspective, the access-and-legitimacy perspective, and the integration-and-learning perspective. The *Harvard Business Review* (HBR) article is a managerial one, introducing the three perspectives with their strengths and weaknesses and giving advice on leadership requirements. The *Administrative Science Quarterly* (ASQ) article is research oriented, studying how the three diversity perspectives are important conditions under which cultural diversity enhances or detracts from work group functioning through intermediate group outcomes such as quality of intergroup relations, degree of feeling valued and respected, and meaning and significance of cultural identity at work.

According to the integration-and-learning perspective on diversity, the skills and experiences employees have developed as members of various cultural identity groups are potentially valuable resources that an organization can use to rethink its primary tasks and redefine its business practices in ways that will advance its mission. This perspective links diversity to work processes – the way people do and experience the work – in a manner that makes diversity a resource for learning and adaptive change.

The access-and-legitimacy perspective on diversity is based on recognition that the organization's markets and constituencies are culturally diverse. It therefore instigates the organization to match that diversity through its workforce as a way of gaining access to and legitimacy with those markets and groups.

The discrimination-and-fairness perspective is characterized by a belief in a diverse workforce as a moral imperative to ensure justice and the fair treatment of all members of society. It focuses on providing equal treatment opportunities in hiring and promotion, suppressing prejudicial attitudes, and eliminating discrimination.

Both articles have strongly influenced my own reflections on the strengths and weakness of diversity management practices, as these three perspectives offer a powerful way to identify the underlying assumptions when approaching workforce diversity. Specifically, the three perspectives differ in terms of (1) rationale for diversifying, (2) value of cultural identity, (3) connection between cultural diversity and work, and (4) indicators of progress, with the integration-and-learning perspective achieving sustained benefits from diversity. This perspective is expected to lead to increased representation of traditionally under-represented groups that have power to change the organization, as there is a shared sense that cultural diversity is a source for learning. In my opinion, this perspective is powerful as it goes beyond the traditional way of managing diversity through cross-cultural training, bias-free selection methods or mentoring. It is crucial that one should integrate cultural differences into the core work and processes as appropriate, leading to change and organizational development.

In addition, the differences among the three perspectives are discussed not only in terms of organizational outcomes, but also in terms of interpersonal and personal ones. Following the integration-and-learning perspective, what is important is open and constructive conflict resulting from cultural differences in point of view, all employees feeling respected and valued for their competence, and racial identity as a source of value for people of colour. Overall, these perspectives offer insights into the type of cognitive frame that is used when interpreting and acting upon the experience of workforce diversity.

Maddy Janssens
Katholieke Universiteit Leuven, Faculty of Business and Economics, Research Centre for Organisation Studies, Leuven, Belgium.

Michael Tonry, 1995. *Malign Neglect: Race, Crime and Punishment in America* (New York: Oxford University Press), 233 pp.

Keywords: *race, crime, punishment, imprisonment*

The combination of race and crime is a key societal issue in many countries, especially in the USA where the rate of imprisonment for blacks, and to a somewhat lesser extent Hispanics, has increased dramatically. It should be noted that the overall rate of imprisonment rose sharply in the 1980s and 1990s, but the difference between blacks and whites stood at seven to one when *Malign Neglect* was written. These ratios led scholars to search for answers in research and policy-makers to provide answers in the headlines. Tonry tackles this thorny issue in a unique manner, taking a look not only at the statistics in terms of who commits crime and who spends time in prison, but also at the nature of the policies that contributed both to decisions regarding the allocation of resources for identifying and prosecuting crimes (e.g., more focus on certain types of drug offences) and to who eventually ends up in prison and for how long.

Tonry's primary argument is that the effects of the wars on drugs and crime – in terms of their disproportionate impact on blacks and Hispanics and others who live in American inner cities – were foreseeable. Tonry holds that the American criminal justice system is not outright discriminatory or biased, in terms of the law as written or in the overall behaviour of police officers and other actors in the criminal justice system, but that the implementation of laws that one could expect to have a highly differential impact represent a passive form of discrimination or, as he terms it, malign neglect.

The argument and evidence presented does not ignore the facts, but encourages the reader to think about the relationship between sentencing policy, crime and the offender in light of the likely consequences of a given policy by taking patterns in criminality into account. Laws that focus on street-corner drug-dealing will, given the make-up of USA cities and differences in dealing by socio-economic class, lead to an increase in arrests of young black and Hispanic males. The provocative aspect of Tonry's argument lies in his focus on the malign neglect of certain groups – minorities and those living in poverty.

The work adds to an extensive literature in the area of race and crime as well as poverty and crime, providing a new perspective on an age-old problem. It focuses on the USA during a period of mass incarceration, but its implications are much broader as it combines the study of offenders with the study of policy, striving to look at both in real and practical terms. We are encouraged not to deny certain realities that arise from individual and societal differences (e.g., high rates of certain types of offending by young black males living in the inner cities), but also to be keenly aware of the disparate impact of laws that are, at least on the surface, not discriminatory. *Malign Neglect* represents a call to take responsibility, as policy-makers and as a society.

Vanja M. K. Stenius
Psychoanalytic Institute for Social Research, Rome, Italy.

Tsvetan Todorov, 1993. *On Human Diversity: Nationalism, Racism, and Exoticism in French Thought* (Cambridge, MA: Harvard UP), 448 pp.

Keywords: *universalism, relativism, humanism, Enlightenment, France*

On Human Diversity challenges the Lévi-Straussian call for cultural relativism on the grounds of three different arguments. From a historical standpoint, it first rejects the notion that the Enlightenment universalism was elaborated as a presentable ethnocentric war machine for Europe. From a consequentialist perspective, it shows that the *doxa* of absolute difference complicates more intercultural, moral judgment and dialogue than it actually protects against intolerance. From a philosophical point of view, it contends that closing the diversity debate satisfactorily implies circumscribing cultural difference within the frame of an overarching, transculturally shared system of meaning which would draw the line between tolerable and intolerable diversities – a moral enterprise that could only be achievable thanks to man's universal ability to reshape his primitive norms. To avoid all risk of ethnocentrism, Todorov insists that this universal feature is "an instrument of analysis, a regulatory principle allowing the fruitful confrontation of differences, and [that] its content . . . is always subject to revision" (p. 390).

The work of Todorov has often been divided into two successive periods – one dedicated to the study of French, Russian and English literature, one rather focused on questions of ethics. This taxonomy renders it difficult to classify *On Human Diversity*. This book is indeed both a philosophical essay on the French intellectual tradition from the sixteenth through the twentieth centuries, and an attempt at prescribing ways of engaging with the diversity debate. Its interest, nonetheless, lies precisely in this in-between. On the one hand, the massive philosophical investigation that it proposes pursuing into the doctrines of Montaigne, Lévi-Strauss, Gobineau, Renan, Tocqueville, Michelet, Barrès, Péguy, Chateaubriand, Segalen, Rousseau and Montesquieu allows one to develop a thorough understanding of the French universalist, racist, nationalist and relativist strains of thought and of their links and interdependencies throughout history. On the other hand, Todorov's invitation to take up with the legacy of the Enlightenment when reflecting on the ways of escaping the cultural diversity predicament shows the utility of enlarging the historical scope of research in this respect. It suggests that, just as this discussion might not be as recent as one could think, perhaps its normative conclusions could be found in the writings of past authors.

Olivier Rousseau
Interdisciplinary Centre for Comparative Research in the Social Sciences, Paris, France.

Alain Touraine, 2000. *Can We Live Together? Equality in Difference*, translated by David Macey (Stanford University Press), 336 pp.

Keywords: *identity, social movements, multiculturalism, nation, democracy*

The more we become a vast global society, the more we break into "identity-based groupings and associations, sects and cults and nationalisms based on a common sense of belonging" (p. 2). Rather than coming together, we are with-drawing into tribes foreign to one other that remind us of the totalitarian state. Meanwhile, "The old answers have become inaudible or inapplicable" (p. 11). How can we live together in such a divided world? We are caught in a dilemma: history "turned into a nightmare and an instrument of domination" (p. 14) when it tried to force individuals into universal orders. At the same time, however, rejection of all forms of unity or unqualified acceptance of difference often leads to segregation or civil war.

The author examines in detail the ways of the past that he considers fundamentalist dead-ends. To be able to live together, he claims, "We have to construct new forms of collective and personal life" (p. 15). "In a world of permanent and uncontrollable change, the individual attempt to transform lived experiences into the construction of the self as actor is the only stable point of reference. I call the individual's attempt to become an actor, 'the Subject'" (p. 13). Furthermore, "the personal subject is our starting-point . . . democracy our goal [and] . . . Inter-cultural communication is the path that leads from one to the other" (p. 301). To live together, we need to "reconcile the unity of society and a diversity of personalities and cultures" (p. 14).

This book guides the reader through a path-breaking criticism of prevailing explanations that question both communitarian/homogenizing schemes and uncritical commitment to diversity. It seeks a new path departing from production of a Subject that is at the same time a critical departure from the past and a social movement to construct the future via intercultural communication. In his words, "Our new battles will be battles for diversity rather than unity, for freedom rather than participation" (p. 304). Unity will not come from imposed universals, but from intercultural communication; democracy will not be about "institutional procedures" (p. 231) or political representation, but about "assertion of personal freedom" (p. 14).

Touraine's analysis and proposals push us out of the old order into production of a new one in which change rather than institutional order is the norm. "The era of order is coming to an end; this is the beginning of the era of change" (p. 12). What I found most helpful was his departure from fundamentalist versions of identity and diversity to versions that operate in the tension between self-assertion and collectivism within a new paradigm of change.

John J. Betancur
University of Illinois at Chicago, Department of Urban Planning and Policy, Chicago, USA.

Enzo Traverso, 2007. *A ferro e fuoco. La Guerra civile europea 1914–1945* (Bologna: Il Mulino), 273 pp.

English Translation of the Title: *With Fire and Sword: The European Civil War, 1914–1915.*

Keywords: *world war, nationalism, war of class, ideology*

The book is based on the idea, largely shared by contemporary historiography, that the two world conflagrations of the first half of the twentieth century and the tormented inter-war period must be considered as a unitary generalized conflict among, at the same time, powers, nation-states, social classes, ideologies and the related *Weltanschauung*. As a result, Europe, namely the epicentre of this total war, lost the world hegemony, conquered during the whole early modern age and arrived at its climax with the starting of modernization in the nineteenth century. Such a perspective, formulated originally by Ernest Nolte (*Der Europäische Bürgerkrieg 1917–1945. Nationalsozialsums und Bolschewismus*, Berlin: 1987) in the frame of the revisionist debate on Nazi Germany, was developed fully, moving from opposite, Marxist bases by Hobsbawn's *The Short 20th Century* in 1994, which extends its analysis to include the post-war period up to the fall of the Berlin Wall.

Traverso has been chosen for the present bibliography because he provides an up-to-date and rather shared version of this latter interpretation, focusing however only on its core period, the first half of the century, without dealing with the more controversial and evolving analyses of the post-World War II period. If in Europe, during the largest part of the nineteenth and the twentieth centuries, the diverse *other* was perceived primarily as one who belonged to a different nation or a different social class, then this perception produced its extreme consequences in the total conflagration of the two world wars, playing a decisive role in the destinies of contemporary history.

Traverso analyses the European civil war from different viewpoints, presenting its forms, its cultural and anthropological aspects, the general historical movements that frame it, as well as its extreme consequences, like the Holocaust, Stalinism or the use of nuclear weapons. The description of the total conflict caused by the radicalization of nationalism and class war contributes to make explicit the tragic echoes that the idea of diversity arises in the memory of the Old Continent, as well as of the many other parts of the world involved in its history.

Francesco Chiapparino
Marche Polytechnic University, Department of Social Sciences, Ancona, Italy.

Jean-Claude Trichet, 2007. "The Monetary Policy Implications of Ageing", *European Central Bank Press*, 1–13. Speech by Mr Jean-Claude Trichet, President of the European Central Bank, at the ABP Conference on Pension Diversity and Solidarity in Europe, Maastricht/Heerlen, 26 September 2007.

Keywords: *ageing, investments, international factor flows, migration*

The monetary policy implications of ageing analyses the impact which demographic development in the Euro Zone has on the macro-economic environment. The article examines two major questions: how ageing will affect our economies through changes in the balance between savings and investment – changes which could well bring adjustments in the real interest rate; and how implications of population ageing will influence monetary policy where domestic savings have higher rates towards those who are young or retired. It analyses how people, once retired, manage to live.

The research shows that population ageing increases the proportion of households in the economy with a relatively lower savings rate and therefore tends to reduce private savings. Furthermore, public savings are negatively affected by the ageing process through higher healthcare costs. Investment in this points to a connection between ageing and technological progress. The question as to whether demographic developments affect capital intensity depends on two main factors: capital stock and the labour force. From the article, it is obvious that ageing does not play a positive role in this economic category. It is presumed that ageing generates a fall in the rate of growth of the labour force, or at least a reduction in its size. Consequently, when investment rates are expected to decrease, the growth rate of capital stock could gradually decline to better accommodate the relatively scarcer labour force.

The international mobility of factors has an influence on ageing as the EU economy gives opportunities to many young people to work abroad for a higher wage. However, this doesn't mean there are no impediments to labour mobility within the Euro Zone. As a consequence, this process causes higher rates of return outside this area. Labour mobility can have a negative impact on the demographic profile when large numbers of highly qualified young people leave developing countries. In general, the migration process will deepen over the following decades, eventually creating a downward effect on demographic factors. The demographic factor is defined through the age of the different world economic areas. The differences in the pace of ageing between Europe, Japan and the USA are even larger. Therefore, if production factors are internationally mobile, demographic factors may lead to sizeable flows between developed and developing economies, owing to significant differences in their demographic paths.

In my opinion, the issue leads to higher estimates regarding budgetary costs related to ageing. As such, the ageing process will be a significant reason for a substantial fall in private and public savings. We must note that population ageing is predicted to generate a faster fall in investment rates than in savings rates in most industrialized economies.

The main challenges resulting from ageing will not be for central banks. Fiscal policies and structural policies are in the forefront, as the most severe problems that ageing will pose for public policies are likely to come in the form of a dramatic deterioration in fiscal positions – owing to mounting pension expenditure – and a considerable reduction in the rate of growth of the labour force.

Iskra Christova-Balkanska
Institute of Economics, Bulgarian Academy of Sciences, Sofia, Bulgaria.

Peter Pericles Trifonas (ed.), 2005. *Communities of Difference: Culture, Language, Technology* (New York: Palgrave Macmillan), 231 pp.

Keywords: *pluralism, difference, critical pedagogy, social aspects of globalization*

This book examines the challenges of "rearticulating the notion of community . . . as communities of difference" (p. xviii). It criticizes the classical divide between *us* and *them* resulting from enactment of (European) universalism and its self-assigned right to decide who belongs and who does not, who is right and who is wrong. Organized into three distinct parts linking difference and community to culture, language and technology, it examines issues as diverse as the war against children, racism in academia, the nation, postmodernism in formal education, crisis of the left, critical pedagogy, love and school, subjectivity and objectivity, the digital technology revolution and the internet from the perspective of social justice – while calling for academics to link knowledge with action.

A couple of citations provide a sense of the tone of the book: "the achieving of information is not benign, but subject to the governance of the means of representation by external forces, mechanical and ideological, though ultimately grounded in the logic of cultural practices" (p. 227), and "the pluralism of any post-modern interpretation of difference, as re-conceptualised through the educational lenses of critical pedagogy, contains the promise to release the subject by freeing the power of identity unto a knowledge of the truth of self. Yet, one is still wont to ask, is this enough or can it ever be?" (p. 162).

The book exposes the nuances and unspoken assumptions accompanying universal notions of community and communitarianism while exploring new paths, new pedagogies, new approaches to democracy, and new foundational ethics of difference. Authors show that criticism plays a major role in the move from a homogenizing framework towards "a democracy to come" (p. 77) on the basis of "a pedagogy to come" (p. xv) and the rescue of the spirit and the heart largely dismissed by totalitarian rational universalism. The book is particularly useful for educators willing to challenge their philosophies of and approaches to teaching and to incorporate new insights and methods into their work.

John J. Betancur
University of Illinois at Chicago, Department of Urban Planning and Policy, Chicago, USA.

United Nations Department of Economic and Social Affairs
(UNDESA), 2004. *World Economic and Social Survey 2004: International Migration* (New York: United Nations), 274 pp.

Keywords: *migration, labour markets, development*

International migration is one of the central dimensions of globalization. Facilitated by improved transportation and communications and stimulated by large economic and social inequalities in the world, people are increasingly moving across national borders in an effort to improve their own and their family's well-being. In the past decades, international movements of people have increased along with expanded international flows of goods and capital. International migration is an increasingly worldwide phenomenon, involving a growing number of states as countries of origin, destination or transit of migrants.

The forces underlying these trends are unlikely to reverse so that these international movements of people will continue – and most probably increase – in the future. The increased mobility of people across national borders has affected not only the migrants themselves, but also the lives and welfare of many peoples and societies, as well as the functioning of specific countries and groups of countries. As with increasing flows of goods and capital, it is necessary for governments – and the international community – to decide how to address this facet of global development.

This publication examines the background to and the nature of the increase in international migration and its wide-range impacts, and identifies the policy challenges posed by these developments. It provides a comprehensive review of developments in international migration, by performing a retrospective analysis starting from the Napoleonic Wars and World War I until the migratory phenomena of today. The paper focuses mainly on the current aspects of migration, providing important information about the characteristics of migrating populations as well as the trends followed with regard to the regions of destination and immigrant status (voluntary, asylum seekers, refugees, etc.), while issues like unauthorized migration are also examined.

What is most interesting about this paper is that it studies the social as well as the economic effects of migration worldwide, as much for the countries of origin as for the countries of destination. The paper examines national migration policies and how they have adapted to address an array of concerns, including the effects of low fertility and population ageing, unemployment, protection of human rights, social integration, xenophobia, national security, brain-drain and brain-gain, remittances, asylum granting and human trafficking.

Finally, what is most useful is that this paper presents existing ways for increasing the benefits and reducing the costs of international migration both for the countries of origin and the countries of destination, and suggests new ways for further improvement.

Lena Tsipouri
National and Kapodistrian University of Athens, Athens, Greece.

Daan van Knippenberg, Carsten K.W. De Dreu & Astrid C. Homan, 2004. "Work Group Diversity and Group Performance: An Integrative Model and Research Agenda", *Journal of Applied Psychology* 89, 6: 1008–1022.

Keywords: *categorization-elaboration model, self-categorization theory, group performance*

Diversity in psychology refers to any characteristics varying among individuals that make them aware of differences between others and themselves. Therefore diversity can comprise an almost infinite number of variables. In research on diversity, mainly two broad categories have been differentiated: diversity in socio-demographic characteristics and diversity in informational/functional characteristics. The former has usually been associated with negative effects like stereotyping, lacking communication, and conflict, while the latter has been related to positive effects like better group performance, including higher creativity, and better decision-making.

Negative effects of socio-demographic diversity within groups have been explained by social identity theory (Tajfel, 1972; Tajfel & Turner, 1986) and self-categorization theory (Turner, 1985): to categorize themselves, people will more easily refer to socio-demographic variables than differences in underlying variables like professional background, because socio-demographic characteristics are visible and therefore highly accessible categories. Given that parts of individuals' identity derive from their membership in social groups (e.g. being a Muslim, being Afro-American, being an artist), they maximize the positive difference between their own groups (in-groups) and other groups to which they do not belong (out-groups): by derogating these out-groups, individuals can feel positive about their in-groups.

Social identity theory and self-categorization theory focus on the relational aspects of diversity and take a critical stance as to the nature of effects. Models on information processing analyse diversity from a task-related point of view and come to more positive conclusions: diversity increases absorptive capacities, requisite variety and network boundaries of workgroups. The higher group members' diversity in terms of information and knowledge, the more knowledgable and flexible workgroups become.

According to Van Knippenberg, De Dreu and Homan, however, relating socio-demographic diversity to negative and informational diversity to positive outcomes does not provide a comprehensive picture on the effects of diversity within workgroups. By developing the categorization-elaboration model, they demonstrate that both types of diversity can trigger positive and negative effects. Moreover, they define a series of process variables and contextual variables that influence the effects of diversity on group performance, creativity and decision-making. Thus the paper integrates established theories and provides a comprehensive theoretical framework which combines seemingly inconsistent research findings on the effects of diversity within workgroups.

Myriam N. Bechtoldt
University of Amsterdam, Department of Psychology, Amsterdam, The Netherlands.

Validation and Certification of Training in the Field of European Cultural Cooperation Project Management (VANIA), 2008. "Teaching Pack for Cultural Cooperation: The selection of most relevant and used tools in teaching cultural cooperation in Europe", *VANIA*, pp. 1–21.

Keywords: *European cultural cooperation project management, cultural field, training, intercultural skills*

The research discussed in this report identifies the concepts and methods of teaching cultural cooperation: how future practitioners are prepared to work together, to co-produce or to mediate (interpret) the products and values of one culture in another cultural context.

Globalization and the new media demand knowledge of diverse material and visual culture and skills of cultural operators. At the same time, cultural operators have to be aware of differences in policy measures as they influence the new local forms of cultural practice.

The report documents efforts which are being made in cultural management education, as well as higher art education, to respond to the needs of cultural operators who work in a climate of mobility and intercultural dialogue. Knowledge and skills addressed as *cultural capital* are required for cooperation and co-production, but also for communication serving intercultural dialogue. The report helps to accentuate existing differences in the conceptualization and teaching of "cultural operation" and cultural diplomacy, outlining practice in basic and postgraduate academic courses and in courses within programmes of lifelong learning.

The report raises a number of questions, such as how cultural managers and other operators are educated to work in different cultural contexts; whether training develops a capacity to understand and to make understandable the expressions of different cultures; whether the traditional training formats and training tools adapt to the needs of new professionals in cultural management and cultural diplomacy; and whether they create the competence and knowledge necessary for international cooperation within Europe – through artistic dialogue, representation and exhibition, but also through mediation and communication.

My personal reasons for mentioning this report are its elaboration on the uses of concepts of *international, European, transnational* and *trans-European* in relation to cooperative activities in culture. International and European are generic concepts, which frequently refer to bilateral and multilateral cultural cooperation of national and subnational units from the point of view of national policies and interests. Transnational and trans-European refer increasingly to cultural cooperation where activities of units, be they small companies, NGOs, networks or individuals, transcend both national borders and objectives. Transnationalism is increasingly used in the case of economic, ethical, environmental or social objectives (Médecins Sans Frontières and Greenpeace), or ideological objectives (political movements). In this report, the authors take these conceptual distinctions into account, but opt for transnational as their preferred term in relation to cultural cooperation projects. The exploration of this term is valuable for research dealing with dialogue through arts in Europe and beyond.

Ljiljana Simic
Oracle – Network of European Cultural Managers, Brussels, Belgium.

Michael E. Veal, 2007. *Dub, Soundscapes and Shattered Songs in Jamaican Reggae*, 1st edn (Connecticut: Wesleyan University Press), 338 pp.

Keywords: *sound, technological innovations, politics, social significance, aesthetics*

Jamaican musicians are well known in today's global popular music culture for their impassioned fusion of popular music, politics and spirituality. Musicians such as Bob Marley, Peter Tosh and Jimmy Cliff are influential icons of what might be called the *conscious party* – the idea that popular music may be enjoyed in a meaningful way that remains mindful of the realities shaping human lives.

What is less well known is that Jamaica has also been extremely influential in terms of the *sound* of today's popular music. *Dub: Soundscapes and Shattered Songs in Jamaican Reggae* examines the Jamaican recording studio as a sonic and cultural institution, tracing its aesthetic evolution from the early years of the 1940s through the current age of digital production. The focus of the book is the roots reggae era of the 1970s and early 1980s – the years when Jamaican recording engineers such as Osbourne "King Tubby" Ruddock, Errol Thompson and Lee "Scratch" Perry defined a unique production aesthetic in which the implements of the recording studio (sound-processing units and the multitrack mixing console) were refashioned as instruments of real-time improvisation. This resulted in the genre known as *Dub*, a bass-driven subgenre of reggae defined by fragmented melodies and lyrics echoing through reverberant sonic spaces. This music is considered both as a local variant of the post-World War II tradition of electronic/experimental music and as a sonic embodiment of post-colonial Jamaican culture. The book also examines the impact that Dub's studio techniques had (and continue to have) on popular music production techniques outside Jamaica. Dub music continues to exert a profound influence on the sound of popular music in the digital age.

In the end, this book explores the differing inflections technology can be given as it is transposed across cultural borders, and presents the idea that we can read a culture and its priorities in a given historical moment through the way it represents itself in musical sound. To a practitioner and researcher of North Indian classical music, Dub opens up a whole new space of sound and rhythm. The traditional *dhrupad* and *khyal* singing in India has evolved over centuries, yet it has remained within prescribed norms. Experiments in sound with the recording studio as a hub are an exciting revelation. It offers a new challenge to listening as well as to the perception of aesthetics. The book opens up a new world. Patronized by kings, princes and elites, classical music in India is asocial, apolitical. India has a rich history of popular music with ever-evolving forms expressing people's aspirations and disappointments; in addition, different forms of religious music reflect diverse strands of socio-cultural norms and customs.

Studies relating this diversity to social and political changes, however, are rare. By analysing the connection between musical innovations and Jamaica's social and political changes, Michael Veal gives challenging insights into the sociology of the music of the region. For scholars studying the sociology of Indian music, this opens up refreshingly new avenues for research.

Alaknanda Patel
Centre for Development Alternatives, Ahmedabad, India.

Alessandra Venturini, 2001. *Le migrazioni e i paesi sudeuropei: Un'analisi economica* (Torino: UTET), 305 pp.

English Translation of the Title: *Migrations and South European Countries: An Economic Analysis.*

Keywords: *southern Europe, motives, consequences, flows, migration policy*

The book provides an economic analysis of the migratory phenomenon. This is studied through motives of migration, consequences for both receiving and original countries, and the type and efficacy of migration policies. The focus is on southern European countries (Portugal, Italy, Spain, Greece) that share a recent and rapid transition from emigration country to destinations of immigration. In terms of the reasons for this change, they are interesting yet not much studied: Venturini tries to fill the gap and to give a common analysis for the whole of southern Europe. The analysis is articulate and complete; Venturini does not support only a single thesis, but she presents the literature, the different perspectives and the main empirical data.

The book is useful for understanding the complexity of the issue and its many interactions on demographic, economic (growth, labour market, remittances), social (social expenditure, retirement system) and institutional (integration/assimilation policies) fields. Therefore it gives diversity a broad meaning, avoiding reductionist interpretations that are simpler and easier but also partial and incomplete, and that are not able to fully understand the real opportunities and dangers connected with migratory flows. The complexity and choices that are present in each human relationship increase in relations with people different by culture and origin: it is useful try to understand the large range of connections that diversity can create and to see its dynamics in depth. The results of these matches could be much diversified: competition, complementarity, apparent waste of resources, and support to the retirement system.

Diversity caused by migration could therefore be an extraordinary instrument of economic and social development, but it could also become a source of stress and conflict. In any case, according to Venturini, it is a process which is complex and difficult to understand. The adoption of an open and long-range perspective and the capacity to see the whole situation and its different interrelations represent an important incentive to better value the challenge of diversity and its opportunities, avoiding any short cut full of prejudices that may seem more attractive but that in practice has no exit.

Gabriele Morettini
Marche Polytechnic University, Department of Social Sciences, Ancona, Italy.

Steven Vertovec, 2007. "Super-diversity and its implications", *Ethnic and Racial Studies* 29, 6: 1024–54.

Keywords: *multiple categories, complexity, urban societies, theory*

Much of the literature on diversity in Europe and Northern America has traditionally focused on specific immigrant and ethnic minorities and the way in which these minorities settle into their new homes, form relations with members of the majority society, and deal with processes of inclusion and exclusion. Such research has been important during times when significant numbers of immigrants originated from the same origin, for example southern Europe, south Asia and the West Indies.

Resulting from this focus, both academic theorizing and policy practice have been shaped by a view of diversity as consisting of few minority groups who are confronted with the majority society. In the last ten years or so, however, we have seen an increasing number of people of different ethnic and national backgrounds migrating. In fact, there has been a *diversification of diversity*, not only in regard to different ethnic backgrounds, but also in regard to other variables such as routes of immigration, legal status, religion, gender, waves of immigration, and educational and socio-economic backgrounds. In his article on these new conditions of current patterns of migration, Vertovec proposes *super-diversity* as a summary term to describe and take into account the coalescence of these different variables which significantly shape patterns of settlement, integration and cohesion.

Vertovec's paper calls for a new view of migration and settlement which also looks at other-than-ethnic categories, and takes a more differentiated view of the nature of immigrant communities, public service needs, patterns of integration, etc. This approach takes into account the fact that today, we can find urban areas where no one group dominates, and where considerable differences among migrants of the same ethnic background can be found in factors such as time of immigration, socio-economic and educational background, and legal status.

Although Vertovec's article primarily draws on material from the UK, we can find such new configurations emerging across European and other cities of the world. Importantly, *super-diversity* not only refers to such new patterns of migration and settlement, but, on a more conceptual level, it calls for the need to apply a multidimensional perspective on diversity by looking beyond the "ethnic lens" when analysing immigration. This more differentiated view of diversity includes multiple affiliations and identifications along axes of differentiation such as legal status, professional identities, age and generation, and especially the interaction of these various axes.

Vertovec's article serves as a refreshing and much needed new approach to the ever more complex configurations of urban societies. But it also raises important methodological challenges resulting from this multidimensional viewpoint. These challenges are to be taken up by the coming generation of qualitative and quantitative social scientists and will hopefully lead to insightful comparative findings on the nature of current and future super-diverse societies.

Susanne Wessendorf
Max Planck Institute for the Study of Religious and Ethnic Diversity, Göttingen, Germany.

Sandra Wallman (ed.), 1982. *Living in South London: Perspectives on Battersea, 1871–1981* (The London School of Economics and Political Science: Gower), 229 pp.

Keywords: *neighbourhood, ethnography, networks, types of social systems*

This book is a classic manual of neighbourhood and household studies in the ethnographic vein, focusing on the London borough of Battersea. Richly annotated with historical and statistical data based on a neighbourhood survey questionnaire, extended interviews, contextual observations and archival research, the text aims to arrive at a depiction of the "style" of integration which gives the neighbourhood its distinctive flair. Living in the inner city involves complex and many-stranded ways of managing livelihood, resources and social relations, and it is one of the observations of this study that, in contrast to the official perspective which classifies a mixed inner-city population in terms of origins alone, classifications of neighbours by neighbours is multipurpose and complex. This is a local study of the local system, local resources, local status, local attitudes, local involvement and local livelihood, tracing networks which connect and criss-cross households within the neighbourhood and the borough.

The immediate neighbourhood is LARA, which during the time of the research contained 446 households. The rich depictions of neighbourhood relations illustrate combinations of structural/material resources (housing, people and services, goods and money) and organizing resources (time, information and identity) which make livelihood feasible. They are set against the style of Battersea politics and its elected politicians, describing the waxing and waning of Battersea identity against the background of Battersea's economic history and demography. What makes this book so useful is its detailed account of methodology, including the selection and training of interviewers, fieldwork management, debriefing of interviewers, and a detailed discussion of the time-line of research. Its many tables and diagrams, including the appended survey questionnaire, reflect the varied and complex data that were collected, from which richly contextualized examples of people and their lives in Battersea emerge, giving the interpretation of the data an animate character.

From a survey of the borough and the neighbourhood to close depiction of the profile of respondents, a picture emerges of how people forge contacts in the locality, make use of local amenities, draw on kin and external relations to bolster and support the household, and generally organize livelihood in ways which allow incomers of any origin to *become insiders* on the basis of residence or active participation in local activities. The open and yet inclusive style of integration, which emerges from the investigation of the management of local networks of social relations, is supported by an equally in-depth study of employment, including unremunerated tasks like housework.

The focus here is not the household, but the individual, and the relationship of the individual's sex, age, social class, ethnic origin and position in the household to a wide range of work activities, documenting patterns of seeking, finding and getting a job which vary with the extent of integration and involvement in the neighbourhood. The findings of this study open a perspective on the organizational options which are active in the creation of local boundaries and identities and which shape the style and scope of local livelihood.

Susanne Küchler
University College London, Department of Anthropology, London, UK.

Li Wei (ed.), 2006. *The Bilingualism Reader* (London: Routledge), 592 pp.

Keywords: *bilingualism*

This volume is a *reader*, its first edition was published in 2000 and this is its second edition (2006). It is a collection of key articles on theories and research in the study of bilingualism that were previously published in different journals and books. The idea is to have a resource book for students so that they can easily access articles dealing with different aspects of bilingualism. The volume is an introductory text and it can be useful not only for students, but also for anybody interested in linguistic diversity.

The volume has an introduction by Li Wei, the editor, who discusses different dimensions of bilingualism. The articles are divided into three parts: Part 1. *Sociolinguistic Dimensions of Bilingualism*; Part 2. *Linguistic Dimensions of Bilingualism*; and Part 3. *Psycholinguistics and Neurolinguistic Dimensions of Bilingualism*. The editor has written a concluding chapter, "Methodological Issues in the Study of Bilingualism", and has added a resource list, a glossary and a bibliography. The volume covers many different topics such as definitions of bilingualism, language choice, the bilingual brain or code-switching. Some of the articles included in the volume were originally published many years ago and are real classics in the study of bilingualism and language diversity, such as "Diglossia" by Charles A. Ferguson or "The description of bilingualism" by William F. Mackey. This volume provides access to key articles in the study of bilingualism and creates the opportunity to read original sources in the case of articles that are not always easily accessible.

The volume is aimed at students and provides study questions and activities for each of the chapters, but it can also be useful to anybody interested in linguistic diversity and bilingualism. It can be particularly interesting for scholars and students focusing on linguistic diversity, because it covers different dimensions of bilingualism and makes classic articles available.

Jasone Cenoz
University of the Basque Country, Donostia-San Sebastián, Spain.

Martin L. Weitzman (1992), "On Diversity", *Quarterly Journal of Economics* 107, 2: 363–405.

Keywords: *ethnic heterogeneity, cultural diversity, indicators*

Much empirical research on diversity uses indices that depend only on the number of types in a population and their relative abundances. This is true, for instance, in biology (to measure the diversity of habitats by the number and relative abundance of species in the habitat), in regional economics (to measure regional specialization by the number and relative employment shares of industries in the region), and in industrial organization (to measure industrial concentration by the number and relative weight of companies in the industry).

This article takes a different approach and provides a theoretically rigorous framework to construct an index of diversity that considers the differences between types.

The article defines a recursive algorithm to calculate the value of diversity function for a population. It starts by defining an arbitrary value assigned to a subset of the population including only one species (arbitrarily chosen). The value of the diversity function of an enlarged subset is then calculated by bringing an additional species (arbitrarily chosen) into the set, and so on. When a type is added, the value of the diversity function is increased by the distance between the new species and the closest already in the subset.

The article shows that such diversity function is uniquely defined only in the case of perfect taxonomy, when the extinction of a type is equivalent to cutting a branch of the taxonomic tree. For the general case, when differences cannot be structured in a taxonomic tree, the article provides an algorithm (based on dynamic programming) that reduces the actual distances into a taxonomic tree. The algorithm proceeds by comparing actual distances between types and clustering the two types with minimum distances. In this way it is possible to represent the differences with a tree. The tree is just an approximation, but it can be shown that it is the "most likely" approximation. The approximation bears a cost; while in the case of perfect taxonomy, the diversity of a subset of types can be inferred from the total diversity (as total length of the branch of the subtree), this is not possible in the general case: the artificial tree will rearrange if a type is eliminated from the original tree.

The article shows how this approach can be used to calculate the diversity of architectures, languages and biological species and to design cost-effective policies for the conservation of biodiversity. It is important in two ways. First, it provides a theoretically rigorous approach to calculating diversity which takes into account the differences between types' characteristics. Second, it shows that this approach can be applied in a variety of cases across many disciplines, highlighting the related similarities, and also the differences.

Dino Pinelli
Eni Enrico Mattei Foundation (Milan, Italy).

Katherine Y. Williams & Charles A. O'Reilly, 1998. "Demography and Diversity in Organizations: A Review of 40 Years of Research", in B. M. Staw & L. L. Cummings (eds), *Research in Organizational Behaviour* (Greenwich, CT: JAI Press), pp. 77–140.

Keywords: *age, gender, ethnicity, tenure, group creativity*

The usual opening of a paper on diversity emphasizes that one of the most dramatic changes facing managers today is the increasing diversity of the labour force. This change has been associated with positive effects, especially with regard to organizational creativity and innovation. For example, the *value in diversity* hypothesis (Cox & McLeod, 1991) asserts that the greater the level of diversity among group members, the greater the chances for divergent viewpoints that are a prerequisite for developing creative solutions to ill-defined problems. Diversity in this regard may refer to age, gender, ethnicity, tenure in teams or personality variables, i.e. to all characteristics individuals draw upon to describe differences between themselves and others.

In this extensive review, Williams and O'Reilly summarize the effects of more than eighty studies "relevant for understanding the effects of demography as it applies to work groups and organizations" (p. 77). Based on their review, the authors draw several conclusions. First, there is substantial evidence both from laboratory and field studies that diversity among group members can have important effects on group functioning. However, the majority of studies suggest that these effects will be negative. Group members in diverse groups engage in more stereotyping and in-group/out-group categorizing. These cognitive processes are disruptive to group functioning, including social integration, communication and conflict management.

One type of diversity, however, seems to be more likely to result in positive effects on group creativity: functional diversity, i.e. differences in information and knowledge. In contrast to socio-demographic diversity, functional diversity denotes task-relevant differences between group members that may increase creativity. Still, the authors conclude that at the micro level, increased diversity decreases the ability of groups to function effectively over time. In contrast to that, there is evidence that team-level diversity is positively related to organizational performance. Therefore the authors call for more research on the effects of specific forms of diversity to understand how successful groups leverage the potential benefits of diversity. This extensive review summarizes forty years of psychological research on diversity in groups. Since it was published, it has become seminal for psychological research on diversity. Although theory on diversity in workgroups has developed considerably since, it is one of the classical psychological readings on the subject.

Myriam N. Bechtoldt
University of Amsterdam, Department of Psychology, The Netherlands.

Elizabeth M. Wilson & Paul A. Iles, 1999. "Managing Diversity – an Employment and Service Delivery Challenge", *The International Journal of Public Sector Management* 12, 1: 27–48.

Keywords: *business case for diversity, case studies, managing diversity, equal opportunity, public sector management*

The authors discuss the reasons behind UK public sector managers' shift of emphasis from the traditional Equal Opportunity (EO) policy to the USA-originated Managing Diversity (MD) programmes, and identify five differences between these two policies. They maintain that (1) EO is externally driven and rests on moral and legal arguments, while MD rests on the business case and is viewed as an investment; (2) EO works at the operational level and is concerned with process, while MD is works at the strategic level, with a focus on outcomes; (3) in EO difference is perceived as problematical and deficit, while in MD difference is perceived as asset and richness; (4) EO focuses on groups, while MD focuses on the individual; and (5) EO is supported by positivist knowledge, while MD is supported by a wider pluralistic knowledge base.

The authors then look closely at the shift from EO to MD in two public sector cases, and provide some recommendations for public sector managers. What policy recommendations do the authors offer for diversity managers in the public sector? They hold that the organization must (1) identify why it wishes to pursue a change in emphasis, which may include failures in previous attempts such as EO, or, more positively, it may wish to include all the workforce in its development programmes; (2) decide what underpins a change in policy, again ranging from pragmatic, instrumental factors to augmenting traditional public sector values such as equity and accountability to wider groups for moral reasons.

The strength of the article lies in its evaluation of EO and MD polices in the public sector, and the five differences on which both policies are developed. The article provides very appropriate arguments for choosing either EO or MD polices, with a focus on the UK. It argues that even in its business case, MD is not limited to private, profit-oriented companies, but is also relevant in the public sector.

Kiflemariam Hamde & Nils Wåhlin
Umeå University, Umeå School of Business, Umeå, Sweden.

Louis Wirth, 1938. "Urbanism as a Way of Life", *American Journal of Sociology* 44 (July): 1–24.

Keywords: *urban sociology, city lifestyle, diversity, migration*

The text is a pilot essay in this first-rate sociological journal. It tries to grasp the main traits of city life and portray the character of a city dweller. Louis Wirth (1897–1952), a leading light of the Chicago School of Sociology, published it in the 1930s, when sociology was fully embodied into the positivistic paradigm. With the help of relatively simple causalities he suggests that the quantity, density and heterogeneity of the city population substantially influence city-dweller identity. Social heterogeneity is, according to Louis Wirth, a permanent trait of the city and a major product of urbanization. It was Louis Wirth who argued that because the city population does not reproduce itself, it must recruit migrants. The city has thus historically been a mixture of races, peoples and cultures, and a most favourable breeding ground of new social hybrids.

Louis Wirth suggested that the city not only tolerates, but also rewards new individual differences. Consequently, the city dweller is a rational person, well educated, relatively tolerant, secular and inventive. He/she is at the same time rather schizoid, beset by segmental roles. The city dweller is a dependent person with numerous superficial social contacts and utilitarian interpersonal relations, suffering from feelings of seclusion. The diversified urbanites' sophistication and cosmopolitanism comes at the expense of acceptance, stability and security. The Wirthian city dweller has many specific positive and negative traits. He/she is not a completely new personality. Since the city is the product of growth rather than instantaneous creation, it bears an imprint of previous folk society. It is difficult for city dwellers to coexist with heterogeneous urbanites. Under such circumstances, competition and formal control mechanisms furnish substitutes for the bonds of solidarity that are relied on to hold a folk society together. Thus the quality of formal rules of interpersonal coexistence is extremely important in a socially diversified society.

In the 1930s, "Urbanism as a Way of Life" was a breakthrough work. The Wirthian concept of urbanites as products of diversified society seemed to be universal. Later on, it appeared to be only one variant of city personality development and the essay was criticized by some, including Herbert Gans. Nevertheless, "Urbanism as a Way of Life" expresses numerous traits of human sociability in a socially diversified environment and retains its classic status up to the present day.

Zdenek Uherek
Institute of Ethnology of the Academy of Sciences of the Czech Republic, Prague, Czech Republic.

Phil Wood (ed.), 2004. *Intercultural City Reader*, Intercultural city series (Stroud: Comedia), 327 pp.

Keywords: *diversity, city, innovation, interculturalism, migration*

The Intercultural City Reader edited by Phil Wood provides a terrific insight into the complex arena of a diverse city. Wood managed to draw together the best of scholarly literature dealing with urban diversity, multiculturalism and interculturalism from a multidisciplinary perspective. The starting point of Wood's understanding of diversity is that he sees it as a source of new thinking, innovation and energy that can lead to the growth and wealth of the city.

Thirty texts selected for the *Reader* tackle a broad range of issues, including historical and geographical context for the study of diversity; ethnicity, identity and immigration; culture; diversity politics; economics, creativity and innovation; diversity in business; intercultural communication; and management of urban diversity.

The *Reader* was produced as part of a wider project exploring ways to turn diversity into a positive force for urban development. It targets a broader readership than a traditional academic one, as it is aimed also at practitioners and policy-makers in urban management, economic and cultural development and diversity management. The book offers exciting reading for anyone who is even slightly interested in the topic of urban diversity – be it as a student, an academic, a city official or a business manager. The fact that there are thirty rather short essays in the book written from different disciplinary angles makes it diverse, fresh and inspirational. The combination of interest in cultural diversity, innovation, interculturalism and city management is innovative itself and worth exploring.

The book brings a lot of new ideas, it challenges and provokes and makes us think beyond the traditional borders of our field. For a scholar it offers a step out of the academic box to an applied science and policy-making approach, which can sometimes be very refreshing and brings us closer to the *real* world. Some academics may find Wood's positive approach towards diversity to be one-sided or even non-objective. When reading the book, however, one must not forget that its main aim is to focus on diversity as an asset and an engine of development – an angle that can inspire urban practitioners in innovative and progressive policy-making.

Alexandra Bitusikova
Matej Bel University, Research Institute, Banska Bystrica, Slovakia.

Stuart Joseph Woolf, 1988. *Porca miseria. Poveri e assistenza nell'età moderna, translated by Paola Querci and Anna Woolf* (Roma-Bari: Laterza), 258 pp.

English Translation of the Title: *The Poor in Western Europe in the Eighteenth and Nineteenth Centuries.*

Keywords: *poverty, social assistance, pauperism, philanthropy, charity*

In this book, the author documents the condition of the poor in Western Europe and especially in Italy, highlighting the economic causes of pauperism. He points out how the endemic poverty of the peasants, but also that of the artisans, who had similar living conditions because of sudden crises due to wars, famines or negative economic circumstances, can generate particularly deep and conflicting forms of social diversity.

A series of chapters set out some aspects that are ascribable to the spread of poverty and its relationship with social structures. In the first chapter, devoted to Eastern Europe, Woolf tries to compare the different forms of poverty present in the contemporary world with those in the past. We can also see the burden of poverty on society as a whole. The author gives an outline of the relationship between the growth of pauperism and the economic system of modern Europe that is characterized by the progressive development of capitalism. The role of the family has also been sketched, both as a basis for a new form of poverty, often dictated by excessive numbers of children, and as an instrument for warding off or absorbing destitution. The author takes into account the different attitudes that have matured towards beggars and wayfarers through the course of the centuries, together with the ways through which institutional charity is expressed.

At the beginning of the modern age, generalized poverty gives way to a real and accurate cataloguing of the poor through a classification of people. The *false* poor are expelled from the cities or are secluded, while the *needy* are helped and given shelter in appropriate institutions such as hospitals, orphanages, almshouses, etc., depending on the case. Among the beggars, a special place is reserved for the *shameful* poor who, due to their social status prior to becoming poor, are ashamed to ask for alms. Finally, the author moves on to the phenomenon of workhouses, and the different forms of home assistance tried out in the past by means of social philanthropy and charity. Some passages have also been devoted to the attitude of the poor towards their own condition and towards charity.

Subsequent chapters are devoted to the Italian context and to the change from the *poor* category to that of the proletariat during the nineteenth century. It is in this phase that new professions come into being that are incapable of overcoming the world of poverty that characterizes the lowest level of the social hierarchy. The problems of the history of pauperism in Italy have also been addressed through statistics and government actions launched during the Napoleonic period.

The book is significant for studying social diversity, as it describes the transformation that takes place through the course of centuries and in particular during the developing phases of the working class.

Augusto Ciuffetti
Marche Polytechnic University, Department of Social Sciences, Ancona, Italy.

Achyut Yagnik & Suchitra Sheth, 2005. *The Shaping of Modern Gujarat: Plurality, Hindutva and Beyond* (India: Penguin Books), 328 pp.

Keywords: *religion, diversity, harmony, politics, violence*

Gujarat, a state on the western coast of India, has a long history of diversity, pride of identity and social harmony as well as conflict. The story of this region is complex and puzzling, for although it is traditionally multicultural and inclusive, it also has pockets of insularity, parochialism and caste barriers. It is one of the richer states of India, but "one-fifth of the population lives below the poverty line" (p. xii); even though the cities are safe for women and the Goddess Shakti (power) is the predominant deity worshipped throughout the year, the female sex ratio gives great cause for concern.

The book is an account of the socio-political scene of this region from ancient times (the time of Emperor Ashoka's edicts, 273 BC) to the present, from early beginnings to the growth of a mercantile ethos, from multiculturalism and communal harmony to the present paradox of a see-saw of peace and extreme violence. It is a detailed study of the plurality that was Gujarat, a plurality that has been widely hailed in its art and literature, a cultural synthesis that was an integral part of the everyday life of its people, and of the presence in contemporary Gujarat of hostility and suspicion between Hindus and Muslims, whether as underlying current or overt riot. Just as Gujarat welcomed the British, the call for independence was also strong in this region. It is noteworthy that both Mohandas Karamchand Gandhi, regarded as the Father of the Nation in India, and Mohammad Ali Jinnah, creator of Pakistan, were from Gujarat. Gandhi's ideas of social uplift had dug deep roots here; remnants are still visible in the various social work projects in many remote corners of the state. Yet there has been a rise in *Hindutva*, an ideology that propagates Hindu supremacy for India.

The authors rightly point out that this *new Hinduism* harks back to a supposedly pure Sanskritic form which excludes not only religious minorities, but also the various syncretic forms with their little traditions, a hallmark of India's multicultural society. Unfortunately, the scholarly tradition of Gujarat has been supplanted in recent times by an "intellectual vacuum" (p. 292) which has allowed the precepts of the new Hinduism to go unchallenged "ideologically, theologically [and] philosophically" (p. 292). The result is a ripped society with demarcated and ghetto-like living space, which symbolizes not just physical but also emotional distancing. There is no longer room for "shared childhood leading to adult bonds of understanding and mutual respect" (p. 293).

The authors' prognosis for the future is not of healing, but of encountering more friction. Gujarat is an enigma; there are too many layers, far too many conflicting attitudes and social norms. The book gives an assessment of the forces that have possibly led to this complexity. It is an insightful history of the region for any researcher, bewildered as this reviewer is by the surge of enmity and violence that has overpowered the traditional wisdom of understanding and compassion in Gujarat.

Alaknanda Patel
Centre for Development Alternatives, Ahmedabad, India.

Patrizia Zanoni & Maddy Janssens, 2004. "Deconstructing Difference: The Rhetoric of Human Resource Managers' Diversity Discourses", *Organization Studies* 25, 1: 55–74.

Keywords: *diversity discourse, power, essentialism, critical discourse analysis, rhetoric*

In this article, Zanoni and Janssens analyse twenty-five interviews on diversity with Flemish Human Resources managers using critical discourse and rhetorical analysis. Through these techniques, the authors contribute to the reconceptualization of diversity in a critical, non-essentialist way, by showing how diversity discourses are linked to existing power relations and how power enters these discourses through the micro-dynamics of language.

First, the article shows how managers see employees as representatives of specific groups manifesting a given essence. Such a construction has specific power effects, as subjects lose their individuality and agency. The article also argues that differences are sometimes constructed as a lack, and sometimes as an added value, and that this is done based on the perceived ability of these differences to help in reaching organizational goals and in respect to the production process of the specific work context. In this way, the diversity discourses can be said to be products of the power relations between management and employees within the organization. Finally, the authors show that the discourses not only reflect, but also reproduce, existing power relations, as they can be used to manage the labour force and make it more compliant. It has to be noted that the authors also found two examples of discourses challenging existing power relations, but here it was only the practices between groups that were addressed, and not the power relations between management and workforce.

This article has been important for me, mainly because it gives a clear picture of how managers think about diversity, supported by rich empirical material. It is interesting, for example, to see how the managers, when asked how they think about diversity, start talking about individual differences (probably in line with practitioner-oriented texts on the subject), but quickly relapse into essentialist, group-based thinking. As this is the kind of reasoning that seems to underlie the way they deal with diversity in practice, this taught me to be critical when managers talk about their individual-based approaches, as this might only be rhetoric.

Moreover, the article clearly shows how diversity discourses are linked to the production process and the organizational context in which they emerge. This again indicates the importance of context in the study of diversity. Furthermore, it is interesting to see how these managers construct their diversity approaches as legitimate, using specific rhetorical schemes and drawing on specific grand discourses. As such, we get a clear, in-depth understanding of how managers talk about this topic and which techniques they use in specific argumentations.

Finally, the article succeeds in showing very clearly how power and diversity discourses are linked, and how these discourses reflect and reproduce existing power relations. As such, this paper is a clear source of inspiration for authors who acknowledge the importance of power in the diversity field and for everyone who wants to combine empirical research on diversity with a critical approach.

Koen Van Laer
Katholieke Universiteit Leuven, Faculty of Business and Economics, Research Centre for Organisation Studies, Leuven, Belgium.

Sharon Zukin, 1995. *The Cultures of Cities* (Massachusetts and Oxford: Blackwell Publishers), 322 pp.

Keywords: *urban culture, diversity, public space, politics*

Sharon Zukin's book brings a new insight into urban culture. Based on the example of the culture capital and global city of New York, Zukin explores how culture is made and negotiated in public spaces – streets, squares, parks, museums, shops, markets or restaurants. She observes the changing nature of culture in the contemporary city and the way it increasingly becomes an important element, and often a battleground of urban politics and economy. Much of the focus of the book lies on the production of space and the production of symbols which are both part of what Zukin calls symbolic economy. Creating public culture involves shaping public space for social interaction and forming visual representations of the city. The main characteristics of urban public space are proximity, diversity and accessibility. Public spaces should be open for all multicultural and socially diverse populations of the city. Are they? Who do these spaces belong to? Who creates and who occupies them? Zukin tries to find answers to these questions. She explores how public space in a diverse society is negotiated over identity, security, social and geographical community, and what is the role of urban politics – public authorities, real-estate developers, civil society and other players in the process of the revitalization of urban space.

The book is highly inspiring, written in a fresh, vivid and easy-to-read style. It makes us look at urban culture, space and population from various angles. For an urban anthropologist used to focusing on one problem or unit – a community, a neighbourhood, a quarter, an ethnic or religious group, a social stratum, space or identity – combining and connecting various categories, such as culture, aesthetics, identity, ethnicity, diversity, space, symbolism, public and private, local and global, politics and economy, is very inspirational, as it is more holistic and leads to better understanding of the complex urban environment of today. It is obvious that the book is not just another publication by a well-known sociologist, but it is also a book written by an urban dweller who cares about her city and loves it.

Alexandra Bitusikova
Matej Bel University, Research Institute, Banska Bystrica, Slovakia.

List of Contributors
and Their Affiliations

Balestrieri, Attilio
Psychoanalytic Institute for Social Research, Rome, Italy

Baker, Walter V.
Holborn Community Association, Bedford House, London, UK

Baycan-Levent, Tuzin
Istanbul Technical University, Dept. of Urban and Regional Planning, Istanbul, Turkey

Bechtoldt, Myriam N.
University of Amsterdam, Dept. of Psychology, Amsterdam, the Netherlands

Bello, Barbara Giovanna
State University of Milan, Cesare Beccaria Department of Law, Milan, Italy

Betancur, John J.
University of Illinois at Chicago, Department of Urban Planning and Policy, Chicago, USA

Bitusikova, Alexandra
Matej Bel University, Research Institute, Banska Bystrica, Slovakia

Bracalenti, Raffaele
Psychoanalytic Institute for Social Research, Rome, Italy

Cattaneo, Cristina
Eni Enrico Mattei Foundation (Milan, Italy) and University of Sussex (Sussex, UK)

Cenoz, Jasone
University of the Basque Country, Donostia-San Sebastián, Spain

Chiapparino, Francesco
Marche Polytechnic University, Department of Social Sciences, Ancona,
Italy

Christova-Balkanska, Iskra
Institute of Economics, Bulgarian Academy of Sciences, Sofia, Bulgaria

Ciuffetti, Augusto
Marche Polytechnic University, Department of Social Sciences, Ancona,
Italy

Cooper, Jasper J.
Interdisciplinary Centre for Comparative Research in the Social Sciences,
Paris, France

Damvakeraki, Tonia
National and Kapodistrian University of Athens, Athens, Greece

De Lobel, Rob
IDEA Consult, Brussels, Belgium

de Ruijter, Arie
Tilburg University, Faculty of Social and Behavioural Sciences, Tilburg, the
Netherlands

Elkadi, Hisham
University of Ulster, School of Architecture and Design, Belfast, UK

Fiorio, Carlo
Eni Enrico Mattei Foundation and University of Milan, Milan, Italy

Galindo-Cespedes, José Fernando
Centre for Research and Promotion of Peasantry, Cochabamba, Bolivia

Giulianelli, Roberto
Marche Polytechnic University, Department of Social Sciences, Ancona,
Italy

Gorter, Durk
University of the Basque Country, Donostia-San Sebastián, Spain

Hamde, Kiflemariam
Umeå University, Umeå School of Business, Umeå, Sweden

Hernández-Sanchéz, Manuela
The Hague University, Academy of European Studies and Communication Management, The Hague, the Netherlands

Heugh, Kathleen
University of South Australia, Research Centre for Languages and Cultures, Adelaide, Australia

Janssens, Maddy
Katholieke Universiteit Leuven, Faculty of Business and Economics, Research Centre for Organisation Studies, Leuven, Belgium

Kendall, Anthony N.
Social Action Radio, London, UK

Knotter, Steven
IDEA Consult, Brussels, Belgium

Krasteva-Vladimirova, Evgenia
Economic and Investment Bank (part of KBC Group), Sofia, Bulgaria

Küchler, Susanne
University College London, Dept. of Anthropology, London, UK

Lo Conte, Rossella
University College London, Dept. of Anthropology, London, UK

McPhillips, Karen
University of Ulster, School of Architecture and Design, Belfast, UK

Montuori, Maria Alessia
Psychoanalytic Institute for Social Research, Rome, Italy

Morettini, Gabriele
Marche Polytechnic University, Department of Social Sciences, Ancona, Italy

Mukherjee, S. Romi
Interdisciplinary Centre for Comparative Research in the Social Sciences, Paris, France

Nilsson, Angela
University of Stockholm, Centre for research in international migration and ethnic relations, Stockholm, Sweden

Patel, Alaknanda
Centre for Development Alternatives, Ahmedabad, India

Pinelli, Dino
Eni Enrico Mattei Foundation (Milan, Italy)

Reymen, Dafne
IDEA Consult, Brussels, Belgium

Rousseau, Olivier
Interdisciplinary Centre for Comparative Research in the Social Sciences, Paris, France

Simic, Ljiljana
Oracle – Network of European Cultural managers, Brussels, Belgium

Sori, Ercole
Marche Technical University, Department of Social Sciences, Ancona, Italy

Stenius, Vanja M. K.
Psychoanalytic Institute for Social Research, Rome, Italy

Tsipouri, Lena
National and Kapodistrian University of Athens, Athens, Greece

Uherek, Zdenek
Institute of Ethnology of the Academy of Sciences of the Czech Republic, v.v.i., Prague, Czech Republic

Van Laer, Koen
Katholieke Universiteit Leuven, Faculty of Business and Economics, Research Centre for Organisation Studies, Leuven, Belgium

van Londen, Selma M.
Tilburg University, Faculty of Social and Behavioural Sciences, Tilburg, the Netherlands

Wåhlin, Nils
Umeå University, Umeå School of Business, Umeå, Sweden

Wallman, Sandra
University College London, Dept. of Anthropology, London, UK

Wessendorf, Susanne
Max Planck Institute for the Study of Religious and Ethnic Diversity, Göttingen, Germany

Note about index pagination

Individual reviews sometimes begin on the same page. Repeated page number references – such as 10–11, 11; or 45–6, 46–7 – indicate that the topic is reviewed in more than one review over the relevant page numbers.

Subject Index

Main Discipline Index

Geographic Area Index

Diversity-Type Index